A GUIDEBOOK for NEW BELIEVERS

Encouraging

WORDS for THE FIRST 100 DAYS

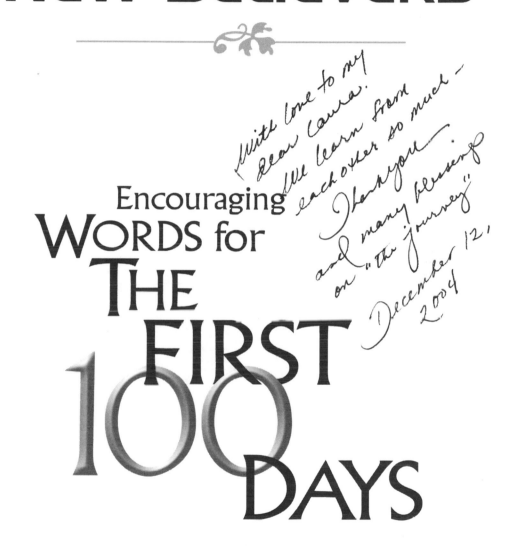

With love to my dear Laura! We learn from each other so much — Thank you. and many blessings on "the journey".

December 12, 2004

BETTE NORDBERG

A GUIDEBOOK for NEW BELIEVERS

Encouraging
WORDS for
THE
FIRST
100
DAYS

AMG *Publishers*

CHATTANOOGA, TENNESSEE

A Guidebook for New Believers

Copyright © 2003 by Bette Nordberg
Published by AMG Publishers
6815 Shallowford Rd.
Chattanooga, Tennessee 37421

ISBN 0-89957-371-1

First printing—April 2003

Cover designed by ImageWright, Inc., Chattanooga, Tennessee
Interior design and typesetting by Reider Publishing Services, West Hollywood,
    California
Edited and Proofread by Robert Kelly, Dan Penwell, and Sharon Neal

Printed in Canada
09 08 07 06 05 04 03 —T— 8 7 6 5 4 3

For

Jeannie St. John Taylor.

May all your investments yield eternal dividends

INTRODUCTION

Not long ago, I went to the store to buy a new telephone. I knew exactly what I wanted: just a handset and a ringer— nothing more. I didn't want auto-dial, or caller ID. I didn't want a message machine or a hands-free headset.

I just wanted a plain old telephone.

When I got to the store, I discovered that no one makes plain old telephones anymore. After more than an hour examining the features included on various models, I bought the simplest one I could find.

It had a 64-page instruction book. Not exactly simple, is it?

I'll never figure out all of the features on my new phone. Undoubtedly, it will limp through life at my house just like our VCR—whose clock still blinks midnight.

Unfortunately, I know too many Christians who live their faith life like my new telephone. They manage the most basic functions—they make it to church and carry their Bible—but they never enter into the depth and richness of the Christian life. Anemic and weak-willed, they never reach their full potential; never know real freedom from sin, or the joy of using their gift in the Kingdom of God. Prayer is an obligation to them, and their only view of community is sitting in the same pew, week after week, waiting for the sermon to end.

Sometimes, weak beginnings lead to early endings.

Unlike my new telephone, I meant this book to be user-friendly. Every day, before you begin, ask God to join you as you read and pray. Then read through a single entry.

Each section begins with a short passage taken from the New Living Bible, already written out for you. Following the passage, you'll find the address or location of the text. After every Scripture, I've included a little story to help you understand the meaning of the text.

The shaded box at the end of the narrative text has prayer suggestions. Use these suggestions to help you pray through the issues in the text and apply them in your life.

In the United States, whenever we elect a new president, we give him the benefit of a 100-day honeymoon. We allow him time to organize his cabinet and find his footing with Congress. Even the press doesn't criticize until the honeymoon is over.

Make the same kind of allowance for yourself. Stick with your new commitment. Don't give up! And when the honeymoon is over, judge for yourself.

By investing only ten to fifteen minutes every day, you will gradually learn more about God, about prayer, the Bible, and the Church. And at the end of the honeymoon, you will be well on your way to experiencing all the wonder of your new life in Christ.

YOU'RE NOT IN KANSAS ANYMORE

So we have continued praying for you ever since we first heard about you. We ask God to give you a complete understanding of what he wants to do in your lives, and we ask him to make you wise with spiritual wisdom. Then the way you live will always honor and please the Lord, and you will continually do good, kind things for others. All the while, you will learn to know God better and better.

We also pray that you will be strengthened with his glorious power so that you will have all the patience and endurance you need. May you be filled with joy, always thanking the Father, who has enabled you to share the inheritance that belongs to God's holy people, who live in the light. For he has rescued us from the one who rules in the kingdom of darkness, and he has brought us into the Kingdom of his dear Son. (Colossians 1:9–13)

When my older kids were teenagers, they loved the Michael J. Fox movie *Back to the Future*. Thanks to videotape, we enjoyed the film over and over. In the story, Fox's character, Marty McFly, must find a way home after being inadvertently sent back in time to the year 1955. When he arrives home, Marty discovers that his presence in the past has changed the present.

Though his parents look and sound the same, they have become entirely different people. Marty's terrifying adversary has become a groveling people-pleaser. Baffled by the changes, Marty struggles to cover his confusion as he navigates the maze of new relationships.

In the same way, you may have experienced some confusion after your recent decision to begin a new life in Christ. Perhaps you've started to question things you once believed to be absolute facts. Your long-held values may already have begun to crumble. Activities you used to do without a second thought now leave a vague sense of uneasiness. Some of your old friends aren't very excited about your new faith.

You haven't lost your mind; there is a reasonable explanation!

Like Marty, you have been transferred to a New Kingdom. Though things look and sound the same, your awareness has broadened. You have a new command center directing the activities and thoughts in your old body. Some folks refer to this change as a heart transplant. Somehow, you must find your way through a maze of changed relationships and displaced beliefs. This new life will take some getting used to.

Nearly three decades ago, I started down this same road. I still remember the shock. I'm no theologian. I don't speak the original languages of the Bible. But I've spent twenty-seven years reading the Word, listening to the best teachers, and finding my way in the New Kingdom. This book is designed to help you begin the journey. It doesn't require that you look up Scriptures or write down answers. You won't have to attend class. But in the end, I hope you'll find yourself yearning for more. You'll want to begin reading your own Bible. You'll have the beginning of a prayer habit. You'll begin to understand some of the most basic terms and principles of Christian living. The ideas here will provide a solid vehicle for the journey.

I'm excited for you. I can say with absolute certainty, I would never go back to my former life! I only regret that I didn't change Kingdoms earlier.

Prayer ideas

Tell your Heavenly Father about the changes you've already noticed in your faith walk. As you begin this new journey, ask God to give you a healthy church and good friends to help you along the way.

THE REAL PROBLEM

Listen! The LORD is not too weak to save you, and he is not becoming deaf. He can hear you when you call. But there is a problem—your sins have cut you off from God. Because of your sin, he has turned away and will not listen anymore. Your hands are the hands of murderers, and your fingers are filthy with sin. Your mouth is full of lies, and your lips are tainted with corruption.

No one cares about being fair and honest. Their lawsuits are based on lies. They spend their time plotting evil deeds and then doing them. They spend their time and energy spinning evil plans that end up in deadly actions. They cheat and shortchange everyone. Nothing they do is productive; all their activity is filled with sin. Violence is their trademark. Their feet run to do evil, and they rush to commit murder. They think only about sinning. Wherever they go, misery and destruction follow them. They do not know what true peace is or what it means to be just and good. They continually do wrong, and those who follow them cannot experience a moment's peace. (Isaiah 59:1–8)

As you begin your new life of faith, perhaps you understand exactly what has happened to you. Or maybe, just maybe, you're feeling a little lost, a bit confused. You know something happened, but you aren't sure quite what. I hope that in these first days I can help you trace the miraculous process that has begun in you.

Think back. Somewhere along life's path, you decided that God is.

You may have looked at the universe and decided that humans are not an accident. Or perhaps you've seen too much design in nature to discount the existence of a designer. Still, as you listened to people talk about God's love, you couldn't quite tap into it. Why not?

What keeps humans from being able to reach God? Sin! Sin makes our relationship with God a bit like a man and woman who meet on the streets of Paris—she, an exchange student from Zimbabwe, he an artist from the United States. Neither can speak the other's language. In Paris, they find no one to interpret for them.

Though the man may find the woman attractive, graceful, fashionable, he cannot get through the language barrier between them. Though she may appreciate his eyes, his smile, his laughter, she cannot truly understand his heart until he speaks and she understands.

Like the man and the woman who cannot speak to one another, so is the relationship between God and man. Unable to reach one another, we are left yearning for contact, wishing for relationship. Instead of a barrier created by different languages, sin creates our barrier with God.

God's justice demands that someone take care of our sin. He cannot wink at our pride, or smile at our self-sufficiency. He cannot tolerate the declaration of independence we express in our determination to go our own way, to live without God, without rules, without restraint.

He can no more excuse our rebellion, selfishness, or pride, than he can excuse Hitler's attempt to annihilate the Jewish people living in Europe. God's economy demands a balancing of the books—a satisfaction for sin. Without it, God and man will never know genuine relationship.

Our sin separates us from God; but God refuses to settle for separation. He has a plan, and long before you were born, he set the plan in motion.

Unfortunately, the plan demands that we recognize our need. Each of us needs a solution for our sin problem. Each of us must come to a place where we recognize our own sinful nature. We must accept God's diagnosis of our problem. Sin leads to separation and death.

Then with the problem clearly in mind, we can celebrate the good news. God has provided a solution! Tomorrow, we'll take a look at the prescription for sin.

Prayer ideas

Can you remember the first time you recognized your own sinfulness? Did you confess your faults to God? Have you thanked God for beginning a new life in you?

✝ ✝ ✝ DAY 3 ✝ ✝ ✝

THE SWAP

Therefore, since we have been made right in God's sight by faith, we have peace with God because of what Jesus Christ our Lord has done for us.... When we were utterly helpless, Christ came at just the right time and died for us sinners. Now, no one is likely to die for a good person, though someone might be willing to die for a person who is especially good. But God showed his great love for us by sending Christ to die for us while we were still sinners. And since we have been made right in God's sight by the blood of Christ, he will certainly save us from God's judgment. For since we were restored to friendship with God by the death of his Son while we were still his enemies, we will certainly be delivered from eternal punishment by his life. So now we can rejoice in our wonderful new relationship with God—all because of what our Lord Jesus Christ has done for us in making us friends of God. (Romans 5:1, 6–11)

On August 3, 2001, police in Afghanistan detained eight Western aid workers and sixteen Afghans working for Shelter Now International. Charged with attempting to convert Muslims to Christianity, the women were put in jail to await trial. Under strict interpretation of the Sharia law imposed by the Taliban, promoting Christianity is a crime punishable by death.

In spite of international pressure to release the women, their time in prison dragged on. Though the Afghan government promised a swift and fair trial, the detained women had few opportunities to meet with a lawyer and prepare their defense.

Over the course of their 105-day imprisonment, police kept the two American women in a total of four prisons. Though they eventually saw International Red Cross representatives, and their own court-appointed attorney, the women had no other contact with Americans or family members until September 1.

On September 11, their situation grew even more desperate. With the attacks on the World Trade Center and the Pentagon, the captured aid workers became pawns of the Afghan regime. The Taliban offered to release the women on the condition that the United States drop its smear campaign against the Taliban and the nation of Afghanistan. It looked as if the two American women, Heather Mercer and Dayna Curry, might not survive their ordeal.

Heather's father, John Mercer, traveled to Pakistan, desperately seeking release for his twenty-four-year-old daughter. At one point, news agencies reported that Mercer asked Taliban officials to accept his imprisonment in exchange for his daughter.

If the reports are true, John Mercer offered to take his daughter's punishment—even though it might mean his own death.

While I haven't been able to track down official records of these negotiations, I do remember being awestruck by this father's determination to save his child. John Mercer refused to let anything keep her from the long and happy life she deserved. In desperation, he offered himself in exchange.

This father, so willing to take his daughter's place—even if it should mean his own death—is a perfect example of our Father's love for us.

Convicted of sin, we face a certain death sentence. But God, like John Mercer, refused to let his children die. He sent his son, Jesus Christ, to take our place. Jesus came to earth, lived a perfectly sinless life, and then offered himself in exchange for the charges against us.

"Take me," he said to my captors. "I will pay the penalty for her sin."

Though the Taliban refused John Mercer's offer, God has accepted the sacrifice of Jesus Christ. His death has fulfilled all the necessary requirements for justice. The penalty has been paid. By his death, the record of your sin has been expunged. By his resurrection you have been offered a new life. A free life—life as a child of God.

While it took a military attack and the toppling of the Taliban government to set Heather Mercer and Dayna Curry free, you have been offered freedom through a simple exchange—Jesus' life for yours. He died. You walk. Hard to believe isn't it?

The offer has been made. Now every human must make his own choice. Have you accepted God's offer? Have you left your prison behind?

Prayer ideas

*I*n your old life, you might have thought of Easter as nothing more than a family holiday. Take some time to consider the exorbitant cost Jesus paid for your freedom. Thank God for the priceless gift of Jesus' death in your place.

WALKING FREE

He is so rich in kindness that he purchased our freedom through the blood of his Son, and our sins are forgiven. . . . All of us used to live that way, following the passions and desires of our evil nature. We were born with an evil nature and we were under God's anger just like everyone else.

But God is so rich in mercy, and he loved us so very much that even while we were dead because of our sins, he gave us life when he raised Christ from the dead. (It is only by God's special favor that you have been saved!) . . .

God saved you by his special favor when you believed. And you can't take credit for this; it is a gift from God. Salvation is not a reward for the good things we have done, so none of us can boast about it. (Ephesians 1:7; 2:3–5, 8, 9)

Imagine for a moment that you are one of the women held in Afghanistan. You face charges of trying to convert Muslims. In truth, you had hoped to accomplish exactly this. You did show a film about the life of Jesus to a Muslim family.

No matter how unfair the law, you are guilty.

Today, you face your scheduled execution. You have enjoyed your last meal and dressed for your own death. Your captors have given you time to make yourself ready. The guard approaches your cell; you hear his sandaled feet on the stone floor.

He opens your door, his keys clanging against the lock, and nods for you to exit. You step into the hallway where other turbaned men wait for you. All eyes avoid yours. Quietly, you follow these men down a dark hallway to a corner of the building. In spite of the heat you feel cold; you shiver and clench your teeth to keep them from chattering.

They open another door.

Suddenly, you are blinded by sunlight. Blinking and confused, you look at the faces around you. From the hallway inside the prison, you hear the noises of the street. You see children playing just beyond the wire fence. You look again to your captors. The one holding the door gestures that you may leave.

Your confusion must show, for a slow smile comes to the face of the man beside you. "An exchange has been made," he says in heavily accented syllables. "You are free to go."

What would you choose?

Some might be so comfortable with prison that they would prefer to stay—even if that meant eventual death. Freedom frightens them. At least they know what to expect in prison. Others, determined to make a point of their lives, choose death. Hoping their martyrdom will convince others to rebel, they walk with pride toward the firing squad.

Some would choose freedom no matter what. These people know the horrors of incarceration. Unwilling to live another moment in captivity, they would risk anything to be free. As the door opens, they rush into the street.

What would you choose?

Without a second glance, you step through the open door and into the blinding sunlight. As you walk through the prison yard, you drop your prison clothes on the ground behind you. Shaking yourself to make certain you are not dreaming, you step through the gate into the street.

Your joy is boundless. You run for a while, anxious to put distance between you and your captors. You rub your wrists, trying to erase the pain of the chains which once held you. You drink water, and beg for food from a street vendor. Then satisfied and free, you rest for the first time in months. Curling up on a park bench, hidden behind a low tree, you try to nap. But your sleep is slow to come, in spite of your exhaustion.

For the first time, you wonder if it was all just a horrible nightmare. And then the question hits you. What will you do with your new freedom?

By your faith in Jesus, you've chosen to leave your prison behind. You have walked away from the sin which held you captive. The initial disbelief and thrill have begun to wear off. Now you face a new and more confusing question.

What now?

Prayer ideas

*T*alk to God about how you felt when you first realized that you had been set free. Don't forget to express your gratitude. Ask Him to show you his plans for your new life.

NEW LIFE

So you should not be like cowering fearful slaves. You should behave instead like God's very own children, adopted into his family—calling him "Father, dear Father." For his Holy Spirit speaks to us deep in our hearts and tells us that we are God's children. And, since we are his children, we will share his treasures—for everything God gives to his Son, Christ, is ours, too. (Romans 8:15–17)

Long ago, even before he made the world, God loved us and chose us in Christ to be holy and without fault in his eyes. His unchanging plan has always been to adopt us into his own family by bringing us to himself through Jesus Christ. And this gave him great pleasure. (Ephesians 1:4, 5)

And now, just as you accepted Christ Jesus as your Lord, you must continue to live in obedience to him. Let your roots grow down into him and draw up nourishment from him, so that you will grow in faith, strong and vigorous in the truth you were taught. Let your lives overflow with thanksgiving for all he has done. (Colossians 2:6, 7)

Remember our Afghan illustration? When we left the story, you had been released from prison and taken a nap in the city park. Your growling stomach wakes you. Rubbing your eyes, you realize the sun is about to set. You sit up and glance around. You recognize nothing. You have no friends. No destination.

Where will you go? What will you eat? Where will you be safe?

You stand up and find your way out of the park onto the still warm sidewalk of the city. Around you, traffic moves quickly as hurried citizens rush home. Lost, and feeling the first pangs of loneliness, you begin to wonder about your choice. *Would I really have died in prison?*

A long black limousine pulls up to the curb. The uniformed driver steps out, walks around the car and opens the rear door. "For you, Madame," he says.

"What?"

"For you," he repeats. "I'm to take you to the summer palace."

Hunger twists your stomach. You shift your weight from foot to foot. Should you go along with him? Shrugging, you step in; you have nothing to lose. During the long drive you drift off to sleep. The driver's voice awakens you.

"We're here," he says, holding the car door. As you step out, the sight of an enormous castle sitting on the edge of a beautiful sea leaves you dizzy. Unwittingly, you draw a deep breath, and bite your lip to keep tears away. Perfectly groomed lawns frame the house, and the sea glows pink in the twilight. "What is this?" you whisper. "Where are we?"

"You're home," the driver says, bowing slightly. "Your father lives here. He sent me to pick you up. The staff is waiting upstairs to help you settle. Then, we'll begin the coronation."

"Coronation?"

"Yes," he bows again. "Today you are to become the Crown Princess. Your father the King has been looking everywhere for you."

What a day! You woke as a prisoner facing the death penalty. Then through unexpected negotiations, you find yourself set free. Later, after wandering away from the prison, you are rescued by your father's emissary.

Before nightfall, you discover that you are part of the ruling family. Wealth, freedom, servants—all will become part of your everyday life. You are a child of the king!

And while the discovery is shocking enough, the reality will take a lifetime of getting used to. Though you may enter the castle and put on the clothes, you may wear the crown and accept your position, you must still grow into your new life. It will take much work, and study and practice.

No matter how comfortable you become in your new surroundings, you must never forget the prison. As you sleep in your silk sheets on your soft feather bed, you must remember the cold prison floor. As you revel in your father's company, you must never forget the loneliness of life inside prison walls.

While you treasure the joy of your new life, you must remember the sorrow of the old. By keeping that memory fresh, you will find yourself overflowing with gratitude for your new father, your new family, your new position.

Such is the new position of every new believer. The swap has been made. We have chosen freedom. Our Heavenly Father has rescued us and given us a new position as a child of the Heavenly King. At first, the severity of the change overwhelms us. Then, we settle into the new position and find ourselves tempted to forget the past.

But we must not let go of the memory of our imprisonment. It fills us with a sense of gratitude so intense that we fall down in praise and thanks for our Father's love.

And in gratitude, we assume our new family responsibility— expressing our thanksgiving with a life that honors the king.

Prayer ideas

Spend a few minutes remembering your old prison, and thank him for your rescue. Ask God to begin to show you the riches of your new position in Christ.

DAY 6

YOU'VE ONLY JUST BEGUN

When I think of the wisdom and scope of God's plan, I fall to my knees and pray to the Father, the Creator of everything in heaven and on earth. I pray that from his glorious, unlimited resources he will give you mighty inner strength through his Holy Spirit. And I pray that Christ will be more and more at home in your hearts as you trust in him. May your roots go down deep into the soil of God's marvelous love. And may you have the power to understand, as all God's people should, how wide, how long, how high, and how deep his love really is. May you experience the love of Christ, though it is so great you will never fully understand it. Then you will be filled with the fullness of life and power that comes from God. (Ephesians 3:14–19)

Every summer our family visits Cannon Beach Christian Conference Center located on the Oregon coast. This summer, on our last evening there, we met an extraordinary couple.

My husband and I had gone to the dining room together, expecting to meet our teenagers. The kids had other plans, and we ended up sitting by ourselves at a table near the back door. Eventually, a young couple joined us.

As we made introductions, we noticed their strong accents and asked where they'd come from. Originally from Russia, the couple had immigrated to Renton, Washington five years ago. In those years, she'd managed to finish her bachelor of nursing degree, while he supported them with minimum-wage work. Now, she works the night shift as a registered nurse while he studies computer engineering at the University of Washington.

As we ate, they began an enthusiastic discussion of the marvels they'd discovered here in the land of opportunity. Though neither of them spoke English when they arrived, they both managed to learn the language as they found their way around the Seattle area. In spite of his background, he obtained work, and managed to climb the ladder of responsibility in a retail industry.

She'd entered nursing school, attending lectures and reading text-books in such difficult subjects as pharmacology and anatomy, even before she became fluent in English. In spite of the difficulty, she finished school and found a job.

At first, they'd both found themselves baffled by our culture, by the breadth of opportunity here. In fact they chose to shop at tiny convenience stores rather than face the startling abundance of food in local grocery stores.

"We'd never seen so much food," the woman told me. "All of it right there, where you can buy it any time you wish. It was overwhelming at first."

The opportunity for work, for advancement, for education, seemed limitless. Even five years later, their voices and expressions betrayed their wonder. They hardly knew where to start in expressing their appreciation for life in the United States.

I asked if they would ever go back—especially when he finishes his degree. "Oh no," she answered, shaking her head. "Things in Russia—even after the fall of communism—are very bad. There is nothing to eat; nothing to buy. No food and no money. We brought both our parents to the United States. This is our home now. We will never go back."

I won't ever forget that meeting. Her enthusiasm for her new home reminded me of today's Scripture. Even though your new life in God might feel just as confusing as moving to a new country, you can put down roots, just as my Russian friends have. Paul wants you to fully explore your new life and take advantage of all the benefits you find in the Kingdom of God.

Just as my Russian friends delighted in the economic benefits, you can revel in the spiritual delights of your Heavenly Father. As you read this book, you're putting down new roots. You are learning to spend time every day with God in his Word. As you do these things, you'll learn more about God and his limitless love for you. By sharing your new life with those you meet along the way, you will grow in gratitude and understanding.

I pray that you will always answer as my friend did. "Oh no, I would never go back to my homeland. This is my home now. In fact, I've brought my family to live with me here."

Prayer ideas

Ask God to show you one new thing about himself today. Ask him to show you one person who would like to hear about your new journey of faith. If you need to, ask for the courage to begin talking about the recent changes in your life.

GOD MADE ALL THINGS

In the beginning God created the heavens and the earth. The earth was empty, a formless mass cloaked in darkness. And the Spirit of God was hovering over its surface. Then God said, "Let there be light," and there was light. And God saw that it was good . . . And God said, "Let there be space between the waters, to separate water from water." . . . And God said, "Let the waters beneath the sky be gathered into one place so dry ground may appear." . . . Then God said, "Let the land burst forth with every sort of grass and seed-bearing plant. And let there be trees that grow seed-bearing fruit . . . And God said, "Let bright lights appear in the sky to separate the day from the night. They will be signs to mark off the seasons, the days, and the years. Let their light shine down upon the earth." . . . And God said, "Let the waters swarm with fish and other life. Let the skies be filled with birds of every kind." . . . Then God blessed them, saying, "Let the fish multiply and fill the oceans. Let the birds increase and fill the earth. ". . . And God said, "Let the earth bring forth every kind of animal—livestock, small animals, and wildlife." And so it was. God made all sorts of wild animals, livestock, and small animals, each able to reproduce more of its own kind. And God saw that it was good . . . Then God said, "Let us make people in our image, to be like ourselves. They will be masters over all life—the fish in the sea, the birds in the sky, and all the livestock, wild animals, and small animals." So God created people in his own image; God patterned them after himself; male and female he created them . . . Then God looked over all he had made, and he saw that it was excellent in every way. This all happened on the sixth day. (Excerpted from Genesis 1)

Most new writers have the same kinds of worries: How do I know if my writing is good enough? Where should I send my manuscript? How long do I have to wait before I find out if the publisher wants my book? But one worry is especially common: What if my idea is so good that they take it and publish it without giving me credit?

New writers often work hard to prevent plagiarism. I've seen them cover their work with elaborate copyright symbols, or send sealed copies to themselves by registered mail. Though plagiarism seldom occurs in publishing, occasionally even experienced writers find their material with someone else's name on it.

Imagine Nora Roberts's surprise in 1997 when she discovered that fellow writer and friend Janet Dailey had lifted complete passages from Roberts's book, *Sweet Revenge,* and published them in her own romance novel, *Notorious.* Since then Roberts has discovered more stolen passages in Dailey's work. "It was like someone had hit me," Roberts is quoted as saying in a 1997 *Time* magazine article. Though Dailey later apologized, her actions have scandalized both the publisher and agents involved.

This must be like what God feels every time we humans give credit to someone or something else for his creation. "No, it was the big bang that got everything going," some assert. Others espouse the Darwinian line, "It was the survival of the fittest."

After pouring himself into the beauty of the world—giving his full attention to the order of atoms, cells, and space—how it must hurt God to see us give an accident or myth credit for creation. While he marches the stars across the sky, sets the limits of the seas, and establishes the patterns of seasons, how he must grieve to have us explain it all away as nothing more than chance.

The Bible leaves no room for doubt. In the opening passages of Genesis, God reveals himself—almost as if he means to say, "I did it! Isn't it wonderful? I made it all myself, for my pleasure. Nature is mine. I have given it order and reason and laws, and now I share it with you as a testament to my power and my character."

But more than that, the creator God, maker of the universe and of heaven and earth, also made you. And it's you he really wants—your attention, your love, your devotion. Celebrate his creation today, by giving him praise for his marvelous work.

Prayer ideas

Express your appreciation for one especially beautiful part of your world. Talk to God about anything that keeps you from giving him full devotion.

THE POTTER'S HANDS

Oh Lord, you have examined my heart and know everything about me.
You know when I sit down or stand up.
You know my every thought when far away.
You chart the path ahead of me and tell me where to stop and rest.
Every moment you know where I am.
You know what I am going to say even before I say it, Lord.
You both precede me and follow me.
You place your hand of blessing on my head.
Such knowledge is too wonderful for me, too great for me to know! . . .
You made all the delicate, inner parts of my body
       and knit me together in my mother's womb.
Thank you for making me so wonderfully complex!
Your workmanship is marvelous—and how well I know it.
You watched me as I was being formed in utter seclusion,
       as I was woven together in the dark of the womb.
You saw me before I was born.
Every day of my life was recorded in your book.
Every moment was laid out before a single day had passed.
How precious are your thoughts about me, O God!
They are innumerable!
I can't even count them; they outnumber the grains of sand. (Psalm
       139:1–18)

Because the Western Washington State Fair takes place here in Puyallup, my husband and I often go several times over the course of its seventeen-day run. Sometimes, we'll run the traffic gauntlet to enjoy an evening concert, or to view the photo exhibit. Once in a while we'll go just to have dinner.

One Friday night, when we found ourselves without teenagers, we decided to celebrate by going to the fair—just the two of us. After a chicken caesar salad, we wandered around the grounds enjoying our favorite displays, ending up in the Artists in Action barn, where my husband, Kim, bought ceramic pins for his office staff.

As he made his purchase, I found myself drawn to a pottery demonstration at the other end of the barn. In front of a mesmerized crowd, an ordinary looking woman punched a baseball-sized lump of clay onto the center of her potter's wheel. With one foot on the pedal and both hands on the clay, she began shaping the lump.

At first, she seemed content to let the clay ride around and around under her fingers. Then, she began to squish the ball into a flat round shape. With one thumb, she pressed a tiny hole in the center. Almost instantly, the sides of the lump rose to form a thick bowl. Then, with two hands, one inside and one outside, she drew the sides higher.

A squirming little boy climbed onto the wall separating her from the crowd. Leaning toward her work, he asked what she was making. Teasingly, she refused to answer. I had no idea what she intended to accomplish. So far, the lump resembled nothing I recognized.

As she worked, she dipped a small sponge into a nearby bucket of water and trickled it onto her clay. Then with delicate, almost deft motions, she shaped the lump. The sides rose still further and she pressed in the center of the shape until a graceful waist formed itself in what now appeared to be a small bowl.

As the shape grew tall and quite thin, I gave up on the idea of a bowl. The sides rose still further. With skilled hands, she drew the clay away from the waist, flaring the shape again and adding more height. The top edge appeared slightly lopsided, and secretly I worried for her. What if she had ruined her work in front of so many people?

While the wheel continued to turn, she took a small scalpel and scored the upper lip of the vessel. Then, as she peeled off the noodle of clay, the top edge became perfectly smooth. She had nearly finished before I identified the slim candleholder she'd created.

When the wheel stopped moving, she slid a string under the vessel, separating it from the wheel. Gently, she lifted the soft clay and moved it to a shelf behind her where it joined dozens of others already waiting their first firing in her oven.

This woman—this artist I'd worried about—knew all along what she wanted to make with her clay. She could see the creation in her mind, long before I recognized it on her potter's wheel. So it is with God.

Long before the creation of the world, he envisioned the person he hopes to create in you. Over time God takes you, a shapeless lump of clay, and sets you onto his wheel. Then patiently, with one hand inside and one outside, he uses gentle pressure to accomplish his purpose. As you change shape, he continues to apply pressure, first here and then there—all the while with a picture of the finished project dancing in his holy imagination.

While others watch, he creates. What appears to be destructive—the cutting edge of a sharp scalpel—creates the perfect finish. He moistens. He pushes. He resists.

Every move God makes has purpose. Every action is part of his plan. Nothing in your life—not a single day, not a single mistake, not a single accident—lies outside of his loving hands. You are on his thoughts every moment of every day.

He is the potter and you are the clay. He created you in your mother's womb. Every day, his work contributes to the beautiful vessel he longs to create in you. Will you yield to the potter's hands?

Prayer ideas

Can you think of ways he has already shaped your life? Ask him to show you his hands in your life today. Thank him for his work in your daily life.

ULTIMATE POWER

Don't put your confidence in powerful people; there is no help for you there.

When their breathing stops, they return to earth, and in a moment all their plans come to an end. But happy are those who have the God of Israel as their helper, whose hope is in the Lord their God. He is the one who made heaven and earth, the sea and everything in them. He is the one who keeps every promise forever, who gives justice to the oppressed and food to the hungry. The Lord frees the prisoners. The Lord opens the eyes of the blind. The Lord lifts the burdens of those bent beneath their loads. The Lord loves the righteous. (Psalm 146:3–8)

He covers the heavens with clouds, provides rain for the earth, and makes the green grass grow in mountain pastures. He feeds the wild animals, and the young ravens cry to him for food. The strength of a horse does not impress him; how puny in his sight is the strength of a man. Rather the Lord's delight is in those how honor him, those who put their hope in his unfailing love. (Psalm 147:8–11)

In 1967, my father sold insurance. On October 11 of that year, he took a check from the bookkeeper for the City of Oak Harbor to insure the new city hall. On Friday, October 12, the most terrible windstorm ever to hit the Pacific Northwest besieged Oak Harbor. They called it the Columbus Day storm and people still talk about it.

My parents planned to go dancing that night. I remember standing on the front porch in my pajamas under the light of a single bulb, saying good-bye to them. I remember them commenting on the unseasonable warmth and stillness of the evening air. My brother had drawn babysitting duty, caring for my five-year-old brother and me.

Two hours later, the power went out. At seven, my fear must have tested my brother's entertainment ability. To comfort us, he lit a roaring fire in the fireplace and opened our living room curtains. He tried to interest us in the magnificent beauty of the storm.

I remember looking out our front window as the wind bent hundred foot fir trees like grass. I saw the huge window flex in the wind, and remember the sound of pinecones and branches slamming against the roof. I can still picture the dark shadows of the trees and the candlelight reflecting off the glass. I didn't find the scene beautiful in the least. We closed the drapes.

Somehow, my older brother got the two of us to bed. Later that night, my mother moved me into another bedroom. As she tucked me in, she said, "You'll be safer on this side of the house, if a tree falls through the roof." Needless to say, I didn't go back to sleep.

In the morning, my father and I drove all over Whidbey Island looking at the damage. The roof of the new city hall had landed unruffled in the fire station parking lot. We marveled at the force it must have taken to make a roof fly. In the city park, oak trees had fallen like toothpicks. Nearly everyone suffered serious wind damage. Insurance companies my dad represented covered most of the damage. For him, the storm symbolized enormous financial loss.

In other parts of Washington, power remained out for nearly a week. Schools were closed, and people moved out of damaged homes. On Saturday after the storm, fire crews were still trying to rescue office workers caught in the elevators of Portland high-rises. Maintenance crews, removing downed trees and power lines, tied up traffic for days. My mother cooked for six children in a pot over the fireplace. We'd come out lucky—cold and bored, but with no real injuries.

This freak storm—packing winds of more than 160 miles per hour—had victimized homeowners from the Canadian border to Salem, Oregon. No one saw it coming.

I am still awed by the power that storm displayed, still amazed at the damage caused by ten hours of hurricane force winds. But the power of the wind is as a breath compared to the power of God. No storm, no earthquake, no avalanche, no tidal wave can compare with his power. The Bible says God controls everything.

Everything in heaven and earth—all things human or natural or spiritual—must answer to God. Think of this the next time a hurricane threatens your home. Whether you face a job loss, a terminal illness, a family crisis or any other threat, remember that He controls all things.

His power extends over everything. And he delights in you.

Prayer ideas

As you pray, consider the extent of God's power—over nature, people, history, churches and governments. Thank him for his power. Confess your dependence on him. Ask God to exercise his power on your behalf.

No Changes Here

Rise up Balak and listen! Hear me son of Zippor.
God is not a man that he should lie.
He is not a human, that he should change his mind.
Has he ever spoken and failed to act?
Has ever promised and not carried it through? (Numbers 23:18, 19)

I am the Lord, and I do not change. . . . Jesus Christ is the same yesterday, today and forever. So do not be attracted by strange new ideas.
(Malachi 3:6; Hebrews 13:8)

Generally, I like change. I think I'd enjoy moving more often. I'd like to decorate a different house, or drive a different car. I sometimes wonder what it might be like to retire to a different part of the world. But don't mess with my friendships.

I've been lucky enough to travel in the same circle of faithful friends for the past twenty years. I've walked every weekday morning with the same bunch of ladies for almost fifteen years now. We know each other so well that we can read one another simply by the shape of our smile, or the rhythm of our steps. We've cried in one another's arms. We've belly laughed until we've had to stop walking and try desperately to remain upright. Sometimes our laughter wakes the neighbors.

We know one another's deepest secrets.

So, you can imagine how difficult it has been for me over the past several years, as older children's college bills have sent most of my walking buddies back to work. Our walking schedule isn't always the same anymore. Sometimes one of us will miss a whole week. Five years ago, one of our members left town for the Chilean mission field. No amount of email replaces the comfort of her presence.

While my friends haven't changed, our circumstances, our schedules, and our availability have. As we've gotten older, I've grieved over the changes life has brought us. While I wanted everything to stay the same, no one listens to me.

While life changes, *God does not.* His proclamations stand from generation to generation. No matter how the world thinks, or dresses or behaves, he does not change. His nature does not change. His purposes do not change. His power does not change. And most importantly, no matter what you do, or what choices you make, his love for you will never change.

As you travel this journey of faith, you'll discover more and more about God. Most of this knowledge will come from the things you learn in the Bible. As you live the faith life, you will experience God. Along the way, you may feel like a beachcomber, carrying your God treasures—this knowledge of the living God—along in your spiritual pockets.

Over time, God will become more familiar to you than a lifelong friend.

But you need never worry about his friendship. Our God will never run out of time for you. He will never have anything more important to do than to be with you.

Our God does not change. And, that's a truth you can rest in.

Prayer ideas

Have you been hurt by change in the past? Have you told God about the hurt? Can you thank him for never changing, never leaving, never taking his love from you?

WHO IS JESUS ANYWAY?

Christ is the visible image of the invisible God. He existed before God made anything at all and is supreme over all creation. Christ is the one through whom God created everything in heaven and earth. He made the things we can see and the things we can't see—kings, kingdoms, rulers, and authorities. Everything has been created through him and for him. He existed before everything else began, and he holds all creation together. (Colossians 1:15–17)

Last year, my daughter's biology class completely frustrated her. The theory of evolution seemed to be the teacher's primary interest. By the time he finished his presentation, he had questioned the intelligence, logic, and emotional stability of anyone who would dare to believe anything other than Darwinian Theory.

Her teacher's confidence in Darwin surprises me, since scientists in many specialties now question the reliability of traditional evolutionary theory. The July 29, 2002 issue of *U.S. News & World Report* states that proponents of Intelligent Design include both biblical literalists and scientists of the highest academic credentials.

In the article, scientists say, "Life's mechanisms—like the flagellum . . . found in some of earth's simplest life forms—are too improbably perfect to have formed by chancy Darwinian evolution alone. The flagellum, as surely as a pop-top on a Coke can, was designed by some unnamed intelligence that might—or might not—be God."

The intractable problems of Darwinism frustrate many scientists—like the fact that no recorded mutation has ever increased the likelihood of an organism's survival. On the other hand mutations, which decrease an animal's chance of survival, happen daily.

Much of the scientific community has begun to question its Darwinian roots. The once indisputable foundation of all biologic science has begun to crumble. Even science has trends. The Bible, on the other hand, leaves no room for fads. The Word of God does not change. It does not respond to the whims of culture. The Bible stands unflinching in the face of popular trends.

Today's passage in Colossians leaves no question of our origin. "God created everything," it says. The passage makes no allowance for interventionist evolution. It leaves no room for creation by space aliens or time travelers.

In the essentials, God makes himself clear. Notice the list of details about Jesus Christ in this passage. He existed before everything else. Through Jesus, everything was created. He is the visible image of the invisible God. He holds all things together.

Make this passage your faith anchor. We know that God, through Jesus, didn't simply create the world and set it spinning off by itself. He continues to hold our world together. Things are under his control.

Your world is under his control. Your family is under his control. The weather is under his control. The powers of government and the powers of terrorists are under his control. As desperate as the front-page news may seem, you can take absolute confidence in this Biblical truth: God is in control.

You need not shoulder the responsibility for the world. You don't have to understand everything. As one of my friends puts it, "There is a God, and you are not him." In that, you can relax a little.

God has everything under control.

Prayer ideas

Have you begun to see God's control in your life? Can you thank him for his work in and around you?

✝ ✝ ✝ DAY 12 ✝ ✝ ✝

A COMPASSIONATE SAVIOR

Her brother, Lazarus was sick. So the two sisters sent a message to Jesus telling him, "Lord, the one you love is very sick."

But when Jesus heard about it, he said, "Lazarus's sickness will not end in death. No, it is for the glory of God. I, the Son of God, will receive glory from this." Although Jesus loved Martha, Mary and Lazarus, he stayed where he was for the next two days and did not go to them. Finally after two days, he said to his disciples, "Let's go to Judea again . . ."

When Jesus arrived at Bethany he was told that Lazarus had already been in his grave for four days. Bethany was only a few miles down the road from Jerusalem and many of the people had come to pay their respects and console Martha and Mary on their loss . . . Now Jesus had stayed outside the village, at the place where Martha met him . . . When Mary arrived, and saw Jesus, she fell down at his feet and said, "Lord, if you had been here, my brother would not have died."

When Jesus saw her weeping and saw the other people wailing with her, he was moved with indignation and was deeply troubled. "Where have you put him?" he asked them. They told him, "Lord, come and see." Then Jesus wept. The people standing nearby said, "See how much he loved him." (Excerpted from John 11:2–36)

Born on Easter Sunday, Melody Carlson arrived fourteen weeks early. In spite of the doctor's efforts, her premature lungs refused to stay open; her tiny blood vessels could not bring enough oxygen to her body to keep her cells fed. When her mother went home, Melody stayed in the hospital.

Melody's mother, my friend Kim, had given birth by Caesarean section. On the day of her discharge, with her husband at work, she asked me to bring her home. The nurse and I put Kim in the wheelchair, stacked her belongings on her lap, and grabbed a box of Kleenex as we left her private room. Before we left the hospital, we stopped by the newborn intensive care.

I'd never seen anything so helpless, so tiny. Melody's little body, eyes covered, tiny hat on her perfect head, seemed to have grown unnatural attachments to beeping monitors and life-giving fluids. Through the portholes of the incubator, Kim caressed Melody, and together we prayed for her life.

For almost three weeks, Melody fought a brave and valiant fight. We believed she would make it. But, in the middle of the night, seventeen days later, Melody died.

Using a pattern I designed from a Cabbage Patch doll, I beaded and embroidered a white dress for Melody's memorial service. She would never have her own wedding; I wanted her to wear a wedding dress celebrating her meeting with her eternal bridegroom. Lying in her casket, Melody looked like a beautiful newborn.

Four weeks later, in the late sunlight of a long summer day, I answered the phone. "Can you come?" Kim asked. "I know it's late, but I need someone."

Together we walked to a nearby school and traipsed for many twilight miles around the cinder track. She talked and I cried. I had nothing to say—no explanations, no divine wisdom, only tears. In fading daylight, we walked back to her house and sat outside on the steps, talking and crying until stars filled the sky and we shivered in the cold night air.

It has been many years since we lost Melody. Her mother is doing well. She looks forward to meeting her daughter again in heaven. And to my surprise, Kim often reminds me of the evening we spent crying together as we walked. Of all the things I did when Melody died, the most valuable seems to have been walking and crying.

I'd have to say, I learned it from Jesus.

During these horrifying days, as we watch Timothy McVey take his madness out on an Oklahoma federal building, as airplanes fall into the Pacific Ocean, and as Twin Towers collapse, I remember my Lord.

When Mary and Martha lost Lazarus, Jesus wept. Our Savior is a man of compassion! When people hurt, Jesus hurts. He knows the unbearable pain of loss.

When we hurt, we can be absolutely certain that he is there with us. We can sense his nearness and feel his anguish. Take comfort in his care for you, and share it with someone who needs you.

Prayer ideas

Ask your Heavenly Father to help you sense his presence when you are hurting. Ask him to show you how to care for others in pain.

LORD OF ALL

One day Jesus said to his disciples, "Let's cross over to the other side of the lake." So they got into a boat and started out. On the way across, Jesus lay down for a nap, and while he was sleeping the wind began to rise. A fierce storm developed that threatened to swamp them, and they were in real danger. The disciples woke him up, shouting, "Master, Master, we're going to drown!"

So Jesus rebuked the wind and the raging waves. The storm stopped and all was calm! Then he asked them, "Where is your faith?"

And they were filled with awe and amazement. They said to one another, "Who is this man, that even the winds and waves obey him?" (Luke 8:22–25)

Twenty-six years ago, on a stormy winter night, we had an urgent phone call from my husband's mother. "The church is on fire," she said. "And the firemen can't get it under control. It's about to take down the new gym."

Obediently we prayed.

When we called the next day, we learned about an amazing miracle. In the dead of night, the sanctuary of Life Center, in Tacoma, Washington had caught fire. The flames spread rapidly inside the dome-shaped building before bursting through the roof. By the time the first fire trucks arrived, the building was already engulfed in flames.

At the same time, a twenty-five knot wind from the south blew the flames and embers onto the roof of the newly constructed gymnasium next door. In a desperate attempt to save the second building, firemen began to hose down the new roof. As news of the fire spread, members of the congregation began to gather in the parking lot. Not only did they face loosing the sanctuary, they also faced the crippling loss of their new gym. If both buildings burned, the congregation would have no place to worship.

There in the midst of streaming water, fire hoses, and bustling emergency personnel, the men of the congregation and the pastoral staff got down on their knees on the wet pavement. With clothes soaked by water, they boldly asked God to still the wind, or to change its direction. Behind them, roof timbers crashed into the sanctuary as the building caved in. More fire engines arrived. Unmoved by the events around them, the men continued in prayer.

And then it happened. An enormous American flag, flying above a nearby parking lot, fell listlessly still—just before it began to fly in the opposite direction. The wind had changed. The flames of the burning sanctuary were blown back on themselves, and the gymnasium completely escaped the inferno next door.

The Jesus of the New Testament had complete control over the elements of nature. He stilled the storm, raised the dead, and healed the sick. Nothing was too difficult for him. In fact, he seemed a little surprised that his own friends didn't expect him to do these things. "Where is your faith?" he asked them.

Nothing has changed with Jesus. He is still in control. Ask for what you need—no matter how outlandish it seems. If you face the flames of destruction in your own life, pray. If you see the floodwaters rising, pray. When you get terrible news from the doctor—pray. You may see the flames of destruction blown back, or the waters recede, or your body healed.

"Where is your faith?" he asks us.

Prayer ideas

Thank God for Jesus' control over nature. Ask boldly for him to accomplish whatever you need from him today.

HANGIN' ON

I am the true vine, and my Father is the gardener. He cuts off every branch that doesn't produce fruit, and he prunes the branches that do bear fruit so they will produce even more. You have already been pruned for greater fruitfulness by the message I have given you. Remain in me, and I will remain in you. For a branch cannot produce fruit if it is severed from the vine, and you cannot be fruitful apart from me.

Yes, I am the vine; you are the branches. Those who remain in me, and I in them, will produce much fruit. For apart from me you can do nothing. Anyone who parts from me is thrown away like a useless branch and withers. Such branches are gathered into a pile to be burned. (John 15:1–6)

I've always admired the human placenta. I'm crazy; I admit it. It seems to me a marvel of physiologic engineering. In fact, according to Dr. Harvey Kliman, M.D., Ph.D., from the Reproductive and Placental Research Unit at Yale School of Medicine, "A healthy placenta is the single most important factor in producing a healthy baby."

This surprising organ manages to protect the incubating infant from immune attack by the mother, remove waste products from the baby's blood, and induce changes in the mother's blood supply to the uterus—all the while producing hormones that govern the biochemical stability of pregnancy.

In a determined effort to provide everything the baby needs for health, the placenta brings oxygen and nutrients to the developing baby, at the same time working as a thermostat to provide the ideal hormonal environment for continued pregnancy. Even when a mother makes poor health choices—choices involving drugs or alcohol—the placenta makes an effort to compensate by becoming more efficient.

You can't have a healthy baby without a healthy placenta.

The unborn child depends completely on the placenta. No matter how determined or creative an infant may be, he cannot scare up his own dinner. Neither can he remove his own waste products. He can't tell mom when it's time for labor and delivery. Everything depends on the placenta. Without it, the only option is death.

I think this kind of dependent relationship—that of branch to vine, of baby to placenta is the kind of relationship we are to have with Jesus. We must look to him as our sole provider. Only he can meet every one of our needs—physical, emotional, and spiritual. He provides every breath our body takes. He gives us every loving relationship, every gentle hug we receive. Every insight, every bit of wisdom and understanding come through him. Without him, we are as productive as a dry branch, or a stillborn baby.

Without him, as my kids would say, "We're toast."

I struggle to keep this focus. I like to think that I'm pretty capable. I willingly accept credit for being well informed, and keeping physically fit. It isn't long before I begin to feel proud of my accomplishments and a little disdainful of those who aren't so energetic or ambitious. Before long my disdain turns to contempt, and my pride becomes arrogance. From here, I'm only a step away from believing that I have no need for Jesus.

Pride whispers quietly, "I can do it on my own." Beware of the voice. Memorize this Scripture. Keep it before you always. Depend fully on the vine.

Only by hangin' on will we produce the fruit he desires.

Prayer ideas

Remind the Lord of your absolute dependence on him. Ask him to protect you from self-sufficiency and pride.

ONE WAY HOME

"Don't be troubled. You trust God, now trust in me. There are many rooms in my Father's home, and I am going to prepare a place for you. If this were not so, I would tell you plainly. When everything is ready, I will come and get you, so that you will always be with me where I am. And you know where I am going and how to get there."

"No, we don't know, Lord," Thomas said. "We haven't any idea where you are going, so how can we know the way?"

Jesus told him, "I am the way, the truth, and the life. No one can come to the Father except through me. If you had known who I am, then you would have known who my Father is. From now on you know him and have seen him!"

Philip said, "Lord, show us the Father and we will be satisfied."

Jesus replied, "Philip, don't you even yet know who I am, even after all the time I have been with you? Anyone who has seen me has seen the Father! So why are you asking to see him? Don't you believe that I am in the Father and the Father is in me? The words I say are not my own, but my Father who lives in me does his work through me." (John 14:1–10)

People say that Seattle has developed into one of the worst three traffic disasters in the entire United States. Having commuted to Seattle during rush hour, I suspect the statisticians are correct. I'd rather give birth than drive in that mess.

But the traffic on Seattle freeways is nothing compared to the traffic flowing through your spinal cord every day. Electrical signals, like cars, travel up and down your spine carrying instructions and information to and from the brain—twenty-four hours a day, seven days a week.

Though we don't often appreciate the wonder of the human spinal cord—in fact we seldom even consider it—without it, we would be unable to complete even the smallest task. Generally, when an injury severs the spinal cord, a blow to the head or legs has fractured the bones in the spinal column driving bone fragments into the cord. These bony pieces slice through the cord—as efficiently as a knife slices through a celery stalk.

The injury need not completely sever the cord in order to render the pathway completely ineffective. I've treated patients with nothing more than cord bruising, who have completely lost the use of their trunk and legs.

Ten years ago Christopher Reeve, famous for his role as Superman, experienced the devastating effects of spinal cord injury. His fracture-dislocation occurred so high in his neck that the nerves which control his breathing no longer signal his diaphragm. He has no ability to cough or breathe deeply on his own. Doctors have restored some function by implanting a small pacemaker in his diaphragm. Without it, Christopher would spend the rest of his life on a ventilator.

So why do I bother you with all this medical mumbo jumbo? Because the harsh reality of human anatomy closely mimics the reality of salvation.

Without the functioning pathway of the spinal cord, the body and the brain cannot talk to one another. Without this vital connection, functioning nerve endings in the hands and feet are unable to tell the brain what they sense. They cannot report burns or injuries. They do not differentiate between a warm bath and scalding death.

There is only one way—one path—for information in the human body to reach the brain. Only one way!

And there is only one way for the human soul to reach the God of all creation—and that way is Jesus Christ.

Jesus makes no apologies for this simple truth. Though other religions may come close to the path—they may mimic the path—they may borrow some of the truths of Scripture—unless they use the one path, the sacrifice and resurrection of Jesus Christ—they have missed salvation.

I like this quote from C. S. Lewis, in *Mere Christianity* (Harper Collins, 1952, 1972), "As in arithmetic—there is only one right answer to a sum, and all other answers are wrong; but some of the wrong answers are much nearer being right than others."

This truth is hard to bear. We long for those who practice other religions to have eternal life. We find it hard to understand how those so fervent could face eternal punishment.

Our Heavenly Father does not expect us to understand. We must simply believe. Jesus Christ is the only pathway to heaven. No one gets to the Father but by him. Without him, we have no hope for eternal life.

You've chosen the path. Have you shared it with others?

Prayer ideas

Do you know someone who has chosen another path to eternal life? Would you spend some time praying for that person? Would you be willing to share your life change with him?

This Ghost Needs No Bustin'

If you love me, obey my commandments. And I will ask the Father, and he will give you another Counselor, who will never leave you. He is the Holy Spirit, who leads into all truth. The world at large cannot receive him, because it isn't looking for him and doesn't recognize him. But you do, because he lives with you now and later will be in you. (John 14:15–17)

When the Spirit of truth comes, he will guide you into all truth. He will not be presenting his own ideas; he will be telling you what he has heard. He will tell you about the future. He will bring me glory by revealing to you whatever he receives from me. (John 16:13, 14)

And when you believed in Christ, he identified you as his own by giving you the Holy Spirit, whom he promised long ago. The Spirit is God's guarantee that he will give us everything he promised and that he has purchased us to be his own people. This is just one more reason for us to praise our glorious God. (Ephesians 1:13, 14)

Over the years, as I've written several novels, I've discovered that you can get most anyone to tell you anything you need to know. You have only to ask.

Not long ago, while developing a book, I spent the summer taking pictures of boats in the San Juan Islands. As I began plotting, I chose the boat best suited for my story. Then I began writing. Before long I realized that I needed to view the inside of a similar very large, very expensive sailing yacht.

On an early summer morning, one year after I took my first pictures, I packed my kids in the car and headed for Yacht Broker Row in Seattle. Randomly, I pulled into a parking lot. "Lord, I need a boat," I prayed. "Show me the right salesman."

We piled out of the car and into the tiny waiting room of a small yacht brokerage. After introducing myself, I showed the salesman my picture. "I need to view the inside of a boat that looks something like this," I said. "I need pictures. I need to be able to imagine life inside a boat in order to write the details of my next novel."

"Where did you get this picture?" the salesman asked. He sounded slightly amazed.

"I took it—in the San Juan Islands, last summer."

"I sold this boat," he said, laughing, "to a professor at the University of Puget Sound."

After thinking for a moment, he consulted his files. "I don't have this exact boat, of course, but one very nearly like it. It's tied up at the dock out back."

"Could I take pictures inside?"

"As many as you need," he said, reaching for the keys.

Leaving both kids in the waiting room, we headed down to the dock. He showed me to the vessel and gave me a walk-through tour. Eventually, when I'd seen everything, he gave me the padlock and asked me to bring it up to his office when I'd finished. "I have work to do," he said. "Take all the time you need."

"I can't believe you're leaving me alone inside this boat. I mean—I'm a perfect stranger."

He laughed again. "Maybe," he said. "But your kids are up in my office. I don't think you'd steal the boat and leave the kids. I'll take them as collateral." With that, he stepped onto the dock and headed back to the office.

I giggled about the whole thing as I shot three rolls of film. The salesman was right. I'd virtually given him my teenage children in promise for the safety of his sailboat.

In the same way, Jesus tells his disciples that his Heavenly Father will give all believers the Holy Spirit as a promise of things to come. As Jesus prepares his friends for his death and resurrection, he tries to comfort them—even before they begin the mourning process. The words in today's passage are his preparatory words.

Jesus seems to say, "Don't sweat it guys. When I leave, the Father will put the Holy Spirit inside you. Even though I'll be gone, you'll never really be alone. Having the Holy Spirit inside you is your promise of salvation and eternal life.

The Holy Spirit living inside believers is a bit like a living engagement ring—a symbol, or a promise of something yet to happen. But, he is more than that. He refuses to be our good luck charm. He won't simply hang around inside believers, hoping for the best. Instead, Jesus promises that the Holy Spirit will play an active role in our growth. He'll spend his time pushing, prodding, reminding. He'll continually correct, guide, help, and comfort.

At the moment you placed your faith in Christ, you received a living Spirit who now resides inside of you. In the days ahead, you'll be looking at some of the implications of this startling revelation.

You are now under new occupancy. Have you welcomed your new guest?

Prayer ideas

Consider the implications of carrying God with you everywhere you go. Talk to him about that. Ask your Heavenly Father to help you recognize the Holy Spirit's prompting in your daily life.

Do You Hear What I Hear?

It was now winter, and Jesus was in Jerusalem at the time of Hanukkah. He was at the Temple, walking through the section known as Solomon's Colonnade. The Jewish leaders surrounded him and asked, "How long are you going to keep us in suspense? If you are the Messiah, tell us plainly."

Jesus replied, "I have already told you, and you don't believe me. The proof is what I do in the name of my Father. But you don't believe me because you are not part of my flock. My sheep recognize my voice; I know them, and they follow me. I give them eternal life, and they will never perish. No one will snatch them away from me, for my Father has given them to me, and he is more powerful than anyone else. So no one can take them from me. The Father and I are one." (John 10:22–31)

After two babies, I'd given up on the idea that I could identify my own newborn's cry among all the other babies at the hospital.

In fact, by the time Maggie was born, I'd let go of most of my theories on child development. Recovering from Maggie's delivery left me too exhausted to think. Chris, my roommate, had chosen to give her baby up for adoption. As I watched her agonize over her loss, her grief occupied most of my thoughts.

Then one morning, a nurse carried Maggie in for a mid-morning snack. After feeding her, I realized that I needed to make a trip to the bathroom. I tried ringing for the nurse, but she seemed to have gone on vacation. What should I do with Mags? I couldn't leave a newborn lying unattended. I certainly couldn't carry her with me to the bathroom.

Though I hated to add to her grief, I asked Chris to hold the baby. As I gave her my wiggling flannel bundle, her eyes filled with tears. I hadn't closed the bathroom door before Maggie started to scream. I tried to hurry—I heard her cries over the roar of the bathroom fan. By the time I opened the door, I'd already begun apologizing for having left Chris with such a cranky newborn. By the time I reached her bedside, Maggie was silent.

"What happened?"

"I don't know," Chris said. "As soon as she heard your voice, she stopped crying."

Maggie lay still in Chris's arms, her head turned toward the bathroom door, her eyes searching intently for the source of my voice.

Then, it hit me. Maggie had been listening to my voice for months. She knew it, trusted it. Though she hadn't begun to recognize my face, she already knew my voice. My voice had calmed her fear. My voice had settled her displaced emotions.

Jesus says the same is true for us. While the Father brings us to birth, he whispers to us. Entices us. Calls us. By the time we are born again, we already know our Heavenly Father's voice. From somewhere deep inside, we recognize it. We trust it.

Jesus promises that we will know our Father's voice.

You've already heard it. Listen for it. Practice responding. As you do, you'll grow more and more confident about your ability to hear and respond. Your love relationship with your Heavenly Father will blossom. Responding to his voice is the secret to the Spirit-led life.

Prayer ideas

Ask your Heavenly Father for help in listening and responding to the Holy Spirit's voice. Ask the Spirit to make himself known to you this very day.

AND WHAT AM I— A TREE?

So I advise you to live according to your new life in the Holy Spirit. Then you won't be doing what your sinful nature craves. The old sinful nature loves to do evil, which is just opposite from what the Holy Spirit wants. And the Spirit gives us desires that are opposite from what the sinful nature desires. These two forces are constantly fighting each other, and your choices are never free from this conflict.

But when you are directed by the Holy Spirit, you are no longer subject to the law.

When you follow the desires of your sinful nature, your lives will produce these evil results: sexual immorality, impure thoughts, eagerness for lustful pleasure, idolatry, participation in demonic activities, hostility, quarreling, jealousy, outbursts of anger, selfish ambition, divisions, the feeling that everyone is wrong except those in your own little group, envy, drunkenness, wild parties, and other kinds of sin. Let me tell you again, as I have before, that anyone living that sort of life will not inherit the Kingdom of God.

But when the Holy Spirit controls our lives, he will produce this kind of fruit in us: love, joy, peace, patience, kindness, goodness, faithfulness, gentleness, and self-control. Here there is no conflict with the law.

Those who belong to Christ Jesus have nailed the passions and desires of their sinful nature to his cross and crucified them there. If we are living now by the Holy Spirit, let us follow the Holy Spirit's leading in every part of our lives. (Galatians 5:16–25)

Though Robert Louis Stevenson wrote *The Strange Case of Dr. Jekyll and Mr. Hyde* in 1885, the questions raised by his novel couldn't be more contemporary. In the story, Dr. Jekyll, aware of the war of good and evil within him, creates a potion to separate these two natures into two distinct personalities—the civilized Dr. Henry Jekyll and the lawless Mr. Edward Hyde.

At first his experiment is only an exploration of good and evil. With time though, Dr. Jekyll begins to enjoy the freedom and base living of Mr. Hyde. Frightened by Hyde's evil nature, Dr. Jekyll chooses never again to take the potion. Though he wants to live a controlled life, two months later Jekyll gives in to his urges. Once again Jekyll becomes Edward Hyde.

At the end of the story, believing that only death can free him from the evil Mr. Hyde, Jekyll kills himself. He leaves a note in which he explains his decision and his inability to resist the evil inside himself. Jekyll writes, "and it fell out with me, as it falls with so vast a majority of my fellows, that I chose the better part and was found wanting in the strength to keep to it."

Most humans would agree. We choose the best things, love, patience, kindness—but we find ourselves too weak to live up to our own expectations. So we try again. We try harder. We try differently. Or, like Jekyll, we give ourselves over to the Mr. Hyde inside of us and live a life of unrestrained evil. There is a better way.

Scripture tells us we don't have to live a life governed by our evil nature. Neither do we have to scrape and strive to cultivate good behavior. When we give control of our lives to the Holy Spirit, he produces bountiful fruit for us. We need not think it out, or fight it out, or waste precious energy as Jekyll did, trying to hold the tide against evil. The Holy Spirit promises to do the work for us, if only we will yield to his leading.

Every day we must choose to follow the leading of the Holy Spirit. We do this moment by moment, all through our day. We cultivate an awareness of his voice, and we learn to respond quickly and obediently to his direction. As we respond, we can rest knowing that he will produce the good things we long to see in our lives.

Prayer ideas

Which of these fruits do you most long to see flourishing in your life? Will you ask God to help you respond quickly to the Holy Spirit today?

OUT BEHIND
THE WOODSHED

"Why do you continue to invite punishment? Must you rebel forever? Your head is injured, and your heart is sick . . . I am sick of your sacrifices," says the LORD. "Don't bring me any more burnt offerings! I don't want the fat from your rams or other animals. . . . For your hands are covered with the blood of your innocent victims. Wash yourselves and be clean! Let me no longer see your evil deeds. Give up your wicked ways. Learn to do good. Seek justice. Help the oppressed. Defend the orphan. Fight for the rights of widows."

"Come now, let us argue this out," says the LORD. "No matter how deep the stain of your sins, I can remove it. I can make you as clean as freshly fallen snow. Even if you are stained as red as crimson, I can make you as white as wool. If you will only obey me and let me help you, then you will have plenty to eat. But if you keep turning away and refusing to listen, you will be destroyed by your enemies. I, the LORD, have spoken!" (Isaiah 1:5, 11–20)

For a while, my husband and I thought that perhaps one of our children would celebrate his sixteenth birthday in Alcatraz.

As a preschooler, whenever we went to a store with this little guy, he came home with something he'd stolen. Always busy, and very curious, he thought that storeowners had placed shelves down low just for him. He thought they wanted him to take all the goodies he could stuff in his little pockets.

We had all the normal parental talks. We explained about paying for things. We kept a much closer watch on him. Still, he came home with things we hadn't paid for. When we knew he understood the concept of stealing, we began adding consequences. Still, this child came home with items he'd picked up along the way.

I began frisking him every time we left a store. I made him take things back and apologize. I escalated the consequences for his stealing. Pretty soon, I cried whenever he got caught stealing.

Thank heaven, he finally got the message.

I'm sure that in the process, folks thought we'd been too hard on him—especially those who observed our struggle near the end. They might have thought us too punitive for such a young child. But in their single glimpse of our struggle, they would have missed the multiple times that a gentler approach hadn't solved our problem.

We escalated the consequences because we knew how desperately our son needed to learn the lesson. Had he continued on his own course, he might have ended up in serious trouble.

In the same way, our Heavenly Father knows exactly what we need to learn. He sees the direction our sin is taking us. He knows the danger we face. And like earthly parents who desperately want to protect their children from error, our Heavenly Father will go to great lengths to correct our course.

While this passage is found in the Old Testament, God's unchanging nature means that the passage still applies to us.

Notice three things about God from today's passage: First, God is not fooled by our outward performance. Though the Israelites went through the traditional religious motions, their hearts were full of evil. While they pretended to love God on the outside, they refused to let him influence their relationships with others. God measures our devotion to him by our behavior and our attitudes toward our fellowman.

God saw through their act, and he despised their pretense.

Second, God offers a solution for our relational problems. Punishment is not his first option. "Here, let me help you," he says. "Let me clean you from your sin." God doesn't sit in heaven shaking his head, and wondering why we don't behave. Instead, God wants to come alongside of us, and help us carry our burden. He wants to remove our sins, and give us the strength to live new and holy lives.

Third, God is willing to let us hurt if the hurt will help us change our mind. Just as my husband and I were willing to let our son hurt in order for him to learn his very important lesson about stealing, God is willing to do anything at all to teach us to change our ways.

God's love is so deep, his ways so wise, his knowledge so complete, that he will do anything to protect us from the greater harm.

Seems amazing doesn't it? God's correction—as painful as it sometimes can be—is also an expression of his divine love for us.

"Let me correct you," God offers. "I can save you from so much pain—if only you will let me correct you." Will you let him?

Prayer ideas

Think of ways you have ignored God's correction in the past twenty-four hours. Ask for forgiveness. Ask the Lord for help in your struggle against sin.

DAY 20

UNDER THE INFLUENCE

So be careful how you live, not as fools but as those who are wise. Make the most of every opportunity for doing good in these evil days. Don't act thoughtlessly, but try to understand what the Lord wants you to do. Don't be drunk with wine, because that will ruin your life. Instead, let the Holy Spirit fill and control you. Then you will sing psalms and hymns and spiritual songs among yourselves, making music to the Lord in your hearts. And you will always give thanks for everything to God the Father in the name of our Lord Jesus Christ. (Ephesians 5:15–20)

Years ago, at a social gathering, someone I trusted drank too much. She didn't stagger or slur her words. She might even have passed a police Breathalyzer test. She laughed and talked like everyone else in our group. Still, she was under the influence.

I had no idea she'd had too much to drink, until she said it.

In the midst of a lively conversation, while we discussed issues of politics and education, this woman betrayed a confidence—something about me that no one else in the group knew anything about. When she finished her little speech, she seemed quite proud of herself, as though she'd clearly explained things just as she meant to. She'd scored a hit. She'd put me in my place.

I was so stunned that I couldn't even respond. The crowd fell silent. Then, after long moments, thankfully someone changed the subject. Later, blinking back tears, I went for a long walk, trying to process what had happened. My hurt turned to anger. How could she say those things? What on earth made her think those words would be acceptable?

My husband joined me later, and we talked about it. "She didn't know what she was saying," he explained. "She didn't mean to say that. It was the beer talking."

For a long time, I didn't care who did the talking. The words had hurt just the same. They could not be taken back. I refused to accept any excuse. It took me several months to forgive her.

When alcohol takes over, our natural inhibitions disappear. We talk louder, laugh louder, and feel slightly invincible. We are under the influence. Alcohol takes over the control center for all our decisions—how fast we should drive, what we should say, and how we should say it. We lose our sense of caution, and agree to things we might never consider under normal circumstances.

These are the reasons I tell my children to avoid alcohol. I want them to make clear-headed decisions, especially in their teen years. I'd like them to live through their mistakes.

In a way, the Holy Spirit wants something completely different for us. Instead of clear-headed lives, he wants to be our control center. He wants us to live under his influence. He wants to decide what we should say, and to whom. He wants us to give all our inhibitions to him, so that he can produce the words, thoughts, and actions that accomplish God's will in our lives.

When you think of the damage done by someone under the influence of alcohol, you can imagine the healing power of one living under the influence of the Holy Spirit. How much encouragement, how much persuasion might we have when he has complete control? Can you imagine what it feels like to live so connected to the Holy Spirit that you respond to him with the same carelessness as one soaked in alcohol?

I want to live like that. I'm going to memorize this Scripture and see what happens as I seek to live under his influence. Will you join me?

Prayer ideas

Ask God to help you find ways to soak yourself in the influence of the Holy Spirit. Think of one thing that makes you resist this idea. Talk with God about your resistance.

CAN'T GET NO SATISFACTION

How grateful I am, and how I praise the Lord that you are concerned about me again. I know you have always been concerned for me, but for a while you didn't have the chance to help me. Not that I was ever in need, for I have learned how to get along happily whether I have much or little. I know how to live on almost nothing or with everything. I have learned the secret of living in every situation, whether it is with a full stomach or empty, with plenty or little. For I can do everything with the help of Christ who gives me the strength I need. (Philippians 4:10–13)

When our kids were younger, we often joined a group of families boating in the San Juan Islands of Washington State. During the nicest summer weather, large numbers of recreational boats travel in and among these small, densely forested islands. The largest boat in our flotilla capped off at twenty-one feet. When we docked, all five of our boats fit in a single slip at the Lopez Island Marina.

One morning in the islands, we agreed to meet at the dock before starting off on a picnic to a local marine park. Steve and I arrived early and loaded our respective boats. Then we stretched out to enjoy the sun and visit while we waited for our families. Our boats had docked in a slip beside a shiny new thirty-eight footer. Sparkling white in the summer sunshine, she looked beautiful bobbing in the water beside the dock.

"Sure is hard to be up here with all these boats," Steve said, pointing at the yacht.

"Makes you think you need one, doesn't it?" I laughed.

"I can't even afford the moorage on one," he said, "let alone the insurance, or the upkeep. But it'd sure be nice."

As we admired the yacht in silence, I felt a catch in my soul. Here in the most beautiful part of the world, enjoying good health, great weather, and a wonderful vacation with close friends, we both felt the insidious onset of dissatisfaction creeping into us.

Discontent. Greed. Suddenly, our boats weren't quite as nice. They didn't ride quite as comfortably. Our summer adventure together had turned slightly sour.

Envy. It drives the Kingdoms of the World. They call it "Keeping up with the Joneses." But in the Kingdom of God, envy will sap your joy. It will consume your energy. It will rob you of opportunities for loving and for being loved. It may even keep you from the joy of generosity, and the sheer thrill of giving away your most valuable stuff.

After twenty-seven years of kingdom living, I still struggle with contentment. There have been seasons in my life that I threw away mail-order catalogues as soon as they appeared in my mailbox. I didn't want to look at the latest fashions, or the newest computer gadgets. I didn't want to ogle the decorations in fashionable living rooms.

I refuse to be driven by what I don't have. I want to be grateful for the good things God has given me. For the good people I know, for the foods I enjoy, for the opportunities the Lord gives me. I want to cultivate a contented and grateful heart.

Kingdom living demands that believers cultivate new values. While the Kingdom of the World encourages us to accumulate, to lust after, to long for, the Kingdom of God tells us to learn the secret of contentment. Like so many kingdom values, our lives are richer when we practice contentment. Can you learn to be satisfied with what you have?

Prayer ideas

Contentment often springs from gratitude. Can you give thanks for the things God has given you? Can you ask God to help you give something away to someone who needs it?

OH LORD, IT'S HARD TO BE HUMBLE

Don't be selfish; don't live to make a good impression on others. Be humble, thinking of others as better than yourself. Don't think only about your own affairs, but be interested in others, too, and what they are doing.

Your attitude should be the same that Christ Jesus had. Though he was God, he did not demand and cling to his rights as God. He made himself nothing; he took the humble position of a slave and appeared in human form. And in human form he obediently humbled himself even further by dying a criminal's death on a cross. Because of this, God raised him up to the heights of heaven and gave him a name that is above every other name, so that at the name of Jesus every knee will bow, in heaven and on earth and under the earth, and every tongue will confess that Jesus Christ is Lord, to the glory of God the Father. (Philippians 2:3–11)

In 1999, our family spent Christmas in Guatemala where my husband does dentistry in a remote village hospital. I'd managed to avoid the trip for two years, under the pretense of staying home with our younger kids. But as the kids got older, my excuse vanished.

We arrived in Guatemala City after a grueling eighteen-hour trip, only to discover that my luggage hadn't arrived. We stayed in town an extra day, hoping for the missing luggage to catch up. When it didn't, we flew into the hills north of the city. Having no clean clothes, I had my husband buy a package of underwear for me in the village market, and one of the women at the mission lent me some clothes. For the first time in three days, I showered and put on clean clothes—dresses made from the homespun fabric of native Guatemalan women.

We'd barely arrived before I went on a guided tour of the hospital grounds. The next day, I taught rehabilitation techniques to nursing students, translated by the director of the mission. My exhaustion grew like water behind a dam.

I have to tell the truth—mission food was exceedingly simple. Our quarters had purified water that dripped into pitchers left for hours under the kitchen faucet. The town, built in city blocks where everyone's front door touched the outside walk, had to be the noisiest village in the world.

I couldn't sleep for the roving packs of dogs, the neighbor's radio, and the crowds of people walking directly outside our bedroom window. The village butcher, who lived on one side of our compound, kept all of his meat alive in the backyard until time to butcher. The noise continued twenty-four hours a day.

I'd packed earplugs, but they were stuck with my luggage, somewhere in south Texas. As I went without sleep, my attitude deteriorated. One night, I crawled into bed with my daughters, desperate for distance from the street noise. Full of self-pity, I cried myself to sleep.

On our last day there, Kim did ten hours of stand-up dentistry in a schoolroom outside of town. His patients sat in stackable chairs, leaning their heads back over piles of seed sacks. Most waited hours in eighty-five degree heat, only to have a decayed tooth extracted. As the sun set, the mission director drove me out to retrieve the dental team. When we arrived they were running late, and I waited for them outside. Eventually, his last patient, an old leather-faced, stooped woman, came out and walked toward me.

With tears running down her cheeks, she took my face in her hands, and spoke long words. The translator said, "She thanks you for bringing your husband to Guatemala." If only she knew.

On Christmas day, as I sat in my chair in our walled compound, I happened to glance down at the switch plate. Tiny ants, as thick as brownie dough, poured through the prong holes. It was the last straw for what I had dubbed the mission trip from hell. I went for a can of Raid and sprayed until the wall dripped with ant killer.

Near tears, I went outside to return the can to the janitor's closet. In the moonlit night, the Lord seemed to speak to me. I think his message went something like this: "You know, Bette, I didn't come to earth because it was beautiful or comfortable. I left heaven, remember? I am the light of the world, and I woke up in the dark of night, living among the animals. I didn't come because I wanted to come. I came because you needed me."

As those words settled in, I felt deep shame. I'd thought only of my own discomfort, my stuff, my clothes, my sleep, my home. I hadn't even considered the mission trip Jesus had made on my behalf. But the Lord wasn't finished with me.

"If I left heaven because you needed me, can't you leave Puyallup because these people need you too?"

I asked the Lord to forgive my attitude, and to create a new heart in me. I want to learn to be uncomfortable for the sake of others. I want to give without hesitation, without resentment. I want to have Jesus' attitude—that though he was God, he gave gladly and freely—thinking more about what I needed than what he rightly deserved.

Humility doesn't come naturally. In a world where self-esteem has become a cultural icon, God asks us to humble ourselves—to think of others as more important than ourselves. God wants to cultivate humility in you. Can you let him?

Prayer ideas

Ask God to help you see the ways your pride keeps you from helping others. Ask for eyes to see the real needs of people around you today.

DAY 23

WHO ME? A SERVANT?

Before the Passover celebration, Jesus knew that his hour had come to leave this world and return to his Father. He now showed the disciples the full extent of his love . . . Jesus knew that the Father had given him authority over everything and that he had come from God and would return to God. So he got up from the table, took off his robe, wrapped a towel around his waist, and poured water into a basin. Then he began to wash the disciples' feet and to wipe them with the towel he had around him . . .

After washing their feet, he put on his robe again and sat down and asked, "Do you understand what I was doing? You call me 'Teacher' and 'Lord' and you are right, because it is true. And since I, the Lord and Teacher, have washed your feet, you ought to wash each other's feet. I have given you an example to follow. Do as I have done to you. How true it is that a servant is not greater than the master. Nor are messengers more important than the one who sends them. You know these things—now do them! That is the path of blessing." (Excerpted from John 13:1–17)

I attended my first writer's conference seven years ago. Too excited for my own good, I spent days preparing for the trip. When I arrived, I found an entire collection of people just like me! Energized by so many other writers, and finding so much to learn, I couldn't sleep. I didn't eat well. On the third day, I paid the high price for my exuberance; I woke with a full-fledged migraine.

Undaunted, I took my medication and limped through the morning. By afternoon, the headache had grown—but I refused to give in. I seriously needed pain medication, but could hardly walk up the hill to my room. Then I met Dave. Driving by in his clattering Subaru, Dave offered me a ride.

"What are you doing?" I asked as I slid into the front seat.

"Oh just ferrying people up and down the hill. Some of these older ladies can't manage the steep path."

I stifled a chuckle. Dave, tall and weathered, had to be nearly seventy years old. "How long have you been doing this?"

"This?" He gave a little laugh and turned his dark brown eyes to mine. "This is what I do," he said. "I just come to drive people up and down the hill."

"Don't you go to classes?"

"Oh yeah. When there aren't any people left to drive, I go to class."

Dave waited while I got my medication, and then drove me back to the main meeting. With genuine gratitude, I thanked him. I'd barely closed the car door before he turned around with another load of passengers. It took me two days to discover that my chauffeur also served as president of Oregon Christian Writers.

In the Kingdom of this World, leaders expect deference, honor, special treatment. In the Kingdom of God, no matter what our position, we care for one another as servants. Where else would the president serve as driver for folks struggling up the steep campus footpaths? Only in the body of Christ.

Dave knew well the concept of foot washing—of serving others with the same dedication and commitment as hired help. Though he was president, he had a servant's heart—meeting needs with humility and kindness. The Kingdom of God demands that believers value a servant's heart. Can you become a servant?

Prayer ideas

Ask the Lord to show you what keeps you from having a servant's heart. Prayerfully commit to serving one person today.

ANYTHING BUT THAT!

But our bodies were not made for sexual immorality. They were made for the Lord, and the Lord cares about our bodies. And God will raise our bodies from the dead by his marvelous power, just as he raised our Lord from the dead. Don't you realize that your bodies are actually parts of Christ? Should a man take his body, which belongs to Christ, and join it to a prostitute? Never! And don't you know that if a man joins himself to a prostitute, he becomes one body with her? For the Scriptures say, "The two are united into one." But the person who is joined to the Lord becomes one spirit with him.

Run away from sexual sin! No other sin so clearly affects the body as this one does. For sexual immorality is a sin against your own body. Or don't you know that your body is the temple of the Holy Spirit, who lives in you and was given to you by God? You do not belong to yourself, for God bought you with a high price. So you must honor God with your body. (1 Corinthians 6:13–20)

In the first chapter of their book entitled, *Every Man's Battle: Winning the War on Sexual Temptation* (Waterbrook Press, 2000), Fred Stoeker and Stephen Arterburn tell this story: "Far from home and without any Christian underpinnings, I descended by small steps into a sexual pit. The first time I had sexual intercourse, it was with a girl I knew I would marry. The next time, it was with a girl I thought I would marry. The time after that, it was with a good friend that I might learn to love. Then it was with a female I barely knew, who simply wanted to see what sex was like. Eventually, I had sex with any-one at any time."

I couldn't make up a better illustration of the danger in sexual impurity. This man's experience shows the strong grip sexual sin can have in our lives. What began as a special circumstance (having sex with his fiancée) became a license for indulgence (having sex with any-one at all). In the end, this man found he had no restraint. With noth-ing more than time and repetition, this man had developed a well-worn sexual habit.

None of us is exempt from this temptation. The wall of sexual restraint can be breached in any of us. And in the end, the sins we think we control—control us.

Sexual sin involves more than intercourse outside of marriage. In our modern culture, sexual images and references inundate us. Television, movies, print media and the Internet provide ready access to pornography for anyone who wants them. Both men and women can fall into the trap.

In these settings, the appetite for sexual stimulation can be satis-fied in the sanctuary of the home, with complete anonymity. The effects of porn—even soft porn—can be both devastating and long last-ing. In his last public interview, convicted serial killer Ted Bundy con-fessed that pornography had fueled addiction for bigger and bigger sexual thrills.

It began, he explained, with magazines he found as a kid. Soon, the magazines weren't exciting anymore. Before he was out of high school, he had moved onto X-rated movies and prostitutes. Not long afterward, the soft-spoken law student from Tacoma, Washington, became our nation's most notorious killer.

No wonder, when talking about sexual temptation, the Scripture uses the verb *run*.

Sexual sin is a way of hurting yourself, the Bible says. No one would consider taking a knife to himself—every day cutting away parts of his flesh and throwing the chunks away. But when we give in to sexual sins, we throw away something far more important—parts of our soul.

God has paid the highest price for you, my friend. More priceless than a rare antique or a vintage wine, you have value beyond mere money. God paid for you with the blood of his son, Jesus Christ. He intends to live inside you—not as a summer home, or a vacation home—

but as a full-time resident. You belong to him—your body, your mind, and your soul. Every part of you must remain consecrated—set apart—for his use.

The Kingdom of the World views sex as nothing more than a natural expression of our humanity. People today expect to enjoy sex with anyone, at any time, without consequence. Our cultural disregard for sexual purity may make this Biblical concept even harder to grasp.

But God longs for us to experience his best. He created sex for us. As we remain sexually pure, we protect ourselves from powerful sexual addictions. We'll never experience the endless pull of pornography or illicit sex. We'll never know the pain of sexually transmitted disease or the emotional emptiness of sex outside of commitment.

In marriage, in the context of sexual purity, we enjoy the enormous satisfaction of healthy sexual expression with none of the devastating consequences.

Your sexuality is a gift from God. He planned for us to remain sexually pure—both for His glory and our good. No matter how you may have abused your sexuality in the past, you can start over. Today is the perfect day to choose a new path. Get help if you need it. Ask for prayer. Confess your temptation to a trusted friend. Don't let passivity rob you of the freedom you want to experience.

Will you commit yourself to sexual purity?

Prayer ideas

*T*alk to your Heavenly Father about your own sexual temptations. Ask for his guidance and strength to eliminate any influence that interferes with your purity.

THROW THE BOOK AT HIM, OFFICER!

Obey the government, for God is the one who put it there. All governments have been placed in power by God. So those who refuse to obey the laws of the land are refusing to obey God, and punishment will follow. For the authorities do not frighten people who are doing right, but they frighten those who do wrong. So do what they say, and you will get along well. The authorities are sent by God to help you. But if you are doing something wrong, of course you should be afraid, for you will be punished. The authorities are established by God for that very purpose, to punish those who do wrong.

So you must obey the government for two reasons: to keep from being punished and to keep a clear conscience. Pay your taxes, too, for these same reasons. For government workers need to be paid so they can keep on doing the work God intended them to do. Give to everyone what you owe them: Pay your taxes and import duties, and give respect and honor to all to whom it is due. (Romans 13:1–7)

I rarely listen to Dr. Laura, but one night with nothing else on the radio, I heard a funny story on her show. She read a letter from a father who'd been called by a police officer who held the man's son in custody. I didn't hear what trouble the boy had gotten himself into. But I did hear this excerpt from the letter:

"When the officer told me that he would release my son to my custody, I'll admit that I was relieved. *Whew*, I thought, *that was a close one.* But then I asked the policeman what would happen if he pressed charges against my son. He told me my son would probably have to wait two years to get his driver's license, and that he would probably have to go to court and be assigned some form of community service. I thought about that for a while, and realized how good that kind of trouble might be for my boy. 'Go ahead and charge him,' I told the officer. 'I think it might be the best thing that ever happened to him.'"

That father realized the danger of letting his son slip through this bit of trouble. Having the boy face his mistake and pay a reasonable price would help him grow into a mature and responsible individual. Though it was a tough choice, the father chose temporary discomfort in exchange for permanent maturity. He recognized the value of order and authority in our society.

Few of us are as wise. We mount radar detectors on our dashboards, hoping to ignore the speed limits. We hide receipts for lunch with friends in our business expense account. We buy equipment for home and deduct it from our business income tax. We resent our taxes, ridicule our politicians, and avoid contact with the police.

In the Kingdom of the World, it isn't popular to think of the government as being God's gift to us—an agent of his care.

But that's how God wants us to think. It will take some getting used to—driving the speed limit even when no one is watching, or obeying the traffic lights in the middle of the night. It won't be easy to pay my taxes without a stomachache. But loving God requires new values.

And if we ask, he will help us change our mind. Are you willing to let him try?

Prayer ideas

Ask God to show you ways that you resent government authority. Ask him to help you change your mind. Pray for the police and firemen in your community.

THE VALUE OF ONE

So Jesus used this illustration: "If you had one hundred sheep, and one of them strayed away and was lost in the wilderness, wouldn't you leave the ninety-nine others to go and search for the lost one until you found it? And then you would joyfully carry it home on your shoulders. When you arrived, you would call together your friends and neighbors to rejoice with you because your lost sheep was found. In the same way, heaven will be happier over one lost sinner who returns to God than over ninety-nine others who are righteous and haven't strayed away!

"Or suppose a woman has ten valuable silver coins and loses one. Won't she light a lamp and look in every corner of the house and sweep every nook and cranny until she finds it? And when she finds it, she will call in her friends and neighbors to rejoice with her because she has found her lost coin. In the same way, there is joy in the presence of God's angels when even one sinner repents." (Luke 15:3–10)

The human body has always fascinated me. In Physical Therapy school, we had many, many classes in anatomy. I loved learning about bones and muscles, organs and systems. In fact, we studied skeletal anatomy more extensively than medical students.

What surprised me though, was this statement by one of my professors. "Now, as we study these parts of the body, I want to make one thing perfectly clear. In this class, we talk only about structure and function. Even when the structure of an organ seems to be ideal for the function of the organ, we will not use the word *design* in this class. As you know, the word *design* implies the presence of a designer."

This teacher clearly wanted to avoid the possibility of a creator God. After all, if design implies the presence of a designer, then wouldn't the designer have some rights concerning the thing designed?

My professor didn't want to face the fact that she might have an obligation to the designer of her soul. Instead, by considering the whole body a fluke of survival, she managed to avoid the issue entirely. And, to maintain her comfort zone, she insisted that all her students speak the same language.

In spite of her objection, the truth is that all human structure shows brilliance in design, function, and structure. In fact the wonder of it would fill an entire volume. Believing that the human body came about by chance takes more faith than believing in a loving designer!

The theory of evolution is a safe way to keep all of us from answering to our Creator. But at the same time, the theory reduces us to nothing more than one small link in the survival of our species. Our lives are governed only by the rules of genetic happenstance. In Darwinian theory, our only purpose is to survive until we reproduce, guaranteeing a stronger gene pool.

The idea that you are nothing more than a cog in the great evolutionary wheel would make anyone depressed. No wonder young people commit suicide! Most humans long to believe that we are important, and that what we do matters.

In this passage, Jesus expresses the enormous value of the human soul. If a shepherd values his sheep, Jesus says, how much more does God value the human he has designed? Our Creator will go to any limit to find and recover a single lost soul. Each human is important. Each has enormous worth. And because every soul is important to him, every soul becomes important to us. The Kingdom of God values every individual.

At one time, you were the lost soul he was looking for. If God would go to so much trouble for one soul, would you?

Prayer ideas

Ask God to help you see people as individual souls today. Ask him for help in expressing his love for just one individual.

A Little White Lie

These wicked people are born sinners, even from birth they have lied and gone their own way. (Psalm 58:3)

The Lord hates cheating, but he delights in honesty. . . . Good people are guided by their honesty; treacherous people are destroyed by their dishonesty. (Proverbs 11:1, 3)

There are six things the Lord hates—no, seven things he detests: haughty eyes, a lying tongue, hands that kill the innocent, a heart that plots evil, feet that race to do wrong, a false witness who pours out lies, a person who sows discord among brothers. (Proverbs 6:16–19)

When I attended Physical Therapy school, we learned a little bit about the process physicians use to diagnose a patient's illness. The physical exam generates the information a patient brings with him to our clinic. In order to understand the information, we studied the process.

Before a physician treats his patient, he must make an accurate diagnosis. Though many disease processes share similar symptoms, the mechanism of the various diseases and their treatment are markedly different.

For instance, a patient may appear at his doctor's office with a complaint of severe headaches. Does he have a tumor in the brain, or does he suffer from migraines? Does he have a pinched nerve in the neck, or a chronic blood sugar problem?

How can the doctor treat the headache until he understands the cause? He begins the sorting process by taking an accurate history. With gentle questions, he lets his patient tell him everything he needs to know about the problem. When did the headaches begin? Where exactly is the pain? How long does a headache last? Does nausea or dizziness accompany the pain? What time of day do they occur? Did something happen—an injury, a fall—just before the patient started having headaches?

The answers to these questions guide the physician to the clues he must study during the physical exam. Next, he pokes, he prods, he tests, he listens . . . to the heart, the lungs, and the gut. When he has looked at all he can see, he asks more questions. These he directs to the body itself by testing the blood, the muscles, the nerves, or the bones.

Finally, when the test results are complete, he considers all the information he has gathered. Only then can the physician make an educated guess as to the cause of the patient's problem. Only then, when the doctor believes that he knows the diagnosis, does he begin to consider a solution. Without the correct diagnosis, his treatment cannot succeed.

I wonder if this is why God values honesty so much? Of course, God is truth. He speaks only truth. And of course he wants us to grow to be like him. God will not tolerate dishonesty. But I believe his commitment reveals more than that. To me, his desire for honesty is based in his desire for our ultimate healing.

Honesty is to God what as an accurate diagnosis is to the physician. Though God knows how desperately sick our hearts have become, without honesty, we have no hope for a cure. Without honesty, we can never admit our need for God.

Suppose your words hurt your spouse. Unless your spouse is honest, you may miss your opportunity to seek forgiveness and mend the rift in the relationship. Suppose your addiction to pornography covers up your desperate fear of close and genuine relationships. Unless you admit—are honest about—your illness (pornography), you have no hope of finding healing in your relationships.

And so it is with every kind of spiritual illness we face. Only honesty leads to a correct diagnosis. Only a correct diagnosis leads to a cure. When we try to blame others for our guilt, we move away from healing. When we make excuses for our misdeeds, we avoid the diagnosis.

My relationship with God depends on my ability to be honest. I must be able to say, "I was wrong." Or, "I am afraid." Or, "I am angry." Or, "I don't believe you, Lord."

My relationship with people depends on honesty too. I must be able to say, "I appreciate your kindness." Or, "I was jealous." Or, "I felt left out." Or, "I stole it." Or, "I need you."

In the Kingdom of the World, we accept half-truths as a necessary evil. We protect ourselves from accountability with lies and innuendo. If the cause is important enough, a lie becomes acceptable.

The Kingdom of God demands nothing less than complete honesty from us—in every area. Only through honesty can we experience the healing touch of God's love, forgiveness, and empowering.

If we hope for healing, we must cling to the truth.

Prayer ideas

Think about your relationships with people. In what ways have you been dishonest? Can you talk to God about your dishonesty? Can you make a commitment to honesty? Ask God to help you keep your commitment.

SPIRITUAL NAKEDNESS

How terrible it will be for you teachers of religious law and you Pharisees. Hypocrites! You are so careful to clean the outside of the cup and the dish, but inside you are filthy—full of greed and self-indulgence! Blind Pharisees! First wash the inside of the cup, and then the outside will become clean, too. (Matthew 23:25, 26)

Someone I love struggles with anorexia. While painfully, dangerously thin, she continues her destructive lifestyle. With less than five percent body fat, her bones poke out behind sallow skin. Still, she exercises endlessly. Her empty refrigerator holds only bottled water. She almost never eats with other people. When she does manage to eat a regular meal, she heads to the bathroom and makes herself vomit.

My friend never intended to become this way. She wanted to be healthy. She wanted to appear attractive. She never intended to live the nightmare that now holds her captive. But somewhere along the way, she valued her outward appearance so much that she became willing to do anything to keep it up—no matter how unhealthy—no matter how dangerous. What she saw in the mirror became more important to her than the risky and bizarre behaviors that keep her looking that way. She has chosen the outside over the inside. Now that her behaviors are habitual, only a miracle will set her free.

I, too, am tempted to let outward appearances dictate my behavior. Writers are often asked to speak at conferences or for small groups.

Sometimes, I teach classes for other writers. As the speaking date approaches, I worry about my appearance. I get a haircut, plan my wardrobe, and hope to lose a few pounds. I've even thought about making a new dress before a special event, though I know that sewing will take time away from my preparation.

Sometimes, when I'm the guest at a large gathering, I find myself imagining what I must look like to other people. I worry about whether I'm being kind enough, or friendly enough, or spiritual enough. Why do I do that?

I wonder if I find it easier to keep up the image than to become the person I ought to be? Is it easier to fake friendliness than to learn to care for other people? Is it easier to appear spiritual than to let the Lord chip away at my hard and resistant heart?

Appearances are always easier.

The "big shots" of Jesus' day had the same problem. They thought if they looked holy on the outside, no one would ever know what kind of people they were on the inside. They thought if they prayed in public, paraded their generosity, and demonstrated their spiritual understanding—no one would ever know the difference. No one would realize that their Oscar-winning performance left them spiritually bankrupt.

The Kingdom of the World always focuses on the outside. Keep up the image. Buy the clothes. Drive the car. Get the girl.

The Kingdom of God warns us against this foolish mistake. Make the inside of your lives your first priority. Value and cultivate a genuine heart. By all means do this before you start teaching others in Bible class. Don't present a false spirituality to others. Remember! Though you may fool others, you will never fool Jesus.

I often repeat a little mantra to myself. Inside first! Inside first! Inside first! It helps to remind me of what the Lord desires. He wants me to clean the inside first.

Prayer ideas

*T*ake a moment during your prayer time to ask the Lord to examine your heart. Listen to his evaluation, and ask him for help to make the changes he desires.

GIVE WHAT?

Remember this—a farmer who plants only a few seeds will get a small crop. But the one who plants generously will get a generous crop. You must each make up your own mind as to how much you should give. Don't give reluctantly or in response to pressure. For God loves the person who gives cheerfully. And God will generously provide all you need. Then you will always have everything you need and plenty left over to share with others. As the Scriptures say,

"Godly people give generously to the poor.
Their good deeds will never be forgotten."

For God is the one who gives seed to the farmer and then bread to eat. In the same way, he will give you many opportunities to do good, and he will produce a great harvest of generosity in you. Yes, you will be enriched so that you can give even more generously. And when we take your gifts to those who need them, they will break out in thanksgiving to God. So two good things will happen—the needs of the Christians in Jerusalem will be met, and they will joyfully express their thanksgiving to God. You will be glorifying God through your generous gifts. For your generosity to them will prove that you are obedient to the Good News of Christ. And they will pray for you with deep affection because of the wonderful grace of God shown through you. (2 Corinthians 9:6–14)

I know a man who, at the end of every year, writes large checks to his favorite Christian ministries. In each envelope he includes a little note of encouragement to the folks who do God's work in his place. He cries as he writes the notes.

People who know him would never suspect that he is able to give away large sums of money. He does not dress well, or drive a fancy car. He does not take expensive vacations. He lives in an ordinary neighborhood; his children attend public school. Only the recipients know about his benevolence.

Though he doesn't flaunt his money, this man is very generous with God's work. I believe that his generosity has brought many blessings into his life—not all of them financial. He has a stable family. His children love the Lord. His adult children seem to be headed in mature and responsible directions.

I know a woman who gives her work away for the various ministries of the church. She doesn't work outside the home; she doesn't need to. But her time and energy and talents are freely given to any ministry who needs them. She tells others that when she gives away what God has given her, her relationship with God flourishes. She has a soft spot when it comes to the things of God. Her generosity isn't financial, but it's just as genuine.

Generosity—the ability to let go of the things we possess and the willingness to share whatever we have with the Kingdom of God—isn't a natural trait. In fact, in the Kingdom of the World, we're taught to horde, to protect, to keep.

The Kingdom of God values generosity. It's a change made deep in the heart of believers. Some who begin this faith walk have no trouble giving themselves and their things away. Others of us have to work at learning to let go. We have to learn to trust that God, who owns all things, will keep his promise to provide for our needs. I've had to struggle with this one. But I'm learning. He promises to give generously to those who give.

In the process, I'm learning to hold money and things, time and talents, loosely. I'm learning to listen carefully for the voice of the Lord. When he whispers, "Give," I'm learning to obey. Can you?

Prayer ideas

*T*alk to God about the things that keep you from being generous. Ask him to show you something you could give away today.

You Want Me to Do What?

And now, dear brothers and sisters, we give you this command with the authority of our Lord Jesus Christ: Stay away from any Christian who lives in idleness and doesn't follow the tradition of hard work we gave you. For you know that you ought to follow our example. We were never lazy when we were with you. We never accepted food from anyone without paying for it. We worked hard day and night so that we would not be a burden to any of you. It wasn't that we didn't have the right to ask you to feed us, but we wanted to give you an example to follow. Even while we were with you, we gave you this rule: "Whoever does not work should not eat." Yet we hear that some of you are living idle lives, refusing to work and wasting time meddling in other people's business. In the name of the Lord Jesus Christ, we appeal to such people—no, we command them: Settle down and get to work. Earn your own living. (2 Thessalonians 3:6–12)

I'm amazed at the number of advertisements on radio and television these days that promise to make the gullible public into millionaires. You've heard ads like these:

- "I'll teach you to make millions in real estate."
- "I can show you how to trade commodities without risk."
- "My simple methods can make you richer than you ever dared to dream. You can live the life you were meant to live."

Get rich quick. It certainly isn't a new philosophy. Men have forever fallen for schemes designed to make them instantly wealthy. This hope fueled the San Francisco gold rush, and the stock market crash in 1929. This same hope fuels sales for lottery tickets, the action at gambling casinos, and the lust for hot stock tips. But what lies behind the hope?

Isn't part of the enticement the idea that wealthy people are free from work?

And then what do they do? How do they spend their time? Are idle people contented people? How would it feel to have so much of your work taken from you that you have nothing left to do but play? Is there such a thing as too much play?

If anyone might expect payment for his ministry, it would be Paul. Instead though, Paul worked days (he made tents) and did kingdom work after hours. Paul did this to show us the right way to live. He earned his own way. He refused to burden anyone.

In the Kingdom of the World, idleness is good. Wealth is admired. But as we look around us, we see a startling number of people falling behind economically. Some are without work. Others are homeless. Many, thanks to easy credit, are living a comfortable life as they spend far more than they earn, week after week, year after year. Eventually heavy debt promises to crush their relationships and demand its final toll.

Though Paul's admonishment won't solve all our money problems, for most of us, it would help us a great deal.

Paul encourages us to value hard work. Refuse to be a burden for others. Pay your own way—even if you must scrimp and save and struggle to do so. As you experience financial freedom, you will find other parts of your life blessed as well.

Hard work is a kingdom ethic. Begin now to cultivate the value of hard work.

Prayer ideas

Talk with God about your work ethic. Do you struggle with laziness? Do you expect others to support you? Ask God to reveal the changes you might make to value work as he does.

THE TRAIL GUIDE

For the word of God is full of living power. It is sharper than the sharpest knife, cutting deep into our innermost thoughts and desires. It exposes us for what we really are. Nothing in all creation can hide from him. Everything is naked and exposed before his eyes. This is the God to whom we must explain all that we have done. (Hebrews 4:12, 13)

I am but a foreigner here on earth; I need the guidance of your commands. Don't hide them from me! . . . Your word is a lamp for my feet and a light for my path. (Psalm 119:19, 105)

An *Esquire* magazine article, "The Lost Boys," tells the tragic story of two young backcountry mountain bike enthusiasts. Chris and Mark arrived in Moab, Utah, on August 4, 1995. In spite of 105 degree temperatures, they looked forward to a three-hour ride in the Slickrock Canyonland. Each boy carried two water bottles and a fanny pack full of energy bars. They planned to be back in town in time for dinner.

Neither of them imagined that some tourist would steal a trail marker for a souvenir.

On their way back down the canyon, they missed a single, unmarked turn. Instead of heading for the safety of the highway parking lot, the two boys found themselves trapped in a maze of cliffs and canyons called The Fins. Realizing their predicament, the boys abandoned their bikes and walked for miles. Their bodies were found one week later, on a cliff hundreds of feet above the rushing water of a nearby river. They died of dehydration.

Of course, if the boys carried more water they might not have died. And, they wouldn't have gotten lost if the trail marker hadn't been stolen. But most importantly, they would have made it safely to their car if they'd only taken along a trail map.

They needed to know where they were and how to get back. They couldn't depend on some inborn sense of direction. They couldn't count on someone else to show them the way. They should have carried a map; but they'd chosen to go out into dangerous territory without one.

The same is true for us. Before you made a commitment to Christ, you may have thought of the Bible as some dusty old volume, perched high on your grandmother's bookshelf. Maybe you tried to read it, but couldn't make any sense of it. It seemed confusing and boring. God meant the Bible for believers. Until you believe, reading the Bible is like trying to read and understand your neighbor's mail. No wonder it seems confusing. Try again!

As of right now the Bible—God's book for you—is your trail map through dangerous and unfamiliar territory. It will keep you safe from deadly cliffs and difficult terrain. It will show you where to find spiritual food and water. It will guide you through hostile territory to a safe place. But you must read it, trust it, and act on it.

The Bible is your living travel guide. Don't leave home without it!

Prayer ideas

Ask God to show you how you can incorporate some Bible time into your everyday life. Ask him to help you commit to reading the Bible all the way through in the next year.

Oops, Where'd You Put the House?

"So why do you call me 'Lord,' when you won't obey me? I will show you what it's like when someone comes to me, listens to my teaching and then obeys me. It is like a person who builds a house on a strong foundation laid upon the underlying rock. When the floodwaters rise and break against the house, it stands firm because it is well built. But anyone who listens and doesn't obey is like a person who builds a house without a foundation. When the floods sweep down against that house, it will crumble into a heap of ruins." (Luke 6:46–49)

Years ago, we celebrated my parents' wedding anniversary near Mt. Baker. In honor of their fifty-five years together, my brothers managed to travel back to Washington for the festivities. With so many guests, my brother Bill borrowed travel trailers and cabins from friends.

Two of my brothers and their wives stayed in a vacation home perched high above a river not far from our campground. They told me the view was spectacular. From the A-frame, perched on an outcropping above Sandy Creek, they could see far upriver. Across the river, a wide valley spread away into the mountains. The spot boasted great fishing, frequent visits by deer, and an occasional bear.

My family stayed in a travel trailer closer to the festivities. For that reason, I never got to see the cabin. I felt a little cheated.

A few years later, the vacation home washed down into Sandy Creek. I called Bill and asked him to explain what happened. It started with heavy logging upstream from the cabin. Somehow debris found its way into the river, blocking the channel. Later, heavy snowfall was followed immediately by a warm front and inches of rain.

Not only did the rain melt the accumulated snow, but so much water fell so quickly, that it backed up behind the debris, building pressure on the riverbank. Eventually, the bank collapsed and water flowed around the debris. In the new channel, rushing water destroyed additional riverbank, until at last the river course lay more than two hundred feet from its original channel below and in front of the cabin.

In the process of changing course, the famous vacation home and three or four others fell into the river. Not only did the river claim the homes, but it took the land and road behind them as well. In the end, nothing at all was left of the original property. It simply vanished. Only the river remained.

The loss of the home devastated the owner. He loved the place, treasured the seclusion and the beauty of the river. When he bought it, he couldn't imagine that little Sandy Creek could cause such rampant destruction. With his home so far away from the river, it seemed perfectly safe.

It's the same with believers. We hear the words of God and choose to go our own way, believing that we can't be in any real danger. Disobedience feels perfectly safe. We rationalize that we've positioned ourselves far enough away from the river to avoid destruction.

We fill the air with excuses. We aren't committing adultery—we're just friends. I'm not stealing from work—just borrowing. I'm not quitting church—just taking a little break. But just like the house built on sand, our disobedience leaves us vulnerable. By disobeying God's Word, we build on an unsteady foundation. When the rains come—and they will—we find our house washed downstream.

So, the choice is ours. Will you build on the shaky ground of disobedience? Or on the strong foundation of God's Word? Where will you choose to live?

Prayer ideas

Ask God to help you be ruthlessly honest with yourself today. Consider the major parts of your life—family, church, God; have you begun to live by Biblical principles? Can you ask God to help you make the needed changes?

WATCH THAT STEP!

Then God instructed the people as follows: "I am the LORD your God, who rescued you from slavery in Egypt.

"Do not worship any other gods besides me.

"Do not make idols of any kind, whether in the shape of birds or animals or fish. You must never worship or bow down to them, for I, the LORD your God, am a jealous God . . .

"Do not misuse the name of the LORD your God. The LORD will not let you go unpunished if you misuse his name.

"Remember to observe the Sabbath day by keeping it holy. Six days a week are set apart for your daily duties and regular work, but the seventh day is a day of rest dedicated to the LORD your God . . . For in six days the LORD made the heavens, the earth, the sea, and everything in them; then he rested on the seventh day. That is why the LORD blessed the Sabbath day and set it apart as holy.

"Honor your father and mother. Then you will live a long, full life in the land the LORD your God will give you.

"Do not murder.

"Do not commit adultery.

"Do not steal.

"Do not testify falsely against your neighbor.

"Do not covet your neighbor's house. Do not covet your neighbor's wife, male or female servant, ox or donkey, or anything else your neighbor owns." (Exodus 20:1–17)

One summer, our daughter worked at the conference center in Cannon Beach, Oregon. There she found herself surrounded by stunning vistas of the Pacific Ocean, best seen from trails through the coastal woods. In such a beautiful location, all the kids spent time hiking. When our family visited her, she gave us directions to one of her favorite sites.

Later that week, as Molly worked, we set off to find the unmarked trail to a spectacularly beautiful outcropping, hundreds of feet over crashing waves.

As soon as we climbed out of our car, we heard water breaking on the rocks far below the highway. We left the car and walked through a steep field of wildflowers and down into a thin forest. At last we came to the edge of a rock cliff.

Molly's descriptions didn't do justice to the raw beauty we found. From that outcropping, the ocean was framed by the bare trunks of giant spruce. At the edge of the precipice, a basalt cliff face dropped vertically into the foaming sea. The view absolutely took away my breath.

Our only problem was that the viewing area sat too far away from the edge to get a picture of both the cliff and the waves. While I stood mesmerized, my husband, who loves photography, stepped over the little fence designed to keep us a safe distance from the drop-off. Moments later I spotted him, crawling on his belly toward the edge, camera in hand, framing the perfect snapshot.

The fear that twisted my stomach hurt all the way to my knees.

I followed behind, blinded by terror. "Honey," I called, struggling to keep my voice from trembling. "Please come away from the edge. I'm so frightened it hurts."

He laughed, and reassured me. "I'm fine here."

It didn't look fine to me. It looked dangerous. Terrified, I wanted to keep everyone else away from that precarious edge. Unable to stop Kim, I turned back up the hill to discover my children climbing over the safety fence. Just as I opened my mouth to shout, my voice caught in my throat.

What I saw choked the words in my mouth. From where they played, they had no clue of what I'd seen. They didn't share my point of view. Unaware, they skipped along the grass above the ocean playing teenaged games with one another. They felt completely safe—nearly twenty feet from the edge of the cliff.

It looked very different from my vantage point. Just under their feet, the cliff had been completely eaten away. Whether by erosion of rain or wind, I could not tell. But what looked to them like a solid grass play area was actually a fragile ledge of sandstone, covered by a thin layer of grass. The whole weakened layer hung gingerly—waiting to crumble hundreds of feet onto the rocks below—with them teasing and chasing one another on top.

Needless to say, I found my voice.

Some people view the restrictions of God as his deliberate effort to thwart our fun. It's almost as if he wants to keep us from the best views, the most exhilarating lifestyles. Today's Scripture includes what most people call the "Ten Commandments." They are by no means the only restrictions God puts on those who lead the faith life. There are many others.

I like to think of God's restrictions as his way of saving us from a terrible fall, and a deadly end. He sees dangers we cannot. In his divine love, he places a fence far away from the cliff. "Go no further," he says, desiring to protect us from the harm on the other side.

How do you look at the restrictions you find in the Word of God? Do you view them as evidence of his loving protection? Will you step over the fence, or stay away from the edge?

Prayer ideas

Ask God to show you how you view the restrictions in the Word of God. Ask him to help you see his Word in a brand new way.

WHAT DROUGHT?

Oh, the joys of those who do not follow the advice of the wicked, or stand around with sinners, or join in with scoffers. But they delight in doing everything the Lord wants; day and night they think about his law. They are like trees planted along the riverbank, bearing fruit each season without fail. Their leaves never wither, and in all they do, they prosper. But this is not true of the wicked. They are like worthless chaff, scattered by the wind. They will be condemned at the time of judgment. Sinners will have no place among the godly. For the Lord watches over the path of the godly, but the path of the wicked leads to destruction. (Psalm 1)

My mother's parents homesteaded in Whitman County, Washington, ten miles outside of Pullman. My father grew up in the same town, and graduated from Washington State University. So, when my daughter chose to go to WSU, in the far southeastern corner of our state, I didn't feel as overwhelmed as most parents who've never even seen Pullman. Every summer of my childhood, I made the long trip from Whidbey Island to Pullman to visit family. I think I could drive across Washington State with my eyes closed.

Still, as many times as I've made the trip—and we've done it even more frequently with Molly there—I've never gotten used to the high desert country east of the Cascade mountains. On the way to Pullman, we travel for nearly one hundred miles through the most arid, useless land anywhere in the United States.

In the summer, the oppressive heat forces travelers to drive at night or in the early morning. In the fall, sagebrush, just like that in old western movies, blows across the highway. Only recently has irrigation from the Columbia River begun to reclaim these millions of acres for agriculture. Now, instead of rocks and sagebrush, you see endless plots of wheat, alfalfa and onions. Black pipes, hundreds of yards long, stand five feet above the ground as self-traveling irrigation systems turn desert into farmland.

Still, irrigation has not yet reached the entire high desert. Where the irrigation systems stop, the desert begins again. Mile after mile of rocks and scrub pass by. And then, when you least expect it, the endlessly straight highway makes a gentle turn and starts down a small canyon. On the right, in the middle of nowhere, is the village of Washtucna.

With only three hundred residents, Washtucna sits just off the main highway. Even in passing, the town appears to have no more than ten or twelve homes along its main street. A drive-in and a gas station serve passing motorists.

But what strikes me every time I make this trip is the startling sight of lush vegetation in the middle of this endless desert. This small town sits under the cool shade of giant cottonwood and locust trees which seem to spring up out of desert sand. I've always wondered where the water came from. My map marks no river running through town. Today, I called the Community Church in Washtucna and asked what brings water to the trees.

"Natural springs—a whole series of them," Dennis answered me. "Washtucna was an Indian watering place even before the first white settlers arrived."

Those trees flourish in the middle of the desert because, like the trees in Psalm 1, they have their feet planted by the water. Though the area around them gets little rainfall, they have an endless supply of water; it comes up out of the ground to nourish them.

In the midst of barren land, the cottonwoods flourish.

We can be just like those trees. When our spiritual feet are planted in the Word of God, we have refreshment and nourishment, even when everyone around us thirsts for water. While we will experience drought, we will never suffer the consequences of it. Our roots go down more deeply than our troubles.

We will remain fruitful, even in times of adversity. We'll prosper, even as others fail. Though the rains may not come, our leaves will remain green and healthy. Our prosperity comes from knowing and doing the will of God. A simple recipe for prosperity, isn't it?

No stocks to buy. No magic formulas. No infomercials. Knowing and doing the will of God will bring us all the refreshment and fruitfulness we'll ever need.

Will you commit to doing the will of God?

Prayer ideas

*I*s there something you know that God wants you to do? What is it? Have you asked him to help you do it? What small change could you make today that might demonstrate your commitment to obedient living?

✝ ✝ ✝ DAY 35 ✝ ✝ ✝

WATCH THAT
NEXT TURN!

I don't want you to forget, dear brothers and sisters, what happened to our ancestors in the wilderness long ago. . . . These events happened as a warning to us, so that we would not crave evil things, as they did or worship idols as some of them did. . . . And we must not engage in sexual immorality as some of them did . . . Nor put Christ to the test as some of them did, . . . And don't grumble as some of them did, for that is why God sent his angel of death to destroy them. All these events happened to them as examples for us. They were written down to warn us, who live at the time when this age is drawing to a close. If you think you are standing strong be careful, for you too, may fall into the same sin. (Excerpted from 1 Corinthians 10:1–12)

Skiing is an expensive sport, especially for a family of six. So, when our kids were little, in order to defray our expenses, both my husband and I taught ski lessons at various ski schools here in the Northwest. In exchange for our two-hour lessons, we both received free lift tickets and a little pocket money.

Teaching got us up on the slopes every week, and kept us growing as skiers. Occasionally during those years, we took weekend trips to destination ski areas. One year, Kim and I visited Whistler Mountain in

British Columbia, where a local guide took us down a little used route she promised would be a great ride. "It's a little secluded, though. You'll have to stick with me," she said as she zipped away.

She kept her promise. Moments later we were skiing on the sweetest snow—fresh and light. When we got to the chair lift she said, "Well, now you can tell everyone you've skied a World Cup run."

I couldn't believe it. On the way up in the chair, I took another, more critical look at the slope. What would it be like to ride that same hill at seventy or eighty miles an hour? I tried to imagine the courage it must take to let your skis go downhill at that speed. I remembered watching our own athletes, standing in the starting gate of the Olympic Downhill competition, swaying as they envisioned the racecourse behind closed eyelids. I remembered seeing them as they watched the other racers, concentrating on every turn, watching for changes in the snow, or wear on the surface, or for unexpected changes in terrain.

You see, in the Olympic Downhill, each competitor only gets one chance at the hill—one breathtakingly fast, tooth-rattling run down the hill. For ski racers, time is everything, but only if they make it down the hill alive.

Living the life of faith is a bit like racing an Olympic Downhill. We only get one chance. By watching those who race before us, we can tweak the odds against us. We can identify the things that trip others going down the same run. We can plan our route to avoid their mistakes. We can visualize making the run with confidence, finishing with success.

God gave the Old Testament to us as a gift. He meant it to be our training video, so to speak, designed to help us succeed. By reading about other believers, we can identify their mistakes. We can plan a different route through the temptations of life. We can learn about our Heavenly Father and the abundant resources he has available to help us on our way.

We only get one run at the life of faith. Though no one times us, others watch. Your brothers and sisters in the Lord cheer as you clear each gate. They hope for you, train with you, and help you all they can. But in the end, it's your race. Will you learn from the training video of the Old Testament?

Prayer ideas

*A*sk Jesus to open your eyes as you read the Old Testament. Ask him to show you something about God that is new to you. Ask him to show you Old Testament principles that will enhance your life today.

ONE OF THE FAMILY

Those who believed what Peter said were baptized and added to the church—about three thousand in all. They joined with the other believers and devoted themselves to the apostles' teaching and fellowship, sharing in the Lord's Supper and in prayer.

A deep sense of awe came over them all, and the apostles performed many miraculous signs and wonders. And all the believers met together constantly and shared everything they had. They sold their possessions and shared the proceeds with those in need. They worshiped together at the Temple each day, met in homes for the Lord's Supper, and shared their meals with great joy and generosity—all the while praising God and enjoying the goodwill of all the people. And each day the Lord added to their group those who were being saved. (Acts 2:41–47)

Is there any encouragement from belonging to Christ? Any comfort from his love? Any fellowship together in the Spirit? Are your hearts tender and sympathetic? Then make me truly happy by agreeing wholeheartedly with each other, loving one another, and working together with one heart and purpose. Don't be selfish; don't live to make a good impression on others. Be humble, thinking of others as better than yourself. Don't think only about your own affairs, but be interested in others, too, and what they are doing. (Philippians 2:1–4)

I've nearly finished reading a book about Lance Armstrong. In the biography, Lance, a three-time winner of the *Tour de France,* and winner of the prestigious Thrift Drug Triple Crown, talks openly about his professional bicycle racing career and his battle with testicular cancer. Though I've never given much consideration to the pro bike circuit before, I've become more interested now that I ride.

In his book, *It's Not About the Bike: My Journey Back to Life* (Berkley, 2000), Lance explains the value of teamwork in racing. "On any team, each rider has a job, and is responsible for a specific part of the race." Some of the slower riders pull the group up hills. They're responsible to block the wind for the riders behind them, conserving the faster riders' energy. By riding in a group, they protect their principal riders from the most perilous parts of the race.

On a steep climb, following behind a rider—letting the lead rider block the wind—can save 30 percent of the energy for the man in the rear. On a windy day, riding behind a teammate might save 50 percent of the energy it would take to ride in the lead.

Lance writes, "Every team needs guys who are sprinters, guys who are climbers, guys willing to do the dirty work. It was very important to recognize the effort of each person involved—and not to waste it."

Early in his career, Lance ignored the teamwork involved in racing. Often, he refused to ride with the group. In the end, he found himself spent and unable even to place in races he might have won. Lance began his career with a "me only" attitude. Once he changed his thinking, he started winning.

In a way, the body of Christ must learn to think like a team of professional bike riders. We must learn to have the same selfless devotion to the cause—winning the race for Jesus Christ. Some of us will pull up the hill. Some of us will sprint and others of us will do the dirty work to protect the lead rider. Few of us will ever cross the finish line in the lead.

But just as Lance did, we must learn that when the team wins, we win.

In today's Bible passage, we see the same sense of selflessness, the same sense of team play operating in the church in Jerusalem. They shared their possessions with a striking generosity. More than sharing their stuff, though, they shared their lives. They ate together, prayed together, and worshiped together. They relinquished their individual plans in order to spend time with the body of Christ. It seems as if all the individuals of the church had blended into a single entity, sharing one purpose—one life.

Individuals in the church aren't all alike—we don't look the same, talk the same, or think the same. But we are instructed to become like-minded. This means we have the same zeal for the work of the kingdom. We have the same willingness to sacrifice, the same determination to do our part, the same earnest desire to help one another succeed in our race.

In the Kingdom of the World, individuals are taught to strive for first place, to be the best, to do whatever it takes to win. The Kingdom of God asks us to sacrifice ourselves for the whole. In so doing we benefit as individuals and as a group. Being part of God's team demands that we identify with a local church, that we attend, and that we participate.

Members of the body of Christ are not cloned. But together we strive for the greater good—the good of winning the race Jesus has set before us.

Have you joined your team yet? Will you help your team win?

Prayer ideas

Have you asked God to help you find the church where you belong? Ask God to help you commit to a specific church. Begin to talk with God about where you can contribute to the work of the church.

WHAT DO WE NEED HIM FOR, ANYWAY?

He is the one who gave these gifts to the church: the apostles, the prophets, the evangelists, and the pastors and teachers. Their responsibility is to equip God's people to do his work and build up the church, the body of Christ, until we come to such unity in our faith and knowledge of God's Son that we will be mature and full grown in the Lord, measuring up to the full stature of Christ. Then we will no longer be like children, forever changing our minds about what we believe because someone has told us something different or because someone has cleverly lied to us and made the lie sound like the truth. Instead, we will hold to the truth in love, becoming more and more in every way like Christ, who is the head of his body, the church. Under his direction, the whole body is fitted together perfectly. As each part does its own special work, it helps the other parts grow, so that the whole body is healthy and growing and full of love. (Ephesians 4:11–16)

I love thighs. Whenever anyone serves chicken, I dive for the thighs. I became chicken crazy long ago, after nutritionists began the big heart-health campaign against red meat. Because my father and brother both have heart disease, I've tried to cut down on animal fat. No longer do we buy half sides of beef. Now, I buy chicken.

Imagine my recent frustration, when a dietician on the Consumer Man's radio show explained that pieces of dark chicken meat have more fat than select cuts of red meat.

Of course I should be used to that frustrated feeling. It's the same way I felt when I found out that margarine is not really more healthy than butter. It reminds me of my disappointment when I found out that Vitamin C wouldn't cure everything—as Dr. Linus Pauling had promised on the Tonight Show.

Who could ever forget the one-inch headlines pronouncing coffee a carcinogenic, followed one week later by headlines promising helpful protection against heart disease with moderate consumption of coffee?

What's a person to believe?

Every year, health reports batter us first one way and then another. Lean red meat is now acceptable. Exercise doesn't count anymore unless you sweat. Confused, I sometimes wonder if I should just stop listening. I think to myself: *I'll order French Fries and forget the whole thing.*

If conflicting information confuses our concept of physical health, how much more confusing are issues of spiritual health? Believe me, over the years the church has weathered many storms of faddish doctrine. In my lifetime, I can think of prayer fads, faith fads, of fads about the roles of husbands and wives. I can think of giving fads, dressing fads, and makeup fads. We Christians are certainly not immune.

God doesn't want us to be tossed about by conflicting traditions and changing fads. He wants us to be anchored, settled, securely living the productive Christian life that brings fruit and grows the body of Christ.

For that reason, he gave gifts to each member. These gifts benefit the church. As each of us exercises our gift, we help the rest of the body to grow more mature. As we mature, we're less susceptible to the changing winds of doctrine, less likely to be carried away by the latest trend.

In order for the body to mature, each one must both give and receive. We must each contribute. And, equally important, we must listen and learn from others. As we do, our roots will grow down deep. Our souls become anchored. And though the winds of fashion may blow, they will not blow us down. We will not be uprooted. When we give and receive, we stand firm. Will you find your gift and use it?

Prayer ideas

Ask God to show you others who are exercising their spiritual gifts. Begin to pray about finding your own spiritual gift. Every member of the body has one; ask God to show you yours.

Who Me, Work?

As God's messenger, I give each of you this warning: Be honest in your estimate of yourselves, measuring your value by how much faith God has given you. Just as our bodies have many parts and each part has a special function, so it is with Christ's body. We are all parts of his one body, and each of us has different work to do. And since we are all one body in Christ, we belong to each other, and each of us needs all the others.

God has given each of us the ability to do certain things well. So if God has given you the ability to prophesy, speak out when you have faith that God is speaking through you. If your gift is that of serving others, serve them well. If you are a teacher, do a good job of teaching. If your gift is to encourage others, do it! If you have money, share it generously. If God has given you leadership ability, take the responsibility seriously. And if you have a gift for showing kindness to others, do it gladly.

Don't just pretend that you love others. Really love them. Hate what is wrong. Stand on the side of the good. Love each other with genuine affection, and take delight in honoring each other. Never be lazy in your work, but serve the Lord enthusiastically. (Romans 12:3–11)

Twelve years ago, my husband and I agreed to serve with four couples on a planting team for a new church in the South Hill area of Puyallup, Washington.

Once a sleepy little valley village, our town has exploded over the past fifty years. Surprisingly, the explosion has occurred on the hill south of the city. Up on the hill, miles of strip malls line the four-lane highway headed toward Mount Rainier. We've watched as mega-stores, discount warehouses, and a regional shopping mall have made hill traffic nearly impassable. One bumper sticker reads, "Pray for me. I drive Meridian."

And though the people moved here in droves, the churches did not.

So as we felt God lead us to plant a new church, we began to meet weekly for prayer. One year later, we began to plan. We chose a name, wrote a constitution, and rented a facility. We invited people to attend a weekly Bible study that grew into the core of the new congregation.

Eventually, we had our first service. Wanting to support our pastor, the team chose jobs. Janet agreed to manage ministry to children. Dave agreed to oversee the facilities. Naomi would handle women's ministries. Eventually, everyone on our committee had a job but me.

Nothing seemed to fit. For a time, I felt left out. Capable, but unused! Discouraged! I knew God had gifted me; I knew I needed to use the gift. But how?

Then, several weeks after we started the church, our pastor asked me to help him with an Easter Service drama production. I'd never trained in drama. I hardly qualified as an actress; yet I agreed.

The week after our performance, the pastor appeared at my back door with a file labeled, "Drama." Smiling, he announced that I'd inherited the dubious responsibility of Director of Drama. I doubt my performance was worthy of this honor.

I started reading about drama in church, and attended a couple of seminars in Kansas. I began writing my own sermon prompters—little sketches designed to pique the congregation's interest in the sermon. I produced everything we did, and took a few roles when other actors weren't available.

I felt like a passenger-turned-pilot, who must land a plane when the pilot suddenly keels over with a heart attack. It was terrifying and thrilling—all at the same time. My friends and co-ministers prayed as I learned. As I stepped into the role, the Lord protected me from many serious mistakes. Over the years, we've made some very funny memories.

But we've experienced wonderful blessings too. A publisher purchased my first full-length production. One of the teens on my lighting team had the joy of seeing his elderly grandfather begin his faith journey because of a Christmas performance. Another year, one of our members saw her husband finally choose to follow Jesus Christ.

Scripture says that God has given every person a gift—an ability, a talent—which he intends for us to use within the body of Christ. Every single one of us, with no exceptions, is expected—even created—to contribute to the church with our own unique talent.

Not every talent is listed in this Scripture. You may play bass guitar, or have a gift with sound equipment. You may have a special talent for calming babies and encouraging new moms. No matter who you are, God gave you something unique to contribute.

Like me, you may have a gift you don't even know about. Be patient. Try things. Think about your passions, your experiences, your education, your ability. Ask yourself questions. What things have you loved doing in the past? What kinds of people do you care passionately about? What things have you done successfully before? Would your mistakes help others?

As you think, ask others for input. They may see a side of you that you would never consider on your own. When you're ready, volunteer to the pastoral staff at your church.

Be prepared to learn from your mistakes and maybe even change your mind. You won't get it right the first time. Still, as you give away your gifts, you will find a joy and satisfaction that warms your soul. If you're working in the right place, you'll bless others. As you find your place in ministry, you'll honor your Heavenly Father. As you use your gift, you'll experience profound growth in your own life as well. Go ahead. Use that gift!

Prayer ideas

*P*ray through the questions in this devotion. Ask God to help you remember things you enjoyed doing, things you do well, and the kinds of people you especially care about. Take time to pray this issue through. Don't give up until you feel ready to try out your gifts.

I Believe in You!

However, some of the believers who went to Antioch from Cyprus and Cyrene began preaching to Gentiles about the Lord Jesus. The power of the Lord was upon them, and large numbers of these Gentiles believed and turned to the Lord. When the church at Jerusalem heard what had happened, they sent Barnabas to Antioch. When he arrived and saw this proof of God's favor, he was filled with joy, and he encouraged the believers to stay true to the Lord. Barnabas was a good man, full of the Holy Spirit and strong in faith. And large numbers of people were brought to the Lord. Then Barnabas went on to Tarsus to find Saul. Then he found him, he brought him back to Antioch. Both of them stayed there with the church for a full year, teaching great numbers of people. [It was there at Antioch that the believers were first called Christians.] (Acts 11:20–26)

A million years ago, when I was a newlywed, our church had a high-energy youth pastor, who'd been saved late in life. Wayde knew no limits. He had enough faith for the entire congregation, and wherever he felt God might be leading him, he followed.

One year, Wayde asked me to teach a high school Bible class. I don't know why he asked me. I'd managed to hide in our large church doing nothing more than singing in the choir. The thought of teaching scared me to death. I'd never done it. In fact, I hadn't even been saved for very long. What did I know about teaching high school students?

Still, I agreed. I prepared carefully and showed up with less experience than an immigrant at Ellis Island. At the end of the evening, Wayde took me aside and told me what a great job I'd done. I didn't believe him. Fear completely erased the lesson from my mind.

The next week, he took me aside again. This time he said, "Have you ever thought about writing?" Of course I hadn't, and I told him so. "You should think about it," he said, nodding his head. "You would be a great writer."

The class lasted only one quarter, but Wayde's encouragement has stuck with me to this day. The Lord used his words to direct me toward a writing ministry. While Wayde had so much on his plate, he noticed someone else's gift. Instead of running out to the car when the evening was over, he took the time to encourage me. His words made a huge difference.

Like Wayde, Barnabas was an encourager. When no one else believed in Paul, Barnabas defended him. "His conversion is genuine," Barnabas reassured the council in Jerusalem (Acts 9:27). "And not only that, he's a great preacher—bold and gifted." Later, when the church at Antioch needed a minister, Barnabas knew just the man. He took the time to travel to Tarsus and find Paul, convincing him to serve in Antioch. Wanting to do more, Barnabas poured his own life into Paul's ministry. Together they ministered with the church in Antioch for a full year, teaching great numbers of people.

The job in Antioch served as Paul's pastoral internship. From there, he received his call to missions and left on his first missionary journey. Once again, Barnabas went along with him.

Barnabas took a risk helping Paul enter ministry. Not only did he believe in Paul, but he also believed firmly in the God who had saved him. Barnabas saw a special gift in the young Apostle, and believed that God intended to use Paul. Barnabas put his belief into action. We could use more men like Barnabas—men who see the gifts in others and who speak risky, encouraging words. We need older Christians who invest themselves in younger, newer believers, teaching them what it means to serve, sharing their lives and their lessons.

Someday, you'll be a Barnabas.

Today though, you're more like Paul. Find someone you can imitate, someone who encourages you, someone who is willing to show you how to serve in the body of Christ. That someone will change your life. And then, some time in the future, if you keep your eyes open, you may find a young Paul who needs your encouragement. Will you be there for him?

Prayer ideas

Ask God for a mentor—someone who can teach you how to serve in the church. Keep asking God to make your area of giftedness clear to you.

OKAY, I QUIT!

We are pressed on every side by troubles, but we are not crushed and broken. We are perplexed, but we don't give up and quit. We are hunted down, but God never abandons us. We get knocked down, but we get up again and keep going. Through suffering, these bodies of ours constantly share in the death of Jesus so that the life of Jesus may also be seen in our bodies.

Yes, we live under constant danger of death because we serve Jesus, so that the life of Jesus will be obvious in our dying bodies. So we live in the face of death, but it has resulted in eternal life for you. (2 Corinthians 4:8–12)

In our church bulletin, I recently read the story of a woman who died on the mission field. It should have been a sad story; she was very young. She hadn't accomplished all she hoped. Still, I found it inspiring.

As a young woman, she desperately wanted to go overseas. But chronic illness forced her to wait. Undeterred, she made the mission field her only goal. She worked for it, fought for it, refusing to consider any work other than mission service. Eventually, she was allowed to travel to a remote Third World country. As a missionary, she wanted nothing more than to befriend women in a predominantly Muslim area. They had no one to tell them about Jesus. She wanted to be the first.

Living in horrible conditions—in complete poverty and poor sanitation—she loved the women there as best she could. Though she hoped some might choose a life of faith, they resisted her. Frustrated, she continued loving and speaking.

A short time later, she became ill. After many tests, doctors discovered a blood-borne parasite harbored in her body. They recommended she leave the country and obtain medical treatment elsewhere in order to survive. Knowing that the relationships she'd established were fragile, and that her chances to reenter the country were small, this woman refused to leave. Without treatment, the disease took her life.

After her death, an outpouring of sympathy overflowed among the women she had contact with. Having lost her physical presence, they suddenly wanted to know more about the God she represented. In her death, many came to believe the Good News.

These kinds of stories are not rare. They occur everywhere, in every corner of the globe. In San Francisco, one pastor of a Christian congregation had his home firebombed. In China, some Christian pastors are jailed and beaten for preaching the gospel. In Pakistan, Muslims shoot Christian ministers, while their churches are burned to the ground.

The word *ministry* means service. When we serve—and we are all asked to serve—we will experience difficulty. Though we may not lose our homes or our lives, we, like Paul, will experience pressure. We will experience conflict. The work of service demands our perseverance, our commitment, and our energy.

At the same time, we can look forward to the abiding presence of God in the midst of our troubles. He promises never to abandon us. He promises to be with us through every difficulty. With his help, we can face trouble with courage and tenacity.

The gospel deserves nothing less.

Prayer ideas

Since you began your life of faith, have you experienced trouble? Have you talked with God about it? Have you observed your fellow Christians suffering as they minister? Ask God how you might encourage those who suffer in ministry.

✝ ✝ ✝ DAY 41 ✝ ✝ ✝

OOOH, REAL FOOD!

This is what the LORD, Israel's King and Redeemer, the LORD Almighty, says: I am the First and the Last; there is no other God. Who else can tell you what is going to happen in the days ahead? Let them tell you if they can and thus prove their power. Let them do as I have done since ancient times . . .

How foolish are those who manufacture idols to be their gods. These highly valued objects are really worthless. They themselves are witnesses that this is so, for their idols neither see nor know. No wonder those who worship them are put to shame. Who but a fool would make his own god—an idol that cannot help him one bit! . . .

He cuts down cedars; he selects the cypress and the oak; he plants the cedar in the forest to be nourished by the rain. And after his care, he uses part of the wood to make a fire to warm himself and bake his bread. Then—yes, it's true—he takes the rest of it and makes himself a god for people to worship! He makes an idol and bows down and praises it! . . .

Such stupidity and ignorance! Their eyes are closed, and they cannot see. Their minds are shut, and they cannot think. The person who made the idol never stops to reflect, "Why, it's just a block of wood! I burned half of it for heat and used it to bake my bread and roast my meat. How can the rest of it be a god? Should I bow down to worship a chunk of wood?" The poor, deluded fool feeds on ashes. He is trusting something that can give him no help at all. (Excerpted from Isaiah 44:6–20)

One weekend, I took two friends to the Seattle Bicycle Expo. The event swarmed with people—many of them clad in Lycra and bike helmets—as they checked out the newest in equipment, accessories, and clothes. These vendors, I expected. But to my surprise, another item featured prominently in the displays. Food!

In fact, it seemed to me that everyone wanted to talk about food—what you should eat before you ride, during your ride, after the ride. It felt as if I'd gotten lost at an Overeaters Anonymous convention.

As I sampled the latest health nutrition bar, I realized that I should have started biking years ago. After all, how could I have missed a sport where food is the most important ingredient?

After looking at displays, we attended a seminar entitled, "Training for Endurance." Once again, the subject of food surfaced, and our speaker exhausted the topic. He covered sports drinks, electrolyte replacement, carbo-loading, and food replacement bars. After his lecture, he answered audience questions. His answer to the last question made me giggle out loud.

An earnest young man had asked, "What should you do when you get tired of all the sports drinks, the Cliff bars, and the protein drinks?"

The speaker paused. The silence swelled and people leaned forward to catch his answer. "Well," he said, suppressing a smile, "when you get tired of all that stuff, you'll just have to eat real food. It has everything you'll ever need. All the enzymes, electrolytes, carbohydrates, and proteins your body needs can be found in real food. You'll just have to choose fruits—like apples and oranges, or juices. You can eat meats, and breads and grains. Everything you need is also packaged as REAL food!

The audience laughed as they realized what he'd said. As bikers, we'd gotten so caught up in the nutritional demand of our sport that we'd forgotten the most basic information. God created food—just to meet our nutritional needs. He planned it all along. And yet, bikers wanted something faster, more convenient—something we could consume without having to slow down.

Isn't that like humankind?

In the Garden of Eden, God gave us freedom of choice and we chose the slavery of sin. God created marriage to meet our sexual needs. But we chose pornography and prostitution so that we could have sex in "convenience food format."

He gave us family, and we chose no-fault divorce, shared custody, and after-school care. He gave us children and we created abortion rights.

Fashioning idols isn't a new phenomenon. We do it too!

Today, some humans make idols of science, sociology, or psychology. For ages humans have chosen convenience versions of God over the reality and truth of a Biblical relationship with our Creator. How it grieves God when we choose substitutes instead of his power and presence in our lives. Decide today! Accept nothing less than the genuine joy of serving the almighty God.

Prayer ideas

Serving the God of the Bible demands that you know him. Tell him about the ways he is different than what you expected. Ask God to show you the things that keep you from giving him first place in your life.

GET ON DOWN!

Without wavering, let us hold tightly to the hope we say we have, for God can be trusted to keep his promise. Think of ways to encourage one another to outbursts of love and good deeds. And let us not neglect our meeting together, as some people do, but encourage and warn each other, especially now that the day of his coming back again is drawing near. (Hebrews 10:23–25)

Our oldest son attended college at the University of Washington. At first, he lived cloistered away as an anonymous freshman in a dorm the size of a small city. Two quarters later, Eric joined the University Christian Union, just off campus.

Two years ago, in the process of moving home for the summer, Eric lost part of a collapsible storage set he uses instead of a chest of drawers. The set, composed of wire squares held together by small plastic connectors, formed cubes where he stored his clean clothes. Somehow, the walls of the cubes came home; but the little circular pieces, which held the walls together, were missing. The whole family searched. Eric drove back to Seattle and looked through his room at the house. He even checked the parking lot where he'd packed his things.

The little connectors had disappeared.

At home Eric realized the wire walls of the cubes were now useless. He had nothing more than fifteen wire squares. Though they began as storage cubes, they no longer worked that way. He bought another full set at Costco.

The church is a little like Eric's storage cube. Together, when connected by our relationships and commitments, we form a strong and useful vessel. Together we carry Jesus to a world which desperately needs to see him.

Without one another, we're nothing more than useless wire squares. Though the potential is there; the strength is absent. The Bible tells us we must commit to meet together regularly. As we do, we have an opportunity to help one another on to bursts of love and good deeds. But we do more than that.

This week, I spent an entire day working on a fifteen-page section of this book. At the end of the afternoon, I sent an electronic copy to a friend and asked for feedback. I cleaned the kitchen and waited for her evaluation. Later, she told me that my ideas didn't work as I'd hoped. Discouragement buffeted me. I felt like I'd wasted the day.

As I thought about her conclusions, I became aware of the ideas flowing through my mind—almost as if listening to someone else's voice. I heard defeated words, deflating words, descriptions of myself that were blatantly untrue. I felt my emotions spiral downward and before long, I found myself eating ice cream with a fork, straight out of the box.

Eventually, I caught hold of myself and called a friend. "Tell me the truth," I said. "Am I a terrible writer? I just feel like giving it all up and eating."

"You aren't a terrible writer. Your life isn't worthless. You won't gain all your weight back," she said. Then she snickered. "You will finish the book on time."

My friend knew all the lies rolling around in my head; she knew exactly where to counterattack. She knew because we'd both committed to be part of the same church. We'd committed to grow together. We shared parts of our lives together. Over the past six years, we'd learned to be honest about the struggles we faced. And in those times when we didn't dare express ourselves honestly, we saw through one another's disguises.

Sometimes, I feel that my friends are the strongest part of my life. They become the voice of Jesus—a voice I can actually hear—telling me the truth about my situation. They encourage me. They correct me. They allow me to vent, to cry, and to laugh. They express God's unconditional love for me in ways I can see and feel.

I am what I am because the body of Christ—the church—has loved me too much to let me quit. They have pushed me too far to let me back down now. They reflect Jesus and show me what it is to become more like him.

Is it easy? No. Is it worth it? Without a doubt! If you want to grow, get on down to a good church!

Prayer ideas

*I*f you have yet committed to a church, ask God what holds you back. Ask Jesus to help you find a healthy church where you can grow into everything he wants for you.

Did You Hear That?

Trust in the LORD with all your heart; do not depend on your own understanding. Seek his will in all you do, and he will direct your paths. Don't be impressed with your own wisdom. Instead, fear the LORD and turn your back on evil. Then you will gain renewed health and vitality. (Proverbs 3:5–8)

I love to cut pictures out of the local newspaper. In Saturday's paper, I found a very special one, depicting a high school freshman as she prepares for a track meet. With shoulder length brown hair, she looks like most runners her age, thin, focused, intent on the race ahead. Undistracted, her face turned downward, she holds one hand at her right ear. In the other, she carries a tiny radio attached to a fanny pack. Nearby her father, Matt McCarthy, speaks into a small transmitter.

Natalie McCarthy, the ordinary looking girl in the picture, sprints both the 100- and 200-meter dashes for her Steilacoom High School track team. It is her almost total blindness that makes her most extraordinary.

So, how does she do it? How does she line up with a group of healthy, sighted teens and dash for a finish line she cannot see?

By radio.

Natalie runs with a single earpiece in her right ear. With her father's voice coming through the tiny transmitter, she hears the course corrections he gives her from the sidelines. With nothing more than trust, and her father's verbal directions, Natalie runs at full speed toward a goal she cannot see, with competitors she can only hear, over obstacles she can only imagine.

Hers is a perfect picture of our race with Christ. For us, the Holy Spirit directs our race. We face challenges we cannot see. We race for a goal we can only imagine. Though we don't hear our coach through a radio earpiece, the Lord promises over and over that he'll guide us in our race for the finish line. He will direct us. We will hear our Heavenly Father's voice. We must trust, as blindly as Natalie does, the whispering in our spiritual ears. We must trust and respond. Change course. Run the race. Your Father is whispering in your ear!

Prayer ideas

Consider how often you hear from the Lord during your day. Do you respond to his small course corrections? Have you thanked him for his guidance? Have you asked forgiveness for the times you've chosen to go your own way instead?

FIRE!

We all make many mistakes, but those who control their tongues can also control themselves in every other way. We can make a large horse turn around and go wherever we want by means of a small bit in its mouth. And a tiny rudder makes a huge ship turn wherever the pilot wants it to go, even though the winds are strong. So also, the tongue is a small thing, but what enormous damage it can do.

A tiny spark can set a great forest on fire.

And the tongue is a flame of fire. It is full of wickedness that can ruin your whole life. It can turn the entire course of your life into a blazing flame of destruction, for it is set on fire by hell itself. People can tame all kinds of animals and birds and reptiles and fish, but no one can tame the tongue. It is an uncontrollable evil, full of deadly poison. Sometimes it praises our Lord and Father, and sometimes it breaks out into curses against those who have been made in the image of God. And so blessing and cursing come pouring out of the same mouth. Surely, my brothers and sisters, this is not right! Does a spring of water bubble out with both fresh water and bitter water? Can you pick olives from a fig tree or figs from a grapevine? No, and you can't draw fresh water from a salty pool. (James 3:2–12)

Not long ago, wildfires consumed the American West. Oregon, Washington, Colorado, and California were especially hard hit. Millions of acres burned. Thousands of men and women risked their lives to protect land and property. Some of these fires expired only when the first snows began to fall.

Three years ago, my brother and his family were evacuated from Leavenworth, Washington, as the Icicle Creek fire exploded over the hill behind the town. After soaking the roof with water, and watering the lawn one last time, Bill, his wife and daughters drove their two cars through a narrow canyon where ashes fell like snowflakes over a landscape blackened by smoke. As they left, they wondered if they would ever see their home again.

How do these fires begin?

In most fire seasons, lightning strikes cause many of these fires. During one recent weekend, twenty-four new fires started from a single storm over central Washington. On the other hand, a forest service employee has been charged with starting the massive 2002 Colorado fire by burning a letter from her ex-husband.

In 1989, the massive Black Tiger Gulch fire burned sixty-seven structures and thousands of acres in Boulder, Colorado. In the ten minutes between the first fire reports and the volunteer response, the fire grew to sixty acres. The steep slope, high summer temperatures, and steady winds blew the fire uphill. Residents literally ran for their lives. The Black Gulch fire began with a discarded cigarette. One of the most devastating fires ever experienced in Orange County, California, began with a spark from a lawn mower.

No one would argue the damage caused by a fast moving fire. In fact, most of us would go out of our way to avoid starting such a fire. Committing Smokey the Bear's motto to memory ("Only YOU can prevent forest fires"), we do our part.

Yet, every day we light matches and toss them out onto the desolate landscape of the human heart. Without a second thought, we curse the woman who steals the parking place for which we waited so patiently. Over lunch in the break room, we assassinate the character of our coworkers. And we don't restrict our damage to strangers.

Tired and stressed, we thoughtlessly rebuke our children. We address our spouse's mistakes with cruel sarcasm, and top it off with heartless criticism. If they don't listen, we turn up the volume.

James tells us we shouldn't do these things. Though we can never tame the tongue, we must commit to using it for God's glory. When others criticize, we can praise. When others yell, we can speak calmly.

When we're tempted to let curses fly, we can choose to keep silent instead. Though we can never tame the tongue, with the help of the Holy Spirit we can prevent the kind of rampant destruction which otherwise comes so naturally. We have a new nature, a new power source.

Only you can prevent forest fires. Can you ask for help with your tongue?

Prayer ideas

*T*he older you are when you begin a faith walk, the more entrenched your verbal habits have become. Ask God to show you one way that you might begin removing destructive words from your daily talk.

SAY WHAT?

Then this message came to me from the LORD: "Son of man, prophesy against the shepherds, the leaders of Israel. Give them this message from the Sovereign LORD: Destruction is certain for you shepherds who feed yourselves instead of your flocks. Shouldn't shepherds feed their sheep? You drink the milk, wear the wool, and butcher the best animals, but you let your flocks starve. You have not taken care of the weak. You have not tended the sick or bound up the broken bones. You have not gone looking for those who have wandered away and are lost. Instead, you have ruled them with force and cruelty. So my sheep have been scattered without a shepherd. They are easy prey for any wild animal. They have wandered through the mountains and hills, across the face of the earth, yet no one has gone to search for them." . . .

This is what the Sovereign LORD says: "I now consider these shepherds my enemies, and I will hold them responsible for what has happened to my flock. I will take away their right to feed the flock, along with their right to feed themselves. I will rescue my flock from their mouths; the sheep will no longer be their prey." (Excerpted from Ezekiel 34:1–6, 10)

Now what's a reader supposed to do with that?

This Old Testament passage is pretty obscure, certainly not a favorite for public meetings. You might even ask why I would bother with strange passages written nearly three thousand years ago? Why don't we just stick with the stuff we understand? We can learn an important lesson from this passage.

The Bible is the living Word of God. Without it, no believer can maintain a healthy relationship with God. The words of Scripture will be your constant source of encouragement, comfort, direction, correction, understanding and wisdom. But to get all these things from the pages of the Bible, you must know how to read it. This passage will teach you how.

How do we read the Bible?

When I began my faith journey in 1974, I bubbled over with enthusiasm for the Bible. In the first summer after I committed my life to the Lord, I read and underlined the New Testament—twice. Since 1979, I can safely say that I've rarely gone more than two days without reading the Bible. Scripture reading is a vital part of my faith walk.

Not all believers have that kind of excitement. For the less enthusiastic, I recommend two things that will bring life to your Bible reading. First, as you open the Bible, ask the Holy Spirit to show you something new about God. Give him permission to teach you anything—and mean it. Second, I ask that you bring these three simple questions to every passage you read:

- What does it say?
- What does it mean?
- What does it mean to me?

What does it say? Go back and reread today's passage from Ezekiel. Take a pen and make a simple list of the statements in the text using as few words as possible. When I do this, I look for the same things a newspaper reporter might include in his opening paragraph: Who? What? Where? When? Why? and How?

My list looks like this: The message is from God. It's written for the shepherds of Israel. The shepherds have taken poor care of the sheep. They've taken advantage of their position as shepherds. They'll be punished for their cruelty and abuse.

As I read, I wonder. Is this passage really about white fluffy animals that eat grass and say, "Baa?"

I don't think so. But, I want to be certain; I scan the text again, looking for clues. I notice this line, "against the shepherds, the leaders of Israel." I think that though the text apparently refers to animals, the passage may have another, deeper meaning. I underline that phrase and consider the new direction.

What does it mean? I have begun to suspect that this passage is really not about shepherds who lead animals on to the next meadow. In fact, I don't think the passage is about animals at all. I'm convinced that Isaiah speaks about the leaders of God's people. I wonder if he means the spiritual leaders of the people.

I look at the list of things that the leaders haven't done. They haven't fed the sheep, or bound up their wounds. They haven't looked for lost sheep. I think these tasks might also refer to the spiritual needs of God's people. Feeding could be teaching. Binding wounds could be helping people deal with disappointments and grief. Lost sheep could refer to people who abandon their faith. The more I think about the passage, the more I suspect that I may be on the right track.

What does it mean? With this question, I think about what the passage may have meant to those who read it first. I believe this passage tells us that God wants his spiritual leaders (the leaders in Isaiah's time) to understand the importance of their job, and the serious consequences of misusing their position.

The last question feels simple, but is profoundly important: **What does it mean to me?** Whenever I read the Bible, I want to take something away with me. Before I begin to apply Scripture, I must answer the first two questions. Only then can I ask the third. Only then can I find meaning in the text for me.

I believe this passage is about the weighty responsibility of leadership. I know that whenever I'm given a position of leadership in the church, I must first focus on caring for the people I lead. I cannot neglect them or let them wander from the faith. I must never take advantage of my position, using it as a platform for wealth or respect. God holds leaders responsible for their actions—good and bad—as they serve him by leading people.

You may have a long way to go before you consider leadership. But someday, if you continue to grow and follow the faith, you will be asked to lead others. Whether you lead the cleanup team or the worship band, remember this passage from Ezekiel.

Remember the high calling of leadership.

Prayer ideas

Ask your Heavenly Father to show you how to use these questions every day as you read the Bible. Consider the weight of leadership now, before you take the role. Ask God to keep you focused on service—not position—as you begin your faith walk. Do you see examples of servant-leadership in your church? Pray for the leaders in your church to become the kind of leaders who please God by caring for his people.

OH NO! NOW WHAT?

So I tell you, don't worry about everyday life—whether you have enough food, drink, and clothes. Doesn't life consist of more than food and clothing? Look at the birds. They don't need to plant or harvest or put food in barns because your heavenly Father feeds them. And you are far more valuable to him than they are. Can all your worries add a single moment to your life? Of course not.

And why worry about your clothes? Look at the lilies and how they grow. They don't work or make their clothing, yet Solomon in all his glory was not dressed as beautifully as they are. And if God cares so wonderfully for flowers that are here today and gone tomorrow, won't he more surely care for you? You have so little faith!

So don't worry about having enough food or drink or clothing. Why be like the pagans who are so deeply concerned about these things? Your heavenly Father already knows all your needs, and he will give you all you need from day to day if you live for him and make the Kingdom of God your primary concern. (Matthew 6:25–33)

As you grow in your Christian walk, you'll build monuments along the way. We have. Twenty years ago, my husband planned to practice dentistry in Goldendale, Washington—a tiny community just east of the Cascade Mountain range. Located above the Columbia River gorge, isolated by rugged terrain, Goldendale needed another dentist. Kim had worked in a clinic there during his last summer in school. He enjoyed the community—

making new friends among his patients. We spent weekends there, getting a feel for rural life. Eventually, we decided we would move immediately after graduation.

We felt so certain of our decision that in the fall of his senior year in dental school, we decided to start a family. At the time, I worked as a Physical Therapist in Bellevue, Washington. Our health care coverage in those days didn't include any maternity expenses. So, we took our meager savings and earmarked it for the delivery of our new baby. We paid particular attention to our instructor during Lamaze classes. Our baby's birth had to be natural; we couldn't afford the extra cost of anesthesia.

As the year progressed, we made plans to move. We rented half of a duplex and sent our nonrefundable deposit to the landlord. We packed our wedding gifts and organized the dental tools Kim had purchased for his practice. In the midst of our preparations, we waited four extra weeks for our overdue baby to arrive.

That spring, six weeks after our son was born, we had a surprise visit from the dentist who invited Kim to Goldendale. To this day, I don't really understand what happened. I didn't hear the conversation. But after he left, Kim told me that our plans had changed. We would not practice in Goldendale after all. Their agreement had fallen through.

I'll never forget the shock of that afternoon. Long after the sun went down, Kim and I sat on the couch in our little rented house and cried. I felt a desolation and confusion I'd never experienced before.

How could we have made such a huge mistake? Hadn't God led us to Goldendale? What would we do now? Without that job, we had no income. Our labor and delivery bills would arrive any moment. We couldn't afford to pay the hospital now.

Kim called another dentist friend to ask to work in his office. Refused again, our tunnel darkened. While I cared for our newborn, Kim started looking for another place to practice. He rented space above an old furniture store near his boyhood home. Eventually, the dreaded hospital bill arrived. Neither of us believed what we read.

Our baby's late arrival gave him a May 5 birthday. Five days before the birth, my insurance coverage was expanded to include labor and delivery costs! The bill we expected to wipe out our savings account never arrived. Because Eric was born late, he was nearly free!

Somehow, in the middle of our misdirection, God met our needs.

As I look back, I can almost feel the doubt and confusion. I still don't understand why we thought we heard Goldendale, when God didn't let us go there. But I'll never forget the deep gratitude and wild jubilation I felt when I opened that bill from the hospital.

God knew about our job situation. He knew about our insurance coverage. He knew when our baby would arrive. And somehow, when things looked completely hopeless, God provided for us—essentially giving us back our savings.

As a couple, we built a kind of spiritual monument around that event. We remember God's faithfulness in our time of need. And in the twenty-four years since Eric's birth, I often remember God's faithfulness as I face new and more frightening needs.

As God meets your needs, build a monument. Keep a notebook. Write it down. And then remember the lilies. If the flowers don't worry, why should I? Why should you?

Prayer ideas

*I*s something worrying you today? Can you talk to God about it? Can you ask God to help you abandon your worry, and trust him to care for you?

You Make Me So Mad!

My dear brothers and sisters, be quick to listen, slow to speak, and slow to get angry. Your anger can never make things right in God's sight.

So get rid of all the filth and evil in your lives, and humbly accept the message God has planted in your hearts, for it is strong enough to save your souls. And remember, it is a message to obey, not just to listen to. If you don't obey, you are only fooling yourself. (James 1:19–22)

Years ago, when my children were very young, I drove an orange Volkswagen Vanagon. On one trip, miles from home, I realized I had an empty gas tank. I searched for a gas station in vain. Eventually, running on fumes, I pulled into a country station as the engine died at the pump. Grateful to make it that far, I got out of the car to fill the tank.

As I held the nozzle in place, a man in a small sports car pulled around my van and parked at the pump in front of me. He got out of the car, slammed his door and began cursing me for not pulling to the forward pump. His angry words continued while I finished filling my tank. Too stunned to reply, I went inside to pay for the gas.

By the time the attendant had run my credit card, I'd started feeling angry too. Who was this guy to yell at me? Hadn't someone been at that pump when I'd pulled into the station? I couldn't have moved forward. The more I thought about it, the angrier I felt.

Just the weekend before, my Sunday school class had talked about humility. A soft answer turns away wrath, I'd learned. As I walked toward my car, I felt the Holy Spirit prompt me to take another tack.

I walked up to the man in the sports car and apologized. "I'm sorry. I was nearly out of gas when I came in. I just dumped the car and filled it. I didn't realize I'd inconvenience you. Please forgive me." The man's face crumpled as I spoke.

"I shouldn't have spoken to you that way," he said, refusing to look me in the eye. "My wife just left me, and I've been out of my mind ever since. I guess I just took it out on you."

I expressed my sorrow for him, and we spoke for a few moments. He drove away reconciled. Because of the Holy Spirit, he had experienced a tiny bit of God's grace.

Though our encounter was brief, I drove away changed. I wondered how many times I've reacted harshly to someone else's anger without taking the time to really find out what might be troubling them. What might have happened at the gas station if I'd launched into a lengthy defense instead of obeying the Holy Spirit?

I don't mean to seem like an angel here. I've acted like the guy in the sports car many times. When I don't get my work finished on time, I bark at the children. When my computer refuses to cooperate, I snap at my husband.

This is the way of the World's Kingdom. We honk when we're cut off in traffic. We speak harshly to grocery clerks when the line is too long. We retaliate when a coworker makes us look bad. We live stressed, hurried, and fatigued lives. In our world, anger is normal.

These things ought not to be, James tells us. We should be slow to speak, and slow to anger. It's not the way of the world. But then, we no longer belong to the world, do we?

We belong to another Kingdom.

Prayer ideas

*I*s anger an occasional or constant problem for you? Do you find it difficult to apologize? Begin your change today. Ask God to help you take a deep breath before you respond in the face of someone else's anger today.

OH, HOW IT HURTS!

All praise to the God and Father of our Lord Jesus Christ. He is the source of every mercy and the God who comforts us. He comforts us in all our troubles so that we can comfort others. When others are troubled, we will be able to give them the same comfort God has given us. You can be sure that the more we suffer for Christ, the more God will shower us with his comfort through Christ. So when we are weighed down with troubles, it is for your benefit and salvation! For when God comforts us, it is so that we, in turn, can be an encouragement to you. Then you can patiently endure the same things we suffer. We are confident that as you share in suffering, you will also share God's comfort. (2 Corinthians 1:3–7)

I never planned to be a writer.

On a lovely winter day, many years ago, I started down the freeway into the Puyallup Valley. The late morning sunrise was glorious, and without thinking I uttered these words, "Oh Lord, I want to know you—not just to know about you—but to really know you."

I didn't think another thing about it, not until later, when my world turned completely upside down. I'd driven to an appointment with my obstetrician, my first visit for this pregnancy—a routine visit before the autumn birth of our third child.

During the exam, a look of concern crossed my doctor's face. He asked me when I thought the baby was due. "I need an ultrasound," he said. "Today!" It didn't take a rocket scientist to know that something didn't add up. I tried to stay calm.

By the end of the day, the doctor determined that our baby hadn't survived the early weeks of pregnancy. In its place, I'd grown a placental tumor, one that had the potential to take my life. Life had catapulted me from happily pregnant into grief and from there into fear.

The days after my appointment were filled by a whirlwind of blood tests, surgery, recovery, and more blood tests. Silently, we waited for the pathology report. None of us could process it all. I cried constantly. For some reason, I wrote my doctor a thank-you letter.

"I'm sure many of your patients say thanks when they hold a healthy baby in their arms," I wrote. "I just wanted to thank you even when the outcome isn't what we expected. You've taken good care of me."

A week later, my doctor called. He asked me to keep a journal of the grief process. "One in ten pregnancies end in miscarriage," he said. "I think you might write something that would help those mothers, something that would comfort them." Though I had my doubts, I agreed to try.

I did nothing more than keep track of the ways the Lord comforted me in my loss. Though my doctor was not a man of faith, I included the Scriptures and comforts the Lord seemed to give me. I wrote about the pain and the sadness. I wrote about the ways my friends encouraged and comforted me. Six weeks later, on Easter Sunday morning, I wrote what I knew would be the last entry. I typed my journal on a manual typewriter and gave it a title.

I took it down to the doctor's office.

"I'm amazed," he said when he called me. "I sat down with a red pen to read it. I thought I'd cross out all the spiritual stuff—but this is so good."

I can take no real credit for the writing. I had only photographed a spiritual event. During the weeks I kept a journal, the Holy Spirit comforted me. He held me as I cried. He spoke to me on the pages of Scripture. He gave me hope. I just happened to catch it all on paper.

My doctor chose to share my work with others. I've gotten letters from women in other parts of the country telling me how much the journal helped them. In the process, I began to understand the power of the written word, and wondered if God meant for me to begin writing more seriously.

God gave me comfort to give away. This is the promise of Scripture. When (not if) we're weighed down with troubles, we'll find comfort in the Holy Spirit. Accept it joyfully—no matter how he delivers it—through the love of your friends, in the words of Scripture, in the music of an artist. Know that it comes from your Father, who loves you. And then, when you find others weighed down with trouble, share what he's given you.

Prayer ideas

Have you experienced God's comfort in a troubling circumstance? Have you been comforted by another believer? Have you thanked God for his kindness? Ask God to show you ways you can share him with others in pain.

WAIT TILL YOUR FATHER GETS HOME!

Don't say, "I will get even for this wrong." Wait for the Lord to handle the matter. (Proverbs 20:22)

And I saw a great white throne, and I saw the one who was sitting on it. The earth and sky fled from his presence, but they found no place to hide. I saw the dead, both great and small, standing before God's throne. And the books were opened, including the Book of Life. And the dead were judged according to the things written in the books, according to what they had done. The sea gave up the dead in it, and death and the grave gave up the dead in them. They were all judged according to their deeds. (Revelation 20:11–13)

Early in 2002, a twelve-year-old girl disappeared from her home in Oregon City, Oregon. Frantic to find her, families, neighbors, and friends combed the area in search of evidence. They put up flyers, and held community meetings and press conferences.

Within weeks, another girl—a neighbor and classmate of the first—vanished as well. The same group of friends and families found themselves again traipsing through woods and fields looking for anything that might lead them to the girls. Pictures of Ashley Pond and Miranda Gaddis ran on the front page of newspapers across the country.

Early in the investigation, frenzied families tried desperately to get local police and FBI to consider a neighbor, Ward Weaver, as a suspect. He had befriended both girls, they said, allowing them to spend time at his home. Just one year earlier he'd been accused of molesting Ashley, they said, though he was never charged in the case.

Eight months after the disappearances, police found the bodies of Ashley and Miranda on Ward Weaver's property. Ashley had been buried in a barrel under a concrete pad Weaver had poured shortly after the girls disappeared.

Imagine for a moment, that you are Ashley's father. Imagine that, for some inexplicable reason, the justice system fails to prosecute Ward Weaver. You are certain that he sexually abused and murdered your daughter. What would you do? What would you want to do?

Most fathers would want to take matters into their own hands. They'd want to buy a gun and use it. They'd want to do the world a favor, and eliminate that kind of person from humanity. They'd want vengeance.

Not hard to imagine is it? Not for any parent, or aunt or grandparent. Not for anyone who has ever loved a child.

But when we enter the life of faith, God asks us to leave vengeance to him. Don't take revenge, he warns us. Let me take care of things. Trust that I keep careful records. Trust that no one gets away with anything—even murder.

In order to let go, we must know something about God's character. He doesn't wink at sin. His standard for us is perfect. God's justice is perfect too. He isn't hampered by rules of evidence, or Miranda Rights. He sees all and knows all. His justice renders the defense team speechless.

In the face of God's eternal judgment, there can be no hung jury, or overturned decisions. His is the final word.

We are not to take our own revenge. No matter what the offense— big or small—from the false accusations of a coworker to the murder of a child, we must depend on God to make things right. Whether he works through the criminal justice system or through the boss at work, or even through circumstance, we can trust him to keep his promises.

Sometimes, we must wait until the final judgment—the great white throne judgment. Yet, no matter how long we wait, we can rest knowing he will eventually settle all the accounts. He will do it fairly, impartially, and perfectly.

Knowing that vengeance belongs to God sets me free. I need not become judge, jury, and executioner. Anger and hatred need not consume me. Memories can't hold me hostage—dragging around behind me like a ball and chain. I can let go of the past and move into the future unencumbered by emotions I was never built to handle.

Can you let go and let God be the judge?

Prayer ideas

*D*o you struggle with the memory of some past hurt? Do you wish you could take revenge? Tell God all about how you feel. Ask for help in letting go of the memory. Express your trust in God's perfect justice.

DAY 50 ✝ ✝ ✝

✝ ✝ ✝

UP, UP, AND AWAY!

I will praise you, my God and King, and bless your name forever and ever. I will bless you every day, and I will praise you forever. Great is the LORD! He is most worthy of praise! His greatness is beyond discovery! Let each generation tell its children of your mighty acts. I will meditate on your majestic, glorious splendor and your wonderful miracles. Your awe-inspiring deeds will be on every tongue; I will proclaim your greatness. Everyone will share the story of your wonderful goodness; they will sing with joy of your righteousness. . . . All of your works will thank you, LORD, and your faithful followers will bless you. They will talk together about the glory of your kingdom; they will celebrate examples of your power. . . . The LORD is faithful in all he says; he is gracious in all he does. The LORD helps the fallen and lifts up those bent beneath their loads. . . .

When you open your hand, you satisfy the hunger and thirst of every living thing. The LORD is righteous in everything he does; he is filled with kindness. The LORD is close to all who call on him, yes, to all who call on him sincerely. He fulfills the desires of those who fear him; he hears their cries for help and rescues them. The LORD protects all those who love him, but he destroys the wicked. I will praise the LORD, and everyone on earth will bless his holy name forever and forever. (Excerpted from Psalm 145)

Some time ago, while writing a novel, I needed information about air search and rescue. By a series of small miracles I came in contact with the director of search and rescue for the

Washington State Department of Transportation, Karl Moore. Karl was kind enough to invite me to training exercises at Harvey Field in Monroe, Washington.

"We'd love to have you come along and watch," he told me. "We like the press to have accurate information about what we do."

So early on a Saturday morning, I joined them and spent the day watching procedures, asking questions and interviewing the members of the team. These dedicated volunteers had flown in from all around the state to train for emergency searches. Together, we sat listening to Karl introduce the make-believe search scenario.

Our task was to locate the wreckage of the plane and send in the ground team. Each person had one specific job, and as soon as Karl finished, everyone went straight to work.

Every flight crew consisted of at least one pilot and spotter. Before long, the room bustled with activity. Intense conversation held over detailed maps, buzzed all over the room.

The head of the CAP group obtained federal clearance for me to fly with Lt. Col. Bill Kennedy, a seasoned Vietnam era pilot. With his steady blue eyes and a full head of silver hair, I trusted him immediately.

Bill gathered our team and reviewed our search assignment. Laying out a map, he showed us our grid and explained what he expected us to see at flight altitude. Moments later, I stumbled out the hangar door behind Bill and climbed into his four-seater Cessna.

Karl Moore had planted ELTs—Emergency Locator Transmitters— in locations all over western Washington. We'd been assigned to a specific grid and told to locate the transmitter hidden there. Within moments of entering the search grid air space, Bill had located the ELT.

"Too easy," he said, grinning over at me. "Let's go do some spotting."

We'd been given locations of several old plane crashes to practice our spotting techniques, and Bill began a search pattern over the forest. We dropped to search altitude and scanned the treetops.

"Let your eyes gaze from window edge to wing tip and back," the spotter in the rear seat advised me. "If you get nauseous, just take a break. Don't feel bad. It happens to everyone."

Before long, I spotted metal debris among the trees. We circled and dropped for a closer look. "Good eyes," Bill said, giving me a thumbs-up signal. "Fuel tanks from a logging operation."

It startled me to realize how much ground we covered as we zipped along over the trees. How much easier it was to search from this altitude than from the ground. No ordinary human could negotiate the dense forest and steep cliffs below our plane. Hundreds of searchers wouldn't see as much from the ground as we could see from this vantage point.

As I flew over the mountainous terrain, I noticed the powerful byproduct of a simple change in viewpoint. By getting up, away from the problem, we'd gotten a wider view. From here, we could see the forest from the airplane crash—so to speak.

And so it is with praise. Praise gets our eyes off our own problems. It gives us much needed perspective. When we focus on God's bigness, we find our own troubles don't look very big anymore. No matter what we face, God is bigger. No matter how much wisdom we need, he has more. Praise is a change in viewpoint. By focusing on God, we see the bigger picture.

God instructs us to praise him—not because he needs our praise—but rather because he knows how desperately we need it. Praise is our airplane—as we focus on God, we're lifted from the hopelessness of our situation. From an altitude of praise, we seek his solutions and receive the power to act on his instructions.

Praise lets you see God in a new light. Will you praise him?

Prayer ideas

*G*et off in a quiet place and read this psalm aloud to God. Stop between phrases and let the words sink in. If you feel like singing a praise song, go for it. If the words of the psalm swell into your own words of praise, let it loose. Praise is one of the most delightful parts of the faith walk. Try it today!

OH NO! NOT A RADAR GUN!

". . . For the Lord disciplines those he loves, and he punishes those he accepts as his children." As you endure this divine discipline, remember that God is treating you as his own children. Whoever heard of a child who was never disciplined? If God doesn't discipline you as he does all of his children, it means that you are illegitimate and are not really his children after all. Since we respect our earthly fathers who disciplined us, should we not all the more cheerfully submit to the discipline of our heavenly Father and live forever? For our earthly fathers disciplined us for a few years, doing the best they knew how. But God's discipline is always right and good for us because it means we will share in his holiness. No discipline is enjoyable while it is happening—it is painful! But afterward there will be a quiet harvest of right living for those who are trained in this way. (Hebrews 12:6–11)

Okay, I'll admit it. Five years ago, on my way from a voice lesson to a teacher's conference, I got a speeding ticket. I don't really think I deserved it. I'd turned left onto a county road at the bottom of a steep hill. As I made the turn, a line of cars appeared—screaming over the hill in my rearview mirror. Frightened, I sped up—right into the radar trap of a waiting county sheriff. Oops.

I took the ticket without objection. But I went to traffic court, armed with photographs and logical explanations. The hill was blind, I explained. I couldn't see oncoming traffic. I'd only sped up to avoid a nasty accident.

The judge, a woman, didn't buy my explanation. Though she lowered my fine, she did nothing about the ticket itself. Now, I not only had a ticket and a fine, but I'd wasted five hours of a beautiful fall day sitting in court with a bunch of traffic violators.

I left the courtroom angry. It took me a few weeks to change my evaluation of what had happened. Though I still felt that particular ticket was unfair, I realized I did have the nasty habit of fudging the speed limit. I used to look at a traffic sign and add five miles an hour to determine my top speed. If I needed to get somewhere in a hurry, I cheated even more.

Don't laugh. I have a sticker on the back of my car that says I'm a Christian.

I started to think about my ticket in terms of heavenly discipline instead of governmental unfairness. In the process, I realized that no matter what happened on the day I got my ticket, my driving didn't honor Jesus. I needed to change. The ticket changed my driving habits.

These days, I watch my speedometer as I drive. I allow enough time between appointments to drive the posted speed limit—not the version I make up along the way. For me, driving defensively no longer means looking for speed traps.

In the process of a natural consequence, the Lord refined my heart.

He did it because he loves me; because I belong to him; and because he wants to create a clean and pure heart in me.

I didn't like it. I didn't like watching my insurance premiums change. I was embarrassed to be stopped by a sheriff where my friends might see me. I never told my husband. But in the end, the experience has changed me. I've become more like my Savior.

Just don't ask about my freeway driving.

Prayer ideas

Think about the discipline you received as a child. Was it loving discipline? How does that memory influence your feelings about godly discipline? Ask God to change your mind about correction. Ask him to help you welcome discipline as a sign of his loving acceptance of you as his child.

OUCH! THAT WAS MY TOE!

So we have continued praying for you ever since we first heard about you. We ask God to give you a complete understanding of what he wants to do in your lives, and we ask him to make you wise with spiritual wisdom. Then the way you live will always honor and please the Lord, and you will continually do good, kind things for others. All the while, you will learn to know God better and better. We also pray that you will be strengthened with his glorious power so that you will have all the patience and endurance you need. May you be filled with joy. (Colossians 1:9–11)

Years ago, with four children under eight, I coerced my husband into taking ballroom dance classes. My parents danced beautifully together, and their dance dates had given them time alone. I thought my husband and I needed some time together thinking about something other than children. Dance class would be just the thing!

Kim wasn't too thrilled with the idea. I don't remember what I promised him for going—but it must have been big. He hated the thought of having to trip over each other as we ran into forty other couples on a high school gym floor.

He agreed though, and soon we were struggling to learn a new dance pattern every week. It wasn't easy. We both like being in charge.

I'd been dancing since I could walk. Kim came from a home where it was considered tantamount to sexual sin. He had a lot of learning to do. So did I.

Dancing requires cooperation. When one person moves, the partner must respond. No matter what direction, forward or back, sideways or straight, turning or twisting, both people must respond to the movements of their partners. Without response, there is only chaos.

We had plenty of chaos. For weeks we wrestled with the steps and then, almost miraculously, we managed to catch on. We didn't talk about it, or analyze it. In fact, we rarely even practiced. But suddenly we settled into a sort of "dancing groove."

This passage from the Apostle Paul talks about a similar groove. Paul wants the Colossian church to learn a sort of spiritual dance. Fortunately for them, they didn't have to go to class. They didn't have to drive to the gym. And neither do you.

It goes something like this: First, the *knowing* step. As we listen to the leading of the Lord in our lives, we'll know what it is that he wants us to do. It can be something simple—reading the Bible—or difficult, reconciling our marriage. Whatever it is, as the Father reveals himself, we learn what he wants of us.

The second step is the *understanding* step. As we consider our assignment, we respond by asking the Lord to show us how to do it. We want to understand how he wants us to obey. We ask questions. Which version of the Bible should I read? Where should I start? Or, how do I go about reconstructing a shattered relationship? Paul prays for the Colossians to have all the wisdom they need to obey him.

Then we take the third step, the *obedience* step. We do whatever he asks—like the dancer responding to his partner. We clear a bit of our daily schedule to be in the Word. Or we make the phone call to see a counselor. Whatever he instructs, we obey.

As we obey, we come to know the one who leads our spiritual dance more intimately. The steps of the dance become easier and easier. Like Kim and I—who did eventually stop stomping on one another's feet—we get to know our partner and leader. As we know the Lord more and more, he asks more and more of us, and in turn we know him better and better. The cycle continues over and over, broken only by our disobedience.

As we learn this dance of obedience, Paul advises us that we need patience, endurance and power to keep moving forward with God. In today's Scripture, Paul shows us how we can pray for ourselves and for one another—that we grow in the dance of obedience. We ask the Lord to make us strong and fit for the dance. And today, we can determine that no matter what happens to us, we'll continue in obedience—that we may come to know our Lord and Savior better and better.

And our dance of grace will be beautiful to see.

Prayer ideas

Have you noticed a cycle of obedience in your faith walk? Can you think of things the Lord has shown you that you have obeyed? How did that make you feel? Did you experience joy? Satisfaction? Have you thanked him for the process? Can you ask God to move you forward in obedience today?

EVERYTHING?

And the Holy Spirit helps us in our distress. For we don't even know what we should pray for, nor how we should pray. But the Holy Spirit prays for us with groanings that cannot be expressed in words. And the Father who knows all hearts knows what the Spirit is saying, for the Spirit pleads for us believers in harmony with God's own will. And we know that God causes everything to work together for the good of those who love God and are called according to his purpose for them. For God knew his people in advance, and he chose them to become like his Son, so that his Son would be the firstborn, with many brothers and sisters. And having chosen them, he called them to come to him. And he gave them right standing with himself, and he promised them his glory. (Romans 8:26–30)

In Lance Armstrong's book, *It's Not About the Bike: My Journey Back to Life*, he says this about riding: "The life of a road cyclist means having your feet clamped to the bike pedals churning at 20 to 40 miles per hour, for hours and hours, and days on end . . . It means gulping water and wolfing candy bars in the saddle because you lose ten to twelve liters of fluid and burn six thousand calories a day at such a pace, and you don't stop for anything . . ."

No one would argue the rigors of professional cycle training. But training involves more than just riding the bike mile after mile. Some days involve nothing but hills. Others involve nothing but sprints. Some involve exercises for coordination and flexibility. Pro cyclists are developed through goal-directed preparation.

On every bike, the pros have a tiny computer monitoring information about the rider's pace, distance, speed, and heart rate. It computes the rider's average speeds and cadence (the number of pedal cycles per minute). At the end of the day, this data is downloaded to a desktop computer, where the trainer uses today's facts to calculate tomorrow's training approach.

Based on the data, the trainer might tell Lance to increase his cadence, or ask him to run a series of sprints, or a series of rapid climbs. Thanks to the trainer and the data, each day's work is carefully planned before it begins.

For each member of the team, every training day has an objective, a clearly defined goal designed to move that rider closer to the winning position.

God has a training objective too.

Our trainer—our loving Heavenly Father—uses everything that happens in our lives to grow in us the character of our Lord Jesus Christ. Everything! The good things. The surprising things. The wonderful things. The sad things. The painful things. God uses every event to create in us our Savior's nature.

Many believers cling to the first half of this Scripture. They love knowing that God causes all things to work together for good. If they lose their job, they use this Scripture to claim a better one. They assume that "for good" means God will give them exactly the things they want, the things they value. But these believers make a critical mistake.

When we read the whole passage, we see that the "good" God intends is character growth. He uses circumstances to help us let go of our earthly nature, and become more like Jesus. God wants us to let go of pride and grow in humility. He wants us to let go of self-importance and grow in patience. He wants us to let go of selfishness and grow in kindness.

God's idea of good is becoming more like Jesus.

It takes a cooperative heart to discover God's good in our everyday lives. Watch for the good God wants to grow in you. The next time someone takes the parking place you've been waiting for, remember this Scripture. And ask God to grow Jesus' character in you.

Prayer ideas

Has a recent disappointment caused you to question God's goodness? Can you talk to God about how you're feeling, and ask him to help you see things his way? Can you see how character growth may help you through the disappointment?

WHAT? IT ISN'T FREE?

He told many stories such as this one: "A farmer went out to plant some seed. As he scattered it across his field, some seeds fell on a foot-path, and the birds came and ate them. Other seeds fell on shallow soil with underlying rock. The plants sprang up quickly, but they soon wilted beneath the hot sun and died because the roots had no nourishment in the shallow soil. Other seeds fell among thorns that shot up and choked out the tender blades. But some seeds fell on fertile soil and produced a crop that was thirty, sixty, and even a hundred times as much as had been planted. . . .

"Now here is the explanation of the story I told about the farmer sowing grain: The seed that fell on the hard path represents those who hear the Good News about the Kingdom and don't understand it. Then the evil one comes and snatches the seed away from their hearts. The rocky soil represents those who hear the message and receive it with joy. But like young plants in such soil, their roots don't go very deep. At first they get along fine, but they wilt as soon as they have problems or are persecuted because they believe the word. The thorny ground rep-resents those who hear and accept the Good News, but all too quickly the message is crowded out by the cares of this life and the lure of wealth, so no crop is produced. The good soil represents the hearts of those who truly accept God's message and produce a huge harvest— thirty, sixty, or even a hundred times as much as had been planted." (Matthew 13:3–8, 18–23)

When I started college, I had high hopes and great expectations. So, I might add, did most of the students who began their college careers alongside me. In my first quarter at the University of Washington, it seemed that nine out of ten freshmen declared themselves to be pre-med majors. While I pursued the prerequisite classes for a degree in Physical Therapy, many of my classmates sneered at my choice. They planned to be the doctors ordering therapy for my patients. I would work for them.

The University of Washington boasts one of the top ten medical schools in the country. With the enormous student population, the university makes no effort to recruit freshmen. In fact the school discourages freshman applicants. Only the best get in. Naturally, among these highly qualified freshmen, one would expect a high number of medical aspirations. Still, by winter quarter, I noticed a significant drop in the pre-med plans among my fellow students. By the end of the first year, only the most serious students remained.

Of course by the time graduation celebrations began, my unofficial survey found few men and women who had actual acceptances to medical school. For the rest, medical school became a vague pipe dream—something they'd considered at one time. Instead, they'd begun careers in education, business, and political science. It was my turn to snicker.

What happened to their earnest ambitions? Did the difficulties of organic chemistry and differential calculus defeat them? Or did they succumb to the passing pleasure of campus parties and unending opportunity for dates?

I can't say with absolute certainty. But many confessed they hadn't been prepared for the intense course work required for medical school admission. As the workload grew, their grades fell. Before long their transcripts eliminated all possibility of medical school acceptance.

Like freshmen headed for medical careers, the Kingdom of Faith has its share of grand plans and false starts. Many who start down the road of faith fail to finish well. Few realize the high cost of following Jesus Christ. Many find themselves distracted by recreation, money, or the pleasure of sin.

To finish well, we must count the cost. We must keep the goal ever before us. We must ruthlessly eliminate anything that would distract us from our task. The goal of finishing well demands our full commitment. Nothing less will do.

Prayer ideas

*A*sk the Lord to show you what distractions keep you from the goal of finishing well. Ask for help to eliminate one of these distractions.

WHERE DID THEY PUT VICTORIA?

Oh, what joy for those whose rebellion is forgiven, whose sin is put out of sight! Yes, what joy for those whose record the LORD has cleared of sin, whose lives are lived in complete honesty!

When I refused to confess my sin, I was weak and miserable, and I groaned all day long. Day and night your hand of discipline was heavy on me. My strength evaporated like water in the summer heat.

Finally, I confessed all my sins to you and stopped trying to hide them. I said to myself, "I will confess my rebellion to the LORD." And you forgave me! All my guilt is gone.

Therefore, let all the godly confess their rebellion to you while there is time, that they may not drown in the floodwaters of judgment. For you are my hiding place; you protect me from trouble. You surround me with songs of victory.

The LORD says, "I will guide you along the best pathway for your life. I will advise you and watch over you. Do not be like a senseless horse or mule that needs a bit and bridle to keep it under control." Many sorrows come to the wicked, but unfailing love surrounds those who trust the LORD. So rejoice in the LORD and be glad, all you who obey him! Shout for joy, all you whose hearts are pure! (Psalm 32)

The Strait of Juan de Fuca lies along the northern coast of Washington State. On the chart, the narrow strip of water looks unimpressive—nothing to be frightened about. However in real life, the straits can be quite a different matter.

On our last trip, we left Gig Harbor early in the morning. Gray clouds covered the southern sound as we journeyed north. Though windy, we made it to Admiralty Inlet easily. As we neared Port Townsend in the late afternoon, we had to make a choice—pull in for the night, or make the jump across the straits to Canada.

The sky ahead looked clear. Sunlight reflected off what appeared to be calm seas. We decided to cross. Not fifteen minutes into the crossing, we began to question our decision. Waves crashed across the left side of the bow, splashing high enough to reach the fly bridge. A hard current pushed the boat to starboard and as we tried to maintain our course, the boat rolled in continual swells. Kim began to get nervous; I could tell by his grip on the wheel.

At one point he said, "I think we'd better wake the kids and tell them to pray."

I laughed. We traveled on. Keeping one eye on our compass and the other on our charts, we finally came close enough to the other side to begin scanning for landmarks. The land looked very different than we expected. Confused, we finally spotted the *Victoria Clipper*, a commercial vessel, zipping across the horizon. It headed west, toward the setting sun.

"How can that be headed for Victoria?" Kim asked, checking his chart again.

"Maybe it's going somewhere else," I said.

Then I pointed to a landform in the distance saying, "That sure looks like Cattle Point." We'd fished for salmon along Cattle Point nearly every summer for years. I studied the chart again. "But it can't be. That would put us somewhere way over here." I pointed at the chart.

Through the combined information from our marina guidebook and our global positioning system, we did eventually identify the cliffs as Cattle Point. I made a hard left turn and headed west. Baffled, it took us a while to figure out how we'd gone so far off course while following the exact compass route we'd plotted.

Nature was the culprit. A little wind here and a little current there—all the while driving us east and north of our intended route. Lucky for us, we recognized the landforms and saw how far off course we'd gone. Otherwise, we'd have been looking for Victoria on the wrong island!

Sin has the same effect on Christians as wind and current have on a boat. You can believe you're making progress while in truth, sin is gradually taking you further and further off course.

By beginning your life of faith, you've already made a big U-turn. Still, you must constantly maintain your new course. When distractions and sin threaten to throw you off, confession and repentance will put you back on course. The only way to deal with sin is confession and repentance. Literally, the word repentance means "turning around."

Don't be lulled into thinking that you are on the right course. Check and recheck your position using all the tools the Lord has given you. Read the Bible. Stay connected with wise advisors. Attend church. Then whenever necessary adjust your course, plot a new course line.

Don't let sin drag you off course!

Prayer ideas

Is something in your life giving you a nagging feeling of guilt? Ask God if your guilt is genuine. If so, ask for help in plotting a new course. Do you need to talk to another believer about it? Ask God to show you how to make a fresh start.

ME? SUBMIT?

And further, you will submit to one another out of reverence for Christ. You wives will submit to your husbands as you do to the Lord. For a husband is the head of his wife as Christ is the head of his body, the church; he gave his life to be her Savior. As the church submits to Christ, so you wives must submit to your husbands in everything. (Ephesians 5:21–24)

When my husband graduated from dental school, only seven of one hundred classmates chose to start a private practice. The other ninety-three entered residencies, began postgraduate studies, or joined existing practices. My husband rented space in Tacoma, and started out on his own.

We spent the summer pounding nails, hanging sheetrock, and painting walls. While I hung wallpaper, he wired and installed the power and vacuum to his second-hand dental chairs. A friend installed vinyl and countertops. Kim did the plumbing himself.

He saw his first patients the week of Halloween. For the rest of that year, we were too busy to keep track of his old classmates. We did everything ourselves—insurance billing, patient scheduling, paying bills, and cleaning the office.

Before long though, we began hearing about Kim's former classmates, who one by one decided to leave the practices they'd so eagerly joined. Why had these relationships failed? Though some had hired on with no more status than a receptionist, others had been promised partnerships, even buyouts when the primary dentist retired.

Kim began asking questions. He noticed that few of his classmates ever signed a contract outlining the arrangements governing the practice relationship. Most of these partnerships had been consummated on nothing more than a handshake. Inevitably, conflict arose. With nothing to govern the decision-making process, hurt feelings escalated into broken business partnerships.

Remember, these practice relationships consisted of equally trained, equally qualified dentists. In many cases, both partners had graduated from the same school.

I wonder if their mutual equality may have actually contributed to the downfall of the relationships. When these partners experienced conflict, both felt equally qualified to make the final decision. In the end, with no structure to resolve the conflict, the partnerships dissolved.

God doesn't want the partnership between husbands and wives to suffer the same fate. And so he gives us guidelines by which we can ensure the maximum health of the husband-wife relationship. God knows that husbands and wives—both equal as persons before the Lord—will have conflict. Bet on it. But our conflict need not dissolve the relationship.

When the word *submit* is used in mixed company, I often see women cringe. Submission isn't a politically correct concept these days. While I can't make the word more culturally acceptable, I can add some wisdom to the mix.

When two persons of equal worth, equal education, and equal qualification have conflicting views about the future, how do they proceed? In business partnerships, in the military, and in the public service sector, the one who has final responsibility must make the decision. Everyone else is expected to support that decision.

Responsibility doesn't automatically make the decision right. But it ends the division caused by disagreement.

I think the Lord gave this instruction to families so that we might avoid the kind of destructive conflict that happens when disagreements get completely out of hand. He loves us too much for that. He assigned ultimate responsibility for the family to the husband. It isn't a position that wives should envy; God holds men highly accountable.

None of Paul's family admonitions will independently salvage a difficult relationship. A loving husband will sometimes find himself with a stubborn wife. And a submitting, supportive wife will sometimes find herself with a self-centered and immature husband.

But, when both husband and wife follow these scriptural instructions about family, their relationship flourishes. I believe that was God's intent—not to devalue women or to prefer men—but to give us a kind of structure that helps humans create strong marriages and families.

He wants that for each of us.

Prayer ideas

As you read this Scripture, how did you feel? If you're a wife, ask yourself how your feelings affect your ability to follow Paul's instructions? Ask God to help you view this passage with new appreciation. Ask him how you can be a more cooperative partner.

✝ ✝ ✝ DAY 57 ✝ ✝ ✝

WHAT? DIE FOR HER?

And you husbands must love your wives with the same love Christ showed the church. He gave up his life for her to make her holy and clean, washed by baptism and God's word. He did this to present her to himself as a glorious church without a spot or wrinkle or any other blemish. Instead, she will be holy and without fault. In the same way, husbands ought to love their wives as they love their own bodies. For a man is actually loving himself when he loves his wife. No one hates his own body but lovingly cares for it, just as Christ cares for his body, which is the church. And we are his body. (Ephesians 5:25–30)

In Seattle, at least, Harry Wampler is famous. A small man, with classic Scandinavian features, blond hair and blue eyes, Harry used to forecast the weather for a local TV and radio station. It seems as if I've watched Harry my whole life.

A couple of years ago, Harry's adult son joined him doing weather. Though we liked the son, Harry held a very special place in Seattle's heart. We thought Harry would never be replaced. Then, one day, he disappeared.

It took me a while to miss him. I assumed he'd taken a long vacation, or that he'd finally retired and I'd missed the farewell show. I was wrong. Harry had taken a leave of absence to care for his dying wife.

In the midst of the hustle and bustle of our culture, the idea of a man leaving work to care for his wife makes tears come to my eyes. Without knowing how long it would take, or how difficult it would be, Harry left the public eye and spent time at home.

He cooked for her, helped with her medicines and doctor's appointments. He spent hours with her, helping when he could, supporting when he could not. Harry left everything that felt comfortable to serve her in her final months. They were Harry's final months also. She died one week before his official retirement date.

I think that makes Harry an extraordinary kind of hero.

But this is the kind of hero God expects of every husband. This command—to love your wives as Christ loved the church—is not as easy as it first appears.

Of course I can love her passionately, you say. I can provide for her, you insist flashing a credit card. I can protect her, you say, flexing your biceps.

But though these expressions of love are necessary, they neglect the most essential element that God demands of husbands—the element of self-sacrifice.

Jesus left his home, gave up his position, his authority, his comfort—all for us. He gave away his very personhood in order to become what we desperately needed. He didn't wait for us to behave well, or understand him, love him enough, or listen to him, or support him. Even before we knew we needed him, Jesus came to earth to give us a new life. And the life we have cost him everything.

This is what God expects of husbands. He wants every husband to love and care for his wife with the same intensity he cares for his own body.

Though this is a difficult command, husbands have divine help. The very God who wrote the command also demonstrated this kind of love for us. He gave up everything for us. At any minute of the day or night, he is available to help. He waits to help you.

Ask him.

Prayer ideas

Ask God to let you see your wife with his eyes. Ask him to show you how to love her the way he does. Ask God to give you one concrete thing to do today that would help you love your wife as Jesus loves the church.

TOO SAD FOR TEARS

Children, obey your parents because you belong to the Lord, for this is the right thing to do. "Honor your father and mother." This is the first of the Ten Commandments that ends with a promise. And this is the promise: If you honor your father and mother, "you will live a long life, full of blessing."

And now a word to you fathers. Don't make your children angry by the way you treat them. Rather, bring them up with the discipline and instruction approved by the Lord. (Ephesians 6:1–4)

Sometimes, something I read leaves me with profound sadness. *Ten Thousand Sorrows*, the story of a Korean War orphan, written by Elizabeth Kim (Harper Collins, 2000), left me with heaviness I could hardly bear.

In Korea, after Elizabeth's American father left for the United States, her disillusioned and starving mother returned with Elizabeth to the family village. Elizabeth's illegitimate birth dishonored her mother's family. At home, both mother and child were so ostracized and hated that villagers pelted them with stones every day, as they went to work in the rice paddy.

Eventually unable to bear the dishonor, Elizabeth's grandfather asked her mother to sell the child into slavery. Her mother refused. In order to avenge the family name, her grandfather murdered Elizabeth's mother as the child watched.

Her grandfather then abandoned Elizabeth in a Christian orphanage. There, with no name and no birth date, the staff kept Elizabeth—

by now a young child—locked in a crib-like cage for four months. Eventually adopted by an American couple, she traveled to the United States.

There, in a small desert community, sick with parasites and unable to speak the language, five-year-old Elizabeth faced unimaginable culture shock. She had never seen carpet or a bed. She had never eaten anything but rice and vegetables. She had never used an American bathroom. Terrified of abandonment, and extremely claustrophobic, Elizabeth faced horrendous treatment from the pastor and wife who adopted her.

They destroyed her toys and demanded that she eat American food. When she did not understand English, they shouted at her. Their determined efforts to change Elizabeth included unforgivable cruelty.

These parents tape-recorded her spankings and played them back at night. Elizabeth writes, "Listening to the tapes later, every slap would come through clearly, along with my sobs. In the background Mom could be heard saying something like, 'Now aren't you sorry you were such a bad little girl? Don't you want to ask Jesus to forgive you?' . . . They got played over and over as I was growing up, and we sat in the living room and listened. My parents loved them. The tape recordings formed the nucleus of our family entertainment."

When Elizabeth entered Junior High, she asked for more fashionable clothing. Her adoptive parents decided she'd developed "worldly desires." As punishment, they forced her to wear the same dress to school every day of the week saying, "If the other kids make fun of you, you should consider it a blessing. You're being crucified with Christ . . ."

About this time, Elizabeth's mother began using her as free help. "She didn't have to pay me but I did all the housework—cleaning, cooking, laundry. I gave her neck and back rubs when she had headaches. I seethed inside, but I did it." Her parents' behavior moved Elizabeth to rage. She directs much of her rage against Christianity.

Before she came to the United States, Elizabeth Kim suffered more tragedy than most of us face in a lifetime. She had been abused, abandoned, and emotionally scarred. As if that were not enough, her adoptive parents added a kind of cruel punishment cocktail that managed to thwart the very objective of their lessons.

As much as they wanted to shape Elizabeth into a godly child, they created an angry and resentful woman. By mixing harsh punishment with emotional neglect, these parents sealed Elizabeth's emotional and spiritual fate. Only God could break the protective shell Elizabeth built in order to survive.

In their eagerness to do the right thing, her parents managed to forget the most important things. They forgot to love their child. They forgot to understand how the world looks from a child's viewpoint. Most importantly, they forgot to use the discipline and instruction approved by the Lord.

In his Word, God demonstrates wise parenting techniques. As he raises his people Israel, you see much affirmation. He frequently reminds them of his love for them—both by words and action. His object lessons surround us—in the wonders of nature, in his protection, in his guidance, in his loving-kindness. His sacrificial love for us is clearly seen in Jesus Christ. Jesus not only told us how to behave; he showed us how to behave. Jesus lived the gospel.

Oh that all parents would learn to parent as our Heavenly Father does.

It comforts me to know that God grieves over Elizabeth Kim's childhood. Because he cares for every child, he holds those who wound children responsible for their actions.

Be careful that your discipline does not move a child to anger. Surrounded by love, backed by example, evidenced by sacrifice, bring your children up in the discipline and instruction of the Lord.

Prayer ideas

Think about your own childhood. Did you experience godly parenting? Ask God to help you let go of the past as you learn new parenting skills.

ISN'T IT JUST A JOB?

Slaves, obey your earthly masters with deep respect and fear. Serve them sincerely as you would serve Christ. Work hard, but not just to please your masters when they are watching. As slaves of Christ, do the will of God with all your heart. Work with enthusiasm, as though you were working for the Lord rather than for people. Remember that the Lord will reward each one of us for the good we do, whether we are slaves or free. And in the same way, you masters must treat your slaves right. Don't threaten them; remember, you both have the same Master in heaven, and he has no favorites. (Ephesians 6:5–9)

I don't keep slaves. Some days though, when the kitchen is a wreck and the dust bunnies acquire the proportion of small Orca whales, I wish I did. In most of the western world, slaves are a thing of the past. The nearest relationship we have is that of employee and employer.

I have a believing friend who runs his own small business, and one evening he made a startling confession. He told me that he wished he could avoid ever hiring another believer.

"It's as if Christian employees think I'll look the other way when they don't show up for work. They want me to make allowances for doing half a job. They even seem to expect all kinds of extra benefits they don't earn."

He sounded bitter; I asked what made him feel that way.

"I know I shouldn't," he explained. "But Christians come in late, and smile as if I'll excuse it because we're both believers. They ask for raises they haven't earned and time off when I have no one else to cover for them."

"Aren't all employees like that?" I asked.

"Not in my experience." He shook his head. "It's as if believers want to take advantage of my kindness. They know what God expects of me, and they want to see just how far I'll bend before I break."

If the report is true, my friend's employees have missed a key scriptural instruction. Christians should be the most outstanding employees—not the laziest or the sloppiest. Our work should reflect our very best efforts—just as if we worked for the Lord himself.

Today's Scripture includes a very important truth. The Lord will reward our work. No matter what your job, or who signs your paycheck, ultimately the Lord determines the value of our work. That encourages me.

Of course all of us have worked for an unappreciative boss, or labored at a dead-end job. I remember one night watching my son retch as he stood outside and took off his work clothes. Eric worked as the head dishwasher at an all-you-can-eat buffet; his clothes were covered with leftover food slop and cooking grease. Poor boy!

We've all had those kinds of jobs. We've been overlooked and underpaid. Even executives in large corporations—even writers—struggle with these feelings. When we see our work as something we do for God rather than for our boss, no one—not the boss, not our coworker, not even the janitor—can steal our pleasure in a job well done.

My work, done enthusiastically, accurately, diligently—whether I'm a dishwasher or a heart surgeon—pleases the Lord.

Honestly, it takes effort to keep this reality in mind. Once in a while I simply want to pound something out, and be done with it. And then I remember that I work for Jesus. I raise my own standard; I work a little longer, a little harder. No matter what you do, your work is important to Jesus. He cares about your work. Do you?

Prayer ideas

Consider your attitude toward work. Ask God to help you see your work differently. Pray about something you might change at work that would bring honor to him.

THANK GOD FOR PASTORS!

Remember your leaders who first taught you the word of God. Think of all the good that has come from their lives, and trust the Lord as they do. . . .

Obey your spiritual leaders and do what they say. Their work is to watch over your souls, and they know they are accountable to God. Give them reason to do this joyfully and not with sorrow. That would certainly not be for your benefit. (Hebrews 13:7, 17)

My pastor is unfailingly human. He detests waiting. He is directionally impaired; he can't find his way out of a paper bag. He hates to be late. Car trips make him desperately sick. He sometimes forgets appointments.

But while his humanity keeps him humble, his leadership makes him a wonderful example for believers in our body. I've learned much from watching and following Art.

Several times every year, Art goes away to pray and ask the Lord for guidance. His questions are frequently the same: What do you require of me, Lord? What direction are you taking our body? What do you want to teach us?

Away from the distraction of ringing telephones and family activity, Art gets quiet and listens. When he comes back, he is stronger, more deliberate, more focused.

Art loves to praise the Lord, and frequently composes music for our worship service. Though he's a gifted musician, it's his heart for worship rather than his musical talent that gives birth to his compositions. His music grows from his own time in praise and worship. It flows from his heart to God's.

Art is committed to prayer. When we gather as a church to pray, Art is always there. He doesn't simply lead in prayer; he participates in prayer. As he prays, he's open to anything the Lord might show him—and sometimes, as we pray together, we see God at work in our pastor.

Art is committed to the Word of God. He reads and memorizes it. He lives by the words and principles he finds in the Bible. When he preaches, he shares God's truth, not man's opinion. As he teaches, he not only shows us how to apply the word—but he demonstrates how to dig out the truth for ourselves. We leave our services better able to feed ourselves.

Over the years, I've had the opportunity to be with Art in times of crisis—a cancer diagnosis, a marriage failure, and a child caught stealing. I've watched him in the heat of sadness, disappointment, and hopelessness. I've watched him love others in the depths of his own despair.

I've watched while Art loved his wife, corrected his children, and laughed with friends. It sounds like I think Art is perfect. I know better. But I do know this: He is genuine, and I can confidently follow his example as he follows our Savior.

In our culture, the media asserts that politicians can be great leaders regardless of the condition of their personal lives. God's Word disagrees. Church leaders should live holy lives—lives that inspire us to greater faithfulness.

God says to watch your pastors; imitate their faith walk. Remember their labor over you. Celebrate their faithfulness. Consider the intense responsibility they carry, and do everything you can to make their job easier, and more pleasant. By doing this, you benefit.

As you begin this life of faith, find a pastor who will let you observe his life. Don't look for a perfect man. He doesn't exist. Instead, find someone who loves the Lord, who is genuine, and who takes his responsibility for you with utmost seriousness. Then watch and follow.

Prayer ideas

Thank God for the man who leads your congregation. Ask God to show you how to pray more regularly and more specifically for him. Consider asking your pastor how he would like you to pray for him. Your commitment to support him in prayer will bless him.

HOLY CONFRONTATION!

"I am a Jew, born in Tarsus, a city in Cilicia, and I was brought up and educated here in Jerusalem under Gamaliel. At his feet I learned to follow our Jewish laws and customs very carefully . . . And I persecuted the followers of the Way, hounding some to death, binding and delivering both men and women to prison. The high priest and the whole council of leaders can testify that this is so. For I received letters from them to our Jewish brothers in Damascus, authorizing me to bring the Christians from there to Jerusalem, in chains, to be punished.

"As I was on the road, nearing Damascus, about noon a very bright light from heaven suddenly shone around me. I fell to the ground and heard a voice saying to me, `Saul, Saul, why are you persecuting me?'

"'Who are you, sir?' I asked.

And he replied, 'I am Jesus of Nazareth, the one you are persecuting.' The people with me saw the light but didn't hear the voice.

"I said, 'What shall I do, Lord?'

And the Lord told me, 'Get up and go into Damascus, and there you will be told all that you are to do.'

"I was blinded by the intense light and had to be led into Damascus by my companions. A man named Ananias lived there. He was a godly man in his devotion to the law, and he was well thought of by all the Jews of Damascus. He came to me and stood beside me and said, 'Brother Saul, receive your sight.' And that very hour I could see him!

"Then he told me, `The God of our ancestors has chosen you to know his will and to see the Righteous One and hear him speak. You are to take his message everywhere, telling the whole world what you have seen and heard. And now, why delay? Get up and be baptized, and have your sins washed away, calling on the name of the Lord.'" (Acts 22:3–16)

Paul, who wrote most of the New Testament, spoke these words before an angry crowd in Jerusalem. This story, which might be considered Paul's testimony (a word Christians use to describe how they came to know Jesus), sounds exciting. Almost unbelievable.

Not everyone has such a dramatic tale. The process that brought you to a life of faith probably had very few cinematic effects. Though yours may be less dramatic, you have a testimony too. Every Christian does.

I grew up in an Irish Catholic home, attending Mass weekly. Until Christmas of my twentieth year, I'd never held a Bible. In fact, I didn't know that ordinary people could read the Bible. I moved to college in 1973 and joined a sorority, where I had my first contact with real Christians.

I accepted an invitation to a Bible study, and was given a small book for our study questions. Though I tried to do the homework, I couldn't answer the questions. I didn't even know how to look up the passages mentioned in the text. For four weeks, I kept my answers covered with one hand so no one would know that I hadn't finished our assignment.

The Christians I met had something I missed. Eventually my sorority sisters explained what it meant to begin a new life in Christ. Their words confused and frightened me.

Then, on an ordinary school night, it happened. I went to my room and knelt by my bed, making my first attempt at real prayer. "Lord, I've really messed up my life. I want to hand it all over to you," I whispered. "And I don't ever want to be sorry for this decision. If you are real, I want you to keep me forever fervent."

Though I didn't understand the concepts of sin or forgiveness, I knew that my life would have to change. I let go without sadness or regret, sensing that something powerful had happened. The next day, my housemates accused me of having a new boyfriend. They said I walked around with a silly grin on my face—all day long.

In a way, they were absolutely right. At twenty, I'd finally found the lover of my soul. My Savior is as exciting today as he was that night in Seattle. He is still the lover of my soul.

So, how did it happen for you? You might want to try to make some notes. Someday, someone will ask you, "How did you come to Jesus?" Your testimony will be something you treasure for all your years on earth. Write it down. Read it often. And then, like Paul, share it!

Prayer ideas

Would you be as bold as Paul in sharing your testimony before a crowd? Why not? Could you ask Jesus to help you smooth out your testimony? Ask him to show you one person with whom you can share it with today.

DON'T KILL THE MESSENGER!

Whatever we do, it is because Christ's love controls us. Since we believe that Christ died for everyone, we also believe that we have all died to the old life we used to live. He died for everyone so that those who receive his new life will no longer live to please themselves. Instead, they will live to please Christ, who died and was raised for them.

So we have stopped evaluating others by what the world thinks about them. Once I mistakenly thought of Christ that way, as though he were merely a human being. How differently I think about him now! What this means is that those who become Christians become new persons. They are not the same anymore, for the old life is gone. A new life has begun!

All this newness of life is from God, who brought us back to himself through what Christ did. And God has given us the task of reconciling people to him. For God was in Christ, reconciling the world to himself, no longer counting people's sins against them. This is the wonderful message he has given us to tell others.

We are Christ's ambassadors, and God is using us to speak to you. We urge you, as though Christ himself were here pleading with you, "Be reconciled to God!" For God made Christ, who never sinned, to be the offering for our sin, so that we could be made right with God through Christ. (2 Corinthians 5:14–21) arly in our marriage, we shared a home with an eighty-year-old man. I made dinner for all of us, and he gave us free rent. One night we watched the news together as reporters covered the conviction of a local serial killer. I don't know why the story moved me so much; but I could not get him out of my mind. He'd been sentenced to life without parole in the state penitentiary.

I went upstairs and wrote a long letter to him, explaining forgiveness in Jesus Christ. I told him I knew what he'd done, but that I believed the power of Jesus' sacrifice covered even murder. "No sin is bigger than Jesus' forgiveness," I told him. When I'd written several pages, I mailed it to the prison.

Ten years later, I happened to catch another report on the news. In a separate story featuring the lives of prisoners, the killer I'd watched earlier had become a model prisoner, leading several Bible studies among the inmates there. Though he had no possibility of freedom, his life had been completely changed by his new life in Jesus Christ.

I'll never know if my letter reached this inmate. Perhaps someone else shared the Good News with him. But in that one experience, I found that the gospel is powerful enough to completely, miraculously change the life of a convicted killer.

Years later, Billy Graham held a crusade in the Tacoma Dome. I volunteered to train as a counselor for the event and took evangelism classes at a local church. Toward the end of our course, we were asked to present the gospel to someone who had never heard about Jesus and his sacrifice on the cross. Writing a letter is one thing—but face-to-face?

It felt like an intimidating task. I'd never tried to explain spiritual things in this way. I visited my retired neighbor and asked for his help with a class assignment. He willingly listened to my presentation, paying close attention to the bridge drawing I made as I spoke. With great care, I explained how he could be made right with God because of Jesus' death on the cross.

When I finished, he said in his strong Boston accent, "I've never heard it explained that way." He paused, scratched his forehead and stared at the little drawing. I noticed his eyes glistening. "But it won't work for me. I was in World War II," he said, as if I'd understand. "No sacrifice could ever pay for what I did over there."

We talked some more, though he remained unconvinced. I didn't plead or argue with him—and we parted good friends. As good friends,

I continued to pray for my neighbor. Five years after the crusade, he died of a massive heart attack. Though I don't know if he made a faith decision, I do know this: He was so moved by the little drawing that he carried it in his wallet for the rest of his life. The gospel made an impact—even when my neighbor chose not to believe.

Whether a person responds to the gospel or not, the Bible charges us with the task of sharing this great truth. Don't ever forget the power of forgiveness in Jesus. The wonder of the Good News is powerful enough to change convicted killers.

It's even powerful enough to overcome our timidity.

Prayer ideas

Ask Jesus to show you the people in your circle who need to hear about Jesus Christ. Begin to pray daily for them. Ask God to give you the opportunity to share the Good News with one of them.

WHO ME? A CHRISTIAN?

When the apostles were with Jesus, they kept asking him, "Lord are you going to free Israel now and restore our kingdom?"

"The Father sets those dates," he replied, " and they are not for you to know. But when the Holy Spirit has come upon you, you will receive power and will tell people about me everywhere—in Jerusalem, throughout Judea, in Samaria, and to the ends of the earth." (Acts 1:6–8)

For I am not ashamed of this Good News about Christ. It is the power of God at work, saving everyone who believes—Jews first and also Gentiles. This Good News tells us how God makes us right in his sight. This is accomplished from start to finish by faith. As the Scriptures say, "It is through faith that a righteous person has life." (Romans 1:16, 17)

I know that you sincerely trust the Lord, for you have the faith of your mother, Eunice, and your grandmother, Lois. This is why I remind you to fan into flames the spiritual gift God gave you when I laid my hands on you. For God has not given us a spirit of fear and timidity, but of power, love, and self-discipline. So you must never be ashamed to tell others about our Lord. And don't be ashamed of me, either, even though I'm in prison for Christ. With the strength God gives you, be ready to suffer with me for the proclamation of the Good News. (2 Timothy 1:5–8)

Most Americans wouldn't recognize the name of Reverend Mehdi Dibaj. We know nothing of the life and death of Pastor Mohammed Bajher Yuseft. We've never heard the names of hundreds who suffered prison and death under the Muslim takeover in Iran. But since 1979, persecution, torture, imprisonment and martyrdom have become normal for Iranian Christians.

Faced with the ultimate punishment, their voices could not be silenced.

The *Book of Martyrs* (Mark Water, Baker Books, 2001) includes the written defense of Mehdi Dibaj, submitted to the Sari Court of Justice in 1993. Charged with apostasy, and facing the death sentence, he wrote this: "I am a Christian. As a sinner I believe Jesus has died for my sins on the cross and by his resurrection and victory over death, has made me righteous in the presence of the Holy God . . . In response to this kindness, He has asked me to deny myself . . . and not to fear people even if they kill my body, but rather rely on the creator of life . . ."

Facing death, Dibaj had the boldness to proclaim the gospel to the very court which would decide his fate. Charged with converting to Christianity from Islam, Dibaj boldly confirmed his conversion.

Some imprisoned American Christians might wallow in self-pity, or call their lawyers crying "discrimination." Not Dibaj. He expressed deep gratitude for his years of isolation and imprisonment. In fact, of his nine-year confinement, he says: "During these nine years, he (Jesus) has freed me from all my responsibilities so that under the protection of His blessed Name, I would spend my time in prayer and study of His Word, with a searching heart and with brokenness, and grow in the knowledge of my Lord. I praise the Lord for this unique opportunity."

Did Dibaj repent for his evangelizing? Never! Facing death, he wrote: "But if one finds a blind person who is about to fall in a well, and keeps silent then one has sinned. It is our religious duty, as long as the door of God's mercy is open, to convince evildoers to turn from their sinful ways . . . Therefore I am not only satisfied to be in prison for the honor of His Holy Name, but am ready to give my life for the sake of Jesus, my Lord . . ."

Unmoved by his eloquent argument, the court sentenced Dibaj to death. Fellow believers both in Iran and in the United States worked hard to secure his release from prison. Iranian authorities eventually bowed to international pressure and released him in January 1994. Five months later, like hundreds of others publicly released from prison, Dibaj was mysteriously abducted and murdered.

In today's passage, Paul tells us he is not ashamed of the gospel. He encourages Timothy, and all believers, to be ready to share the Good News of forgiveness in Jesus. Sound scary? Don't let the idea frighten you.

Before he returned to heaven Jesus assured his friends that believers have a supernatural ability to tell others about Jesus. This help comes from the Holy Spirit living inside us. No matter where we go, we can be certain to have divinely scheduled appointments to share the truth with others who need to know about God.

We must not avoid our responsibility. We must never let the response of others determine our willingness to speak. You and I will probably never face imprisonment or death for sharing the gospel. Considering the enormous risk—that persons we meet might suffer an eternity in hell—what might keep us from sharing the gospel with others? Embarrassment? Discomfort?

I take courage from stories like those of Mehdi Dibaj. Knowing that others shared the Good News in the face of death, I refuse to let fear close my mouth.

If the Good News really is good news, why wouldn't we want to share it?

Prayer ideas

Are you ashamed of or embarrassed by the gospel? Do you know why? Ask Jesus for boldness to share the truth. Ask him to help you find ways of bringing Jesus into conversations with strangers and friends, to see and take advantage of opportunities as they arise.

WHAT DO I DO NEXT?

And so, dear brothers and sisters, I plead with you to give your bodies to God. Let them be a living and holy sacrifice—the kind he will accept. When you think of what he has done for you, is this too much to ask? Don't copy the behavior and customs of this world, but let God transform you into a new person by changing the way you think. Then you will know what God wants you to do, and you will know how good and pleasing and perfect his will really is. (Romans 12:1, 2)

I admit it; I love writing novels. And at this very moment, I have one hatching in the back of my brain. Whenever I discover myself in this state of Artistic Pregnancy, I begin reading—mostly nonfiction—about whatever subject I'm considering for my next work.

Lately, I've been thinking about HIV-AIDS. I just finished a book by Dr. Abraham Verghese, entitled, *My Own Country: A Doctor's Story*. Verghese, a specialist in Infectious Disease, finished his residency at about the same time that AIDS arrived on the medical scene. The virus that has changed the world shaped his early medical career. According to the book, the AIDS phenomenon nearly managed to break his heart and destroy his marriage.

Verghese was born in Ethiopia to Indian parents, both physics teachers. Though he grew up in Africa, he spent time in Birmingham, England, went to medical school in India, and completed his residency in rural Tennessee. He finished his specialty training in Boston,

Massachusetts. His ability to blend in with any culture came from vast experience.

From his childhood, Verghese never had a real home, never completely fit in anywhere. As a result, he taught himself not to stand out. Verghese became the ultimate human chameleon.

In Tennessee, his nimble tongue entertained the nursing staff with the subtle differences in the regional accents of India. The staff, determined to turn Abraham into a southerner, taught him to enjoy southern food—possum stew, squirrel, and hominy.

He learned to say, "How y'all doin'?" without a hint of Indian accent. Except for his skin color, Abraham Verghese transformed himself into a good ol' boy.

While this ability to blend in helped Verghese find a home in Tennessee, the Scripture warns us against being transformed by the culture around us. We're not to take on the world's values, ideas, or behaviors. Instead, we are to be transformed only by the values, thinking, and behaviors found in the Word of God. As we do, we'll become less and less like the people around us, more and more like Jesus Christ.

Christians are meant to stand out—rather than blend in.

This passage in Romans promises one other thing. As we let the Scriptures transform us, we'll discover more and more about God's will for our lives. As our values fall in line with his, we'll recognize his good plans for us.

As you look at the world around you, how much do your opinions and values match the prevailing culture? Does your thinking reflect the words on the opinion page of the local paper, or the words on the pages of Scripture?

Are you willing to let yourself be transformed by the Word? Will you immerse yourself in Scripture? When will you begin?

Prayer ideas

Ask God to show you how much you have conformed to the ideas of your generation. Ask him to use the Word of God to change your heart. Ask him to help you spend time every day in the Scriptures.

I Don't Like You Much, Either!

"When the world hates you, remember it hated me before it hated you. The world would love you if you belonged to it, but you don't. I chose you to come out of the world, and so it hates you. Do you remember what I told you? 'A servant is not greater than the master.' Since they persecuted me, naturally they will persecute you. And if they had listened to me, they would listen to you! The people of the world will hate you because you belong to me, for they don't know God who sent me. They would not be guilty if I had not come and spoken to them. But now they have no excuse for their sin. Anyone who hates me hates my Father, too. If I hadn't done such miraculous signs among them that no one else could do, they would not be counted guilty. But as it is, they saw all that I did and yet hated both of us—me and my Father. This has fulfilled what the Scriptures said: 'They hated me without cause.'" (John 15:18–25)

One weekend, our church bulletin told the story of Christians in Guinea who had taken a public stand against traditional animistic rituals. Natives there trust these rituals to protect them from the gunfire of rebel forces.

Believers who refuse to participate suffer intense persecution. Some have been imprisoned. Others have been whipped. Still other Christian families are denied access to the marketplace. Standing up for their faith, these believers suffer intense retaliation.

Faith-filled Americans rarely experience such severe consequences. No one who disagrees with us will burn down our house, or destroy our business. But once you are identified with Jesus, you can expect non-believers to reflect some of the same hostile emotions.

Last winter, I took a public stand against an event celebrated at my daughter's high school. My letter to the editor, published in a regional paper, generated many angry responses from readers. But the worst response came from one of my daughter's friends.

This teenager typed a three-page letter and sent it to me. Her anger took the form of harsh words and unfair accusations. Over and over she asked me, "Who do you think you are to inflict your beliefs on this community? Who are you to tell us what is right and what is wrong?"

This girl didn't hate me; she hated my Christian viewpoint. Maggie, my daughter, wanted me to blast her with a reply; I chose not to. My unwillingness frustrated Maggie. She didn't understand that the letter reflected a normal response from those in the world. When we reflect Jesus and his values to the people around us, they won't start a fan club.

Jesus told us we could expect to be hated.

As I prayed about my response to the letter, I felt the Lord ask me to keep the lines of communication open—no matter how much anger the writer had expressed. Continuing an argument about the issue would not solve our dispute. *Who knows,* the Lord seemed to be saying, *when she will need to talk to someone who knows me?*

I wrote to my daughter's friend and thanked her for taking the time to let me know how she felt. Though we might not agree on issues, I assured her we could remain friends. She didn't burn my house down. But she didn't answer my letter either.

Expect the world to reject you because of me, the Lord says. They hated me; how much more they will hate you. Don't let it throw you. Let them hate God's goodness in you.

Prayer ideas

*T*hink about how others have responded since you've begun your life of faith. Have you noticed hostility? Have the reactions of others hurt you? Ask Jesus to make you strong enough to stand up to the world's hatred. Ask him to make himself known in you, more and more as you follow him.

HE WORKS AND I WORK

Unless the Lord builds a house, the work of the builders is useless.

Unless the Lord protects a city, guarding it with sentries will do no good.

It is useless for you to work so hard from early morning until late at night anxiously working for food to eat; for God gives rest to his loved ones. (Psalm 127:1, 2)

I'll never forget my first Guillain Barré patient. I met Sara in the intensive care unit at Overlake Hospital. After I introduced myself, I began the therapy that would keep her joints and limbs flexible over the long course of her illness. Gently, I removed the covers and lifted her flaccid limbs, moving each joint through its proper range of motion.

Though I spoke to her through the entire session, Sarah kept her eyes closed while we worked. She couldn't blink or squeeze her hands. She had no voluntary motion anywhere in her body. We weren't sure how much she understood of the conversations around her.

A week or so before I met her, Sarah had come down with what she thought was a cold. Her fever and sore throat developed into progressive paralysis. I found her in an ICU bed, waiting for her body to return to her.

Just below her voice box, doctors had inserted a breathing tube into her throat. Beside the bed, a machine wheezed and puffed, blowing air into her lungs. Through another tube turquoise fluid dripped into her stomach, providing the nutrients her body needed. Glucose dripped from the IV bag into her forearm, while another tube snaked out from beneath the blankets and disappeared into a bag below the bed.

Guillain Barré is a remarkable disease. Scientists know little about what causes the syndrome. There is no way to prevent it, nor is there a commonly successful cure. Scientists believe it may be an autoimmune disease, caused when the immune system attacks the myelin sheaths (like the insulation on electrical wire) of the body's nerves. The brain finds itself disconnected from the muscles in the body, which produces the progressive paralysis.

GBS often occurs after an upper respiratory or intestinal infection, and can progress very quickly. Symptoms can begin with "crawling skin" and move to complete paralysis within seventy-two hours. Not everyone gets as sick as Sarah.

She spent nearly eight weeks completely dependent on hospital personnel for every facet of her life. Machines breathed for her, ate for her, and monitored her heart while the staff kept her alive. Doctors, nurses, and therapists watched her progress and altered her care as the course of her disease progressed.

Spiritually speaking, we're very much like Sarah was in the peak of her illness—though we rarely see our condition that clearly. Psalm 127 tells us how completely dependent we are on our Heavenly Father—for every detail of our lives. We succeed at work because he helps us. We have happy homes because he blesses us. We're safe because he protects us.

No amount of hard work can overcome his absence in our lives.

Every good thing comes from him. We should take no more pride in our success than Sarah did in her breathing while connected to the machine in the ICU.

Sara rested completely in the care of the folks around her. We'd do well to rest just as completely in the care of our Heavenly Father. No amount of striving could ever make up for his loving care. We can depend on him. He cares for us.

Prayer ideas

*A*re there particular issues you have trouble trusting the Lord with—finances, marriage, work? Take these issues to God in prayer. Talk about how you feel and ask him to help you trust his ability to care for you.

YOU SHOULD SEE THE INSIDE!

The next day Jesus' mother was a guest at a wedding celebration in the village of Cana in Galilee. Jesus and his disciples were also invited to the celebration. The wine supply ran out during the festivities, so Jesus' mother spoke to him about the problem. "They have no more wine," she told him.

"How does that concern you and me?" Jesus asked. "My time has not yet come."

But his mother told the servants, "Do whatever he tells you."

Six stone water pots were standing there; they were used for Jewish ceremonial purposes and held twenty to thirty gallons each. Jesus told the servants, "Fill the jars with water." When the jars had been filled to the brim, he said, "Dip some out and take it to the master of ceremonies." So they followed his instructions.

When the master of ceremonies tasted the water that was now wine, not knowing where it had come from (though of course the servants knew), he called the bridegroom over. "Usually, a host serves the best wine first," he said. "Then when everyone is full and doesn't care, he brings out the less expensive wines. But you have kept the best until now!" (John 2:1–10)

As I write this, I'm floating in Maple Bay, a tiny protected cove on the east coast of Vancouver Island, British Columbia. We've taken our boat north this summer, and are working our way slowly up the coast.

Last night I discovered that a medicine bottle I'd brought from home had shattered. Apparently, during our trip across the Strait of Juan de Fuca, the case with the medicine took a bad bounce. Inside, I found tiny shards of glass everywhere. Though I tried to wipe out the case, glass clung to the inside seams; I decided to rinse the case outside.

In the dark of night, I stepped quietly onto our swim step and bent over the black water. Then, dipping the case in the water, I began to stir. What I saw was completely magical!

The moving water began to glow—almost as if a brilliant floodlight shone just below the swim step. Even the air bubbles glowed with a neon-like intensity. I was so surprised that I nearly dropped my make-up case. I stepped back in wonder.

What was that?

Looking around in the water behind our boat, I noticed the tiny fluorescent trails of moving fish and I realized what I'd seen. Phosphorescence (bioluminescence) is a quality of many living things. In this case, the light came from single-celled algae living in seawater. As I stirred, the moving water caused an electrical current to sweep through the algae emitting visible light.

Bioluminescence is in the water all the time—both day and night. But humans can only see the light when competition from sunlight is completely eliminated.

When Jesus changed water into wine, the outside of the pots remained the same. Only by tasting the contents could the master of ceremonies see that something miraculous had occurred.

The presence of the Lord in our lives causes a change very much like the change inside the pots, or the light in the water. Your decision of faith began with changes on the inside too. Since you chose to follow Jesus, you haven't gotten taller or thinner or more attractive. On the outside—unfortunately—everything looks the same. The real change is on the inside.

At first, you can't really see much. Under the right conditions though, like the phosphorescence in seawater, the change can be clearly observed. When trouble or conflict stirs you, the presence of the Lord will begin to glow. When darkness surrounds you, those nearby will clearly see the light of his presence in you. Be patient.

Watch for the glow of the Lord in your life.

Prayer ideas

*M*ake a list of the changes you've detected since you began your faith walk. Thank the Lord for what he has done. Think about the events that stir you up. Have you seen a glow from the Lord's presence? Ask him to help you glow with Jesus when you are stirred—whether the stirring be trouble, or stress or illness.

A MONSTER OF A WEAKLING!

I don't want anyone to think more highly of me than what they can actually see in my life and my message, even though I have received wonderful revelations from God. But to keep me from getting puffed up, I was given a thorn in my flesh, a messenger from Satan to torment me and keep me from getting proud.

Three different times I begged the Lord to take it away. Each time he said, "My gracious favor is all you need. My power works best in your weakness." So now I am glad to boast about my weaknesses, so that the power of Christ may work through me. Since I know it is all for Christ's good, I am quite content with my weaknesses and with insults, hardships, persecutions, and calamities. For when I am weak, then I am strong. (2 Corinthians 12:6–10)

In 1967, while swimming in a local lake, seventeen-year-old Joni Eareckson dove from a small raft into the murky water below breaking her neck and driving bone fragments into her spinal cord. What began as a normal summer day, laughing and playing with friends, ended with Joni lying paralyzed in a hospital bed, wearing stainless steel rods driven through her skull.

The injury devastated Joni emotionally and physically. She could not imagine how God would allow something so horrible to happen. Over the next two years, she struggled with her emotions, eventually giving up her anger and turning her life over to God. Still, she wanted to be healed, and continued to seek prayer for a miraculous recovery.

The recovery never came.

Eventually at peace with her disability, she wrote the book *Joni*. Since then, Joni has married and gone on to form a Christian ministry, *Joni and Friends*—dedicated to extending the message of Jesus to people in the disabled community. Having written more than thirty books, she has received both the Gold Medallion from the Evangelical Christian Publishers Association and a C. S. Lewis Silver Medal.

Would any of these things have happened without the accident?

Late in 1997, a Chinese physician, newly paralyzed by a diving accident of his own, read *Joni*—a twenty-year-old English-language copy provided by his therapist. As he read, he realized his need for God. After reading Joni's book, Dr. Zhang Xu began his own faith journey.

Later, he realized the great value in the words Joni shared. He longed to translate the book and make it available to others in China. Eventually, Dr. Xu managed to translate *Joni,* and with the permission of Zondervan Publishers, found a Chinese government press willing to print copies of the book.

Today, *Joni* is the only Christian book being printed by the Chinese government. Its title, translated roughly as, "Where Is God? Finding the Limits in Man's Strength," expresses the truth both Dr. Xu and Joni discovered in their illness.

In Joni's weakness with paralysis, God wanted to do something marvelous, something more far-reaching than a simple physical healing. In Dr. Xu's weakness, God managed to bring the message of Jesus to an entire nation.

Of the translating process, Dr. Xu later said this, "At that time, I was still very weak, but I could work until late every day. I wondered how that could happen. Later I realized that God had been watching out for me, and gave me strength and wisdom."

Truly, weakness—our illness, our fatigue, and our sorrow—brings out our dependence on God. Only in our weakness do we proud humans humble ourselves enough to ask for his strength. When we do, we find his mighty strength more than adequate to meet our needs.

When I am weak, he is strong. Who could ask for more?

Prayer ideas

Are you especially aware of your own weaknesses? Have you talked with God about it? Have you asked him for strength?

I Have to Tell You What?

Are any among you suffering? They should keep on praying about it. And those who have reason to be thankful should continually sing praises to the Lord.

Are any among you sick? They should call for the elders of the church and have them pray over them, anointing them with oil in the name of the Lord. And their prayer offered in faith will heal the sick, and the Lord will make them well. And anyone who has committed sins will be forgiven.

Confess your sins to one another and pray for each other so that you may be healed. The earnest prayer of a righteous person has great power and wonderful results. (James 5:13–16)

Not long ago, while creating a costume for a Christmas play, I ran a sewing machine needle through my index finger. In and out—a quick injury, followed by intense and long-lasting pain. I wrapped my fingertip in an ice pack and sat on the couch crying.

I managed to finish the costume, attend rehearsals, and put on a relatively successful show. But nearly a week later, continued pain, along with marked swelling and redness told me I had an infection.

I visited my doctor who checked my inoculation record and started me on a course of antibiotics. Fortunately, the infection cleared up without complication.

Had I ignored my regular vaccinations, or worse yet, ignored the symptoms of illness, I might have contracted tetanus—commonly known as lockjaw. I might have experienced muscular rigidity, convulsions, and eventually death by respiratory paralysis. Tetanus is caused by the bacterium *Clostridium Tetani,* whose spores are everywhere. Contrary to popular myth, any scratch can become the source of a fatal infection.

Interestingly, all *Clostridium* are anaerobic—meaning they grow only in environments without oxygen. This characteristic makes puncture wounds especially vulnerable to infection. The body covers the surface of the wound quickly, leaving a deep dark hole—completely without oxygen—where the bacterium can flourish.

Even superficial wounds, when not sufficiently cleaned, can leave enough residual dirt to infect the tissue with *Clostridium.* When injured tissue blocks oxygen—voila! Tetanus.

Sin infects a believer in the same way that *Clostridium* infects a wound. It grows in the dark. It multiplies and gains power. The more we try to cover our sin, the more destructive and powerful it becomes. The more we ignore the damage sin causes, the stronger its foothold.

Eventually, the foothold begins to feel more like a chokehold.

We must bring sin out in the open. Exposed to the air, *Clostridium* dies. Exposed to the light of Jesus, and the caring of other believers, sin dies.

James tells us that in the context of community, something mysterious happens. By exposing our struggles with sin, with life, and with other people, we find healing. When we pray for one another, we clean out the source of sin, exposing our soul damage to the light of Jesus. Only then can the healing process begin.

No one can explain how or why all of this happens—any more than we can explain why *Clostridium* likes dark covered places.

We bring healing when we practice community. We must develop safe relationships where we can honestly expose our difficulties. Then, we follow up with prayer. Together with other believers we pursue holiness, knowing that something miraculous happens when we confess and pray. Who among us couldn't use a miracle now and then?

Prayer ideas

Have you found a small group where you can be honest about your progress in the Christian life? Ask the Lord about finding one. Ask him for courage and commitment to go. Make being part of a small group a big part of your faith life.

DAY 70

I KNEW IT DIDN'T MAKE SENSE!

For Christ didn't send me to baptize, but to preach the Good News—and not with clever speeches and high-sounding ideas, for fear that the cross of Christ would lose its power.

I know very well how foolish the message of the cross sounds to those who are on the road to destruction. But we who are being saved recognize this message as the very power of God. As the scriptures say:

I will destroy human wisdom and discard their most brilliant ideas.

So where does this leave the philosophers, the scholars, and the world's brilliant debaters? God has made them all look foolish and has shown their wisdom to be useless nonsense . . . God's way seems foolish to the Jews because they want a sign from heaven to prove it is true. And it is foolish to the Greeks because they believe only what agrees with their own wisdom. So when we preach that Christ was crucified, the Jews are offended, and the Gentiles say it is all nonsense. But to those called by God to salvation, both Jews and Gentiles, Christ is the mighty power of God and the wonderful wisdom of God. This foolish plan of God is far wiser than the wisest of human plans, and God's weakness is far stronger than the greatest of human strength. (1 Corinthians 1:17–25)

I've heard it said that no one, having once stepped inside a restaurant kitchen, would ever eat out again. Of course the speaker generally refers to the cleanliness—or lack thereof—of the counters, sinks, and floors. Few ever talk about the folks who work behind the scenes in local restaurants.

In my last year of college, I waited tables at Bell's Restaurant, in Seattle, Washington. Bell's was the kind of old-fashioned place where retired people lined up around the block to eat dinner at 4:30 in the afternoon—saving three bucks a plate by ordering dinner from the lunch menu. We waitresses wore green gingham aprons over black skirts. Most of us wore nursing shoes. The shifts were exhausting; the crowds were endless. We worked without breaks.

Back in the kitchen our head cook reigned supreme. Tony considered the entire area around the kitchen his domain, and refused entry to the rest of us. He ridiculed any waitress who dared to let his food cool before serving it to his customers. His language was crude and his hygiene nearly nonexistent. But his tongue was sharp enough to cut glass.

Tony hated the waitresses, though I never could figure out why. I don't think we'd ever done anything terrible to him. At the time, I thought his bad attitude forced him to systematically dump on all of us. Now though, I think his animosity was tied to our commitment to Christ. The restaurant owners both professed Jesus; they handpicked the waitresses from their church.

While I was learning the ropes, Tony ridiculed my faith. At first I made the mistake of trying to defend Jesus. To his delight, I lost every argument. The harder I tried—arming myself with Scripture, and examples from books I'd read—the more he derided me. I felt discouraged and humiliated. Shouldn't I be able to persuade him to change his mind?

Later that summer, I read today's Bible passage and found great encouragement in those words. I finally realized what bothered Tony so much. Our gospel was foolishness to him—not because of my inadequacy, or my poor debate skills. Tony's antagonism was only proof that he'd chosen the road to destruction. Nothing I could do would ever change his mind.

It wasn't that the Good News was foolish, rather, that the gospel was foolish *to him*. Until the miracle of transformation occurred, Tony remained caught in a net of misunderstanding and pride. Only the Holy Spirit can break through that wall.

I learned not to take Tony personally. When I gave up arguing, the war of the kitchen began to subside. When I returned to school, Tony had not yet made a faith decision. We'd become friends of a sort. And I told my friend the truth.

Salvation is a work of the Holy Spirit. We can leave the convincing to him.

Prayer ideas

*H*ave your friends or family belittled your faith decision? Have you taken your hurt to Jesus in prayer? Ask God to open that person's eyes to the wisdom of salvation.

I GIVE UP!

It seems to be a fact of life that when I want to do what is right, I inevitably do what is wrong. I love God's law with all my heart. But there is another law at work within me that is at war with my mind. This law wins the fight and makes me a slave to the sin that is still within me. Oh, what a miserable person I am! Who will free me from this life that is dominated by sin? Thank God! The answer is in Jesus Christ our Lord. So you see how it is: In my mind I really want to obey God's law, but because of my sinful nature I am a slave to sin.

So, now there is no condemnation for those who belong to Christ Jesus. For the power of the life giving Spirit has freed you through Christ Jesus from the power of sin that leads to death. The law of Moses could not save us, because of our sinful nature. But God put into effect a different plan to save us. He sent his own Son in a human body like ours, except that ours are sinful. God destroyed sin's control over us by giving his Son as a sacrifice for our sins. (Romans 7:21—8:3)

I passed my certification test for scuba diving in 1991—but nearly drowned doing it. Late on a warm September morning, five of us, clad in wetsuits and scuba gear, entered the water determined to complete several simple assignments on our last dive together.

A borrowed wetsuit made one of my classmates too buoyant, unable to get below the surface of the water. Before we began skill testing, our instructor took some of my lead weights and put them on her weight belt. Eventually, she went under—though we still had to fill her vest pockets with rocks. The extra work put us behind schedule; the tide began to change.

One of our safety skills required us to remove our BC vests and put them back on. These cumbersome vests carry the air tanks which enable scuba divers to breathe underwater. With limited peripheral vision, the clasps and armholes of these inflatable vests are difficult to find—especially for a beginner. My classmates had no trouble.

When my turn came, I couldn't take my vest off. When I finally did, the flowing water of the changing tide ripped the vest from my hands. It quickly floated away, out of my reach—my air tank attached. With nothing left to hold me above water, I went under like a rock.

I still remember the feeling of complete surprise as I sank so quickly. Desperate for air, I kicked as hard as I could and managed to rise seven feet for a quick gasp of air. Before I could get a second breath, my weight belt dragged me down again; I managed to scream just as the water closed over my face.

Kicking desperately, I watched the water go by as I sank. My weight belt (carrying twenty pounds of lead) dragged me to the bottom. If I wanted to live, I had to drop the belt. But for some crazy reason, I wouldn't do it. *It's rented*, I thought. *I don't want to pay for losing a weight belt.*

Fortunately, my dive master dove after me. Grabbing my vest, he re-inflated his own, compensating for the lead still attached to my waist. Together, we bobbed to the surface as though nothing had happened. He laughed, and I sputtered. Without his quick reactions, I'd have drowned.

Over the years, I've continued diving. Thankfully, my skills have grown. But I'll never forget the overwhelming pull of lead weight, or the absolute certainty of my own death. Without help, my weight belt would have taken my life.

In the Kingdom of the World, no one talks much about sin. Rather, people accept it, make excuses for it, or wink at it as though sin were perfectly acceptable behavior. In the Kingdom of the World, you hear expressions like "boys will be boys," or "when you lie down with dogs you wake up with fleas." In the world, folks don't fight sin; they accept it.

But in the Kingdom of God, sin can't be ignored. Calling it what it is, we confront sin head-on—with no excuses. We know that living with sin is like trying to float while wearing lead weights. It can't be done. In our life of faith, we are not excused from our struggle with sin. We become more aware of sin, more determined to fight against it.

Though I can't explain it, I know this: Only Jesus can remove the weight of sin from the human soul. In Jesus, we can stay afloat.

Prayer ideas

Are you frustrated by a sin you can't seem to overcome? Have you talked with God about your frustration? Are you tempted to just give in? Have you told Jesus? Ask Jesus to give you a friend who can help you with the battle you face. Ask Jesus to give you enough strength to keep from surrendering the battle.

TAKE IT ALL OFF!

Since you have heard all about him and have learned the truth that is in Jesus, throw off your old evil nature and your former way of life, which is rotten through and through, full of lust and deception. Instead, there must be a spiritual renewal of your thoughts and attitudes. You must display a new nature because you are a new person, created in God's likeness—righteous, holy, and true.

So put away all falsehood and "tell your neighbor the truth" because we belong to each other. And "don't sin by letting anger gain control over you." Don't let the sun go down while you are still angry, for anger gives a mighty foothold to the Devil. If you are a thief, stop stealing. Begin using your hands for honest work, and then give generously to others in need. Don't use foul or abusive language. Let everything you say be good and helpful, so that your words will be an encouragement to those who hear them.

And do not bring sorrow to God's Holy Spirit by the way you live. Remember, he is the one who has identified you as his own, guaranteeing that you will be saved on the day of redemption. Get rid of all bitterness, rage, anger, harsh words, and slander, as well as all types of malicious behavior. Instead, be kind to each other, tenderhearted, forgiving one another, just as God through Christ has forgiven you. (Ephesians 4: 21–32)

I'll bet you've been caught in the old computer glitch before. You need a new application, or a new type of hardware. But as soon as you install it, all the other parts—the old parts that used to work—suddenly decide to go on vacation. You find yourself with a lovely beige box that makes a lot of noise, and produces nothing.

Frustration doesn't begin to describe the feeling.

I use two computers—both a desktop and a laptop—accomplishing much of my work in the car or while waiting for the kids. Some time ago, my laptop took on a terminal illness. As it was already old enough to become a boat anchor, I decided to buy a new one, which came with a different operating system than my desktop.

This, of course, made my desktop computer completely obsolete; the two machines refused to have anything to do with one another. In spite of my best efforts, the disks created in the laptop were unreadable by the desktop.

I considered calling in a counselor.

It seemed I had no choice. I had to install the new operating system on the desktop computer as well. What I got was a huge mess. After four days of intense work, I now have two machines who share files.

But the whole terrible event reminds me of the confusion new believers experience when the Holy Spirit installs a new operating system on the hard drive of our souls. Paul doesn't call it an operating system; he calls it a new nature. Still, the Holy Spirit doesn't erase the hard drive of our old nature before the new system goes in.

He doesn't do what computer gurus call a "clean install."

Instead, all the old stuff remains—clouding up our minds and hearts—refusing to let the new system take hold and run smoothly.

Defragmenting the human soul is a lifelong process. Day by day, in cooperation with the Holy Spirit, we find the old files—the old life instructions—and delete them. Though it takes years, we find the instructions that say, "Boil over when someone cuts you off in traffic," and we delete them. Then, we find the old instructions that say, "Think of your own needs first," and we delete them.

But we can't stop there; we don't just remove the old instructions. As we erase our old files, we must install new behaviors and habits that reflect our new life in Christ. Instead of thinking of our own needs first, we might greet our spouse on Saturday morning with a phrase like this: "What can I do for you today?"

I lost four days to the frustrating task of reconfiguring the desktop operating system. I didn't display the kind of patience I would have liked. I found myself short-tempered with the whole world; my family noticed. Now that things are running—well actually, sort of running—I'm feeling better.

But four days are nothing to the lifetime we must invest in changing our soul's operating system. The Scripture calls the process "taking off" and "putting on." Whatever you call it, the process requires that believers actively participate.

Over time, our new system will begin to operate more smoothly. We'll experience fewer crashes and freezes. With time, we'll forget how the old system did things, and find the new behaviors more and more natural. Will you commit to a lifetime of debugging your soul system? Will you diligently replace the old habits with new ones? Though I've followed Christ for nearly thirty years, I'm still debugging the system. Have patience with me, and I promise the same for you.

Prayer ideas

Ask the Lord to make you especially aware of you old habits. Ask him to help you to stop and rethink your response to stressful situations. Ask for new behaviors that reflect the reality of your freedom from sin, and the presence of the Holy Spirit living in you.

DAY 73

AH, THE JOY OF A BATH!

Have mercy on me, O God, because of your unfailing love. Because of your great compassion, blot out the stain of my sins. Wash me clean from my guilt. Purify me from my sin. For I recognize my shameful deeds—they haunt me day and night. Against you, and you alone, have I sinned; I have done what is evil in your sight. You will be proved right in what you say, and your judgment against me is just. For I was born a sinner—yes, from the moment my mother conceived me. But you desire honesty from the heart, so you can teach me to be wise in my inmost being.

Purify me from my sins, and I will be clean; wash me, and I will be whiter than snow. Oh, give me back my joy again; you have broken me—now let me rejoice. Don't keep looking at my sins. Remove the stain of my guilt. Create in me a clean heart, O God. Renew a right spirit within me. Do not banish me from your presence, and don't take your Holy Spirit from me. Restore to me again the joy of your salvation, and make me willing to obey you. Then I will teach your ways to sinners, and they will return to you. Forgive me for shedding blood, O God who saves; then I will joyfully sing of your forgiveness. Unseal my lips, O Lord, that I may praise you. You would not be pleased with sacrifices, or I would bring them. If I brought you a burnt offering, you would not accept it. The sacrifice you want is a broken spirit. A broken and repentant heart, O God, you will not despise. (Psalm 51:1–17)

After my senior year in Physical Therapy, I interned at the Harborview Burn Center in Seattle, Washington. My patients, people of all ages, suffered extensive burns caused by a wide range of injuries. Some had been in car accidents. Others used gasoline to start their barbecues. Many were firefighters, injured in the line of duty.

No matter how they were burned, they faced a common healing process. First, they had to be medically stabilized. That sometimes took weeks. Then, before healthy tissue could be grafted onto the wound, all of the dead and burned tissue had to be completely removed.

In those days, the debridement process involved lengthy soaks in sterile tanks. Nurses followed this with exacting procedures to remove tissue. Sometimes, a high-pressure stream of water shot directly at the burn washed off chunks of dead tissue. Other times, the injured skin—dried onto the dressings—was torn away as nurses removed gauze from the injury. Frequently, the last bits of tissue had to be removed one tiny piece at a time with sterile forceps and gauze.

Needless to say, the procedure was excruciatingly painful. As soon as I opened their hospital doors, my patients often greeted me with vile cursing. They knew what I'd come to do, and they dreaded it. Rightfully, they associated my presence with intense pain. Still it had to be done. No skin graft would ever grow on anything less than healthy, well-vascularized tissue. We paved the way for healthy new skin by removing the dead stuff.

Letting sin flourish in our lives is like leaving the dead tissue on a burn wound. Instead, when we're open about our mistakes with God, when we freely confess and ask his forgiveness, he removes the death that sin brings. Confession leaves our spirits clean and healthy, ready for new growth, new opportunity, and new fruit. Though God doesn't always remove the consequences of our sins, he does promise to restore us to right relationship with him.

Maintaining a right relationship with God requires that we commit to honesty, always sensitive to his assessment about the condition of our lives. In the rich soil of honest confession, we cultivate great harvests of spiritual fruit.

Prayer ideas

How honest are you about your mistakes? Would your family and coworkers agree with your assessment? Ask the Lord to make you sensitive to your own sin. Then, ask for help confessing your faults. Start with the little things. Experience the freedom and health of frequent forgiveness.

I WEIGH HOW MUCH?

Therefore, since we are surrounded by such a huge crowd of witnesses to the life of faith, let us strip off every weight that slows us down, especially the sin that so easily hinders our progress. And let us run with endurance the race that God has set before us. We do this by keeping our eyes on Jesus, on whom our faith depends from start to finish. He was willing to die a shameful death on the cross because of the joy he knew would be his afterward. Now he is seated in the place of highest honor beside God's throne in heaven. Think about all he endured when sinful people did such terrible things to him, so that you don't become weary and give up. After all, you have not yet given your lives in your struggle against sin. (Hebrews 12:1–4)

One summer, a friend of mine challenged me to ride the Seattle to Portland Bicycle Classic. This ride is a Northwest legend. Every year nearly eight thousand riders take two days to make the 200-mile journey along country roads through rural farmland. I've always loved biking, and this seemed like a great opportunity to do this ride with a group of friends.

In October, we rode together for the first time. I had an old mountain bike, and as we started down the Interurban Trail, I could barely keep up with the other ladies. Though they were ten years younger than I, I hated falling behind. I changed gears and pedaled harder. Still, I couldn't keep up. Later that evening, I soaked myself in Tylenol and collapsed on the couch. We'd only ridden ten miles.

I realized I needed a lighter bike, and began the search while still riding my old clunker. I grew stronger. In January, I managed to locate a frame small enough for me. I bought a road bike with comfort handlebars, ten pounds lighter than my old bike. Finally, I could keep up with my riding partners.

We began participating in organized rides in early spring. On our first ride, my riding partner's chain came off her bike several times; one of those nearly made her fall. She and her husband decided to give up on their mountain bikes and buy new road bikes. One week later, with both of them on shiny new bikes, I struggled again to keep up.

It seemed clear that I couldn't go on buying new bikes forever. I went back to my dealer. "I want to ride faster," I said. "My partner is six feet tall. She has a fifty-eight centimeter frame and I just can't keep up."

We discussed the options, and decided to narrow my handlebars to match my shoulder width. Then, we lowered their position on the bike. We hoped to make me more aerodynamic and thus more efficient as I cut through the air.

Several rides later, I still struggled to keep up. I could climb hills easily, but I fell behind going downhill and on the flats. On hilly terrain, I could fall five or more minutes behind very quickly. After one very hilly ride, I went home determined to strip every single extra ounce of weight from my bike.

I removed reflectors from my wheels, and a signal bell from the handlebars. I went through my tool kit and took out the chain tool; I don't know how to fix a chain anyway. I dumped my extra tire wrench. I threw away the boxes my tubes came in. I even decided to carry only one water bottle at a time. That saved twenty ounces. I wanted the bike as light as I could possibly make it.

Though I wasn't racing to Portland; I knew that every ounce of extra weight made my work harder. I didn't want to set a record. I wanted to keep up. I wanted to finish strong.

If only I felt as passionately about my faith race. Somehow that goal seems more obscure, the finish line harder to imagine. If only I were as willing to cut away anything that might keep me from finishing my race with Christ.

Instead, I cling to sin. I long for the comfort of having my own way, letting my emotions make my decisions. I let my pride grow wild, instead of plucking it from the garden of my soul.

Spiritually, I'm like the bike rider who pedals down the road on an antique bicycle, dragging lead anchors behind me. I wonder why I'm tired. I wonder why I make so little progress.

Let us cut away anything that holds us back. Don't let sin slow you down. Don't let it make you work so hard. Cut it away. Finish the race!

Prayer ideas

When your spiritual life feels a little harder than normal, consider this Scripture. Is sin holding you back? Are you holding on to sin? Ask God what might be slowing your progress. Ask for help in cutting away the weight.

GO AHEAD AND CRY!

I am no longer sorry that I sent that letter to you, though I was sorry for a time, for I know that it was painful to you for a little while. Now I am glad I sent it, not because it hurt you, but because the pain caused you to have remorse and change your ways. It was the kind of sorrow God wants his people to have, so you were not harmed by us in any way. For God can use sorrow in our lives to help us turn away from sin and seek salvation. We will never regret that kind of sorrow. But sorrow without repentance is the kind that results in death.

Just see what this godly sorrow produced in you! Such earnestness, such concern to clear yourselves, such indignation, such alarm, such longing to see me, such zeal, and such a readiness to punish the wrongdoer. You showed that you have done everything you could to make things right. My purpose was not to write about who did the wrong or who was wronged. I wrote to you so that in the sight of God you could show how much you really do care for us. (2 Corinthians 7:8–12)

I love a map as much as the next guy. I just never realized how important they could be until I started participating in the training rides for the Seattle to Portland bicycle race. On my first ride with the Cascade Bike Club, they handed us a photocopy of a Seattle street map and sent us on our way. The dumb thing hadn't even been enlarged.

Somehow, with nothing more than this unmarked collection of lines and spaces, we were expected to find our way from the old

Sandpoint Naval Air Station around Mercer Island and back to the bike club—a route of more than thirty-five miles. When I found myself at the tail end of a group of much faster riders, I began to worry about losing my way. What if I lost sight of the riders ahead of me? Would I ever find my way back to the car?

Though I tried to keep them in sight, I soon found myself hot and thirsty and thoroughly alone. The group dropped me—bike talk for being left in the dust. I kept riding, hoping I hadn't made a wrong turn somewhere. Eventually, by God's great grace, I found other riders heading back to the club, and tagged along behind them. One of these riders rode the Mercer Island route regularly. She didn't need a map.

At one point, the group ahead of me swerved into a residential area I didn't recognize. I kept going, thinking they'd made a mistake. A block later, I found myself alone again. The other riders didn't come back. Though I felt certain they'd made a mistake, I turned around and headed back for the intersection. Five blocks later I caught up. I should have known they knew the way.

Repentance is a little like getting lost on your bike. You can slow down. You can recheck the map. You can hope your route catches the correct one somewhere up ahead. But once you realize you're headed the wrong way, there is only one solution.

You must turn around.

The same is true of sin. You can try to slow down. You can hope your route will lead you back to the way of faith. You can talk about it. You can explain it, or excuse it. You can even ask for forgiveness. You can blame it on your background or someone else's behavior. But there is only one way to undo the damage of a wrong turn into sin.

You must turn around.

You must do whatever it takes to stop the wheels of your life, and change direction. Don't talk about it. Don't consider it. Don't wink at it. Don't flirt with it. Don't pray for strength against it. You must walk away from the sin that grabs you, and run—or ride—in the opposite direction as quickly as your little legs will carry you.

This is the true meaning of repentance: changing direction.

The Corinthian church had made a wrong turn. They'd chosen to overlook sin that had invaded the body of Christ. Paul wrote his first letter to the Corinthians to point out their need to turn around. His words were direct, almost brash; he cared more about their spiritual health than he did about their feelings. To his delight, they responded. They felt great sorrow for having allowed sin to gain a foothold in their lives.

And that sorrow—because it led to a change of direction—was a good thing for these believers. So, while you may want to avoid sorrow, and you might want to run from pain, take a lesson from Paul. Sometimes, sorrow helps us realize we are headed in the wrong direction. And in the end, only a change of direction will bring us safely home.

Prayer ideas

Have you found yourself heading down a wrong road? What have you done to change direction? Ask Jesus if there is something more you might do. Is your change of direction genuine—do you really want to turn back? Or, are you trying to ease your guilty conscience? Ask Jesus to make these issues clear to you. Then, ask for strength to obey.

OH, SCARY!

As Jesus was climbing out of the boat, a man who was possessed by demons came out to meet him. Homeless and naked, he had lived in a cemetery for a long time. As soon as he saw Jesus, he shrieked and fell to the ground before him, screaming, "Why are you bothering me, Jesus, Son of the Most High God? Please, I beg you, don't torture me!" For Jesus had already commanded the evil spirit to come out of him. This spirit had often taken control of the man. Even when he was shackled with chains, he simply broke them and rushed out into the wilderness, completely under the demon's power.

"What is your name?" Jesus asked.

"Legion," he replied—for the man was filled with many demons. The demons kept begging Jesus not to send them into the Bottomless Pit. A large herd of pigs was feeding on the hillside nearby, and the demons pleaded with him to let them enter into the pigs. Jesus gave them permission. So the demons came out of the man and entered the pigs, and the whole herd plunged down the steep hillside into the lake, where they drowned.

When the herdsmen saw it, they fled to the nearby city and the surrounding countryside, spreading the news as they ran. A crowd soon gathered around Jesus, for they wanted to see for themselves what had happened. And they saw the man who had been possessed by demons sitting quietly at Jesus' feet, clothed and sane. And the whole crowd was afraid. Then those who had seen what happened told the others how the demon-possessed man had been healed. And all the people in that region begged Jesus to go away and leave them alone, for a great wave of fear swept over them.

So Jesus returned to the boat and left, crossing back to the other side of the lake. The man who had been demon possessed begged to go, too, but Jesus said, "No, go back to your family and tell them all the wonderful things God has done for you." So he went all through the city telling about the great thing Jesus had done for him. (Luke 8:27–39)

When my daughter studied education at Washington State University, she took a class in children's literature. Everyone had to write about the "Harry Potter Controversy." She asked for my help. Over Thanksgiving, we researched public opinions on this best-selling children's series. Vaguely aware of the swirling arguments, I found the various opinions informative:

"No one should comment about witches until they take the time to understand them."

"Christians shouldn't read anything at all about wizards."

"What difference does it make? It's only a story."

"There's no such thing as demons or devils, anyway."

We found plenty of material for Molly's paper. And though I've never read the Harry Potter books, I have read the Bible. From today's passage—about a naked man in a cemetery—I know a great deal about the world of demons and humans:

1. If the Bible is true, then demons do desire to control humans. We can't dismiss the idea as fantasy, or foolishness. Neither can we assume that all our problems stem from demonic interference. In this story, Jesus accurately discerned the source of the man's problem. Only then did he help him.
2. Demons don't like to share power. When they get involved with humans, they want complete control. Uninhibited by chains or ropes, these guys took complete control over their victim.
3. When demons overcome humans, humans lose. This poor guy lived completely isolated from his friends and family. Jesus found him homeless and naked—living in the middle of a cemetery.
4. Not only do demons like control, they resist change. These demons liked living inside this poor man, and they didn't want Jesus to change things.

5. Jesus wanted to set the man free. He knew the man would be better off without a legion of demons living inside of him. Seems like a simple conclusion, but in this day and age, this kind of wisdom seems beyond the general population. "What can be wrong with a few demons?" people ask.

6. Jesus had absolute power over a "legion" of deadly demons. We need to keep this one fact foremost in our mind. Jesus is in absolute, complete control. When he says, "Go," they go. Demons must obey the Commander of the Universe. We can be secure in his control, never fearing the work of demons.

In gratitude for new life, this man begs Jesus to go along on the boat. "No," Jesus responds. "Tell others about what I have done for you." His command is as important to us as it was to the man he set free. If each of us would tell others about Jesus' work in us, we could spread the Good News more effectively than any of our modern evangelistic techniques. So, tell me, what has Jesus done for you?

In the Kingdom of the World people wink at the reality of Satan, placing him in the same category as the Tooth Fairy, and the Easter Bunny.

In the Kingdom of God, we acknowledge that we have a real enemy, whose intentions for us include control and destruction. And, we rejoice in our Savior whose unlimited power exceeds Satan's every meager effort.

Prayer ideas

What did you think of demons before you were saved? Has your thinking changed? Ask Jesus to show you how you might not be taking the reality of an enemy seriously enough. Spend some time praising the Lord for his power over every other spiritual force in heaven and on earth!

GUERILLA WARFARE

Be careful! Watch out for attacks from the Devil, your great enemy. He prowls around like a roaring lion, looking for some victim to devour. (1 Peter 5:8)

He canceled the record that contained the charges against us. He took it and destroyed it by nailing it to Christ's cross. In this way, God disarmed the evil rulers and authorities. He shamed them publicly by his victory over them on the cross of Christ. (Colossians 2:14, 15)

While working to finish my last fiction project, I researched the Vietnam conflict. In the process, I made new friends—men who served in Vietnam, forever altered by their experience in Southeast Asia. Dropped by helicopter into the thick of war, these men faced an enemy unlike any the United States had ever encountered.

Essentially invisible, the North Vietnamese had no qualms about firing through innocent bystanders to reach U.S. troops—their bullets sometimes slicing innocent school children in half. Masters of the unexpected and without value for human life, the North Vietnamese hid grenades in the rice baskets of grandmothers. They strapped explosives to the chests of children. In humid jungles, rice paddies, rivers, and caves, our displaced troops fought the enemy in his own backyard—an enemy who played by rules we could not understand.

Guerilla warfare defied traditional fighting techniques. After battling for days to defend ground, this bizarre enemy would suddenly vanish into the jungle, as though losing ground didn't matter. American soldiers had no "front lines," no safe place, no real rest. As a result, our boys had no downtime. Twenty-four hours of every day, for thirteen solid months, our soldiers faced imminent death.

Though the French spent years trying to manage Vietnam, they never really succeeded. Even with new goals and techniques, we didn't do much better. Nine years after the first American soldiers entered Vietnam, we withdrew in humiliation.

Today, Christians face an equally deadly enemy, just as crafty, just as invisible. Satan uses tactics we haven't seen before. He puts no value on human life. In fact, he delights in death. He'll stop at nothing to accomplish his goals—wanting more than anything to separate families, split churches, destroy friendships, and disable ministries.

The Bible says we must be vigilant, always watching, expecting his divisive approach. Though we cannot blame every dark moment on our enemy, we certainly know that he exists and his plan for us is evil.

Why does Satan continue to harass believers? Even though he has been defeated by Jesus' death on the cross, he continues to fight. He continues to distract. Perhaps he hopes to keep us from sharing the Good News. By recognizing his work, we can stand against him.

Our enemy must give in. He has no strength against the Commander in Chief, Jesus Christ. Recognize and resist the enemy. He has no power over you.

Prayer ideas

How does it feel to know that Satan is a defeated foe? Ask God to help you recognize the benefits you've gained over this relentless enemy. Consider the ways Satan might be trying to distract you. Ask the Lord to help you stand against him.

WHO ME? FIGHT?

A final word: Be strong with the Lord's mighty power. Put on all of God's armor so that you will be able to stand firm against all strategies and tricks of the Devil. For we are not fighting against people made of flesh and blood, but against the evil rulers and authorities of the unseen world, against those mighty powers of darkness who rule this world, and against wicked spirits in the heavenly realms.

Use every piece of God's armor to resist the enemy in the time of evil, so that after the battle you will still be standing firm. Stand your ground, putting on the sturdy belt of truth and the body armor of God's righteousness. For shoes, put on the peace that comes from the Good News, so that you will be fully prepared. In every battle you will need faith as your shield to stop the fiery arrows aimed at you by Satan. Put on salvation as your helmet, and take the sword of the Spirit, which is the word of God. Pray at all times and on every occasion in the power of the Holy Spirit. Stay alert and be persistent in your prayers for all Christians everywhere. (Ephesians 6:10–18)

We are human, but we don't wage war with human plans and methods. We use God's mighty weapons, not mere worldly weapons, to knock down the Devil's strongholds. (2 Corinthians 10:3, 4)

When I asked my friend, Vietnam veteran Chuck Dean, about the weapons of earthly warfare, he wrote this response, "In Vietnam we never went on patrol without all our equipment and the necessary items to survive combat. As soldiers we became keenly aware of the importance of being prepared and protected before entering critical situations. Being in God's army is no different . . ."

So what did Chuck and his fellow soldiers carry along on patrol?

- An M-16 or assigned weapon with one hundred rounds of ammunition.
- A steel helmet, with camouflage cover.
- A flak jacket.
- Jungle boots, with steel shank.
- Pistol belt, with all their necessities hung by suspenders.
- Bayonet.
- Canteens.
- Ammo pouches.
- First Aid pouch.
- Hand grenades.
- Pack with dry socks, C-rations, poncho liner (to keep off rain or bugs), mosquito repellent, and empty sandbags.

These soldiers knew that staying alive while fighting the enemy depended on being well prepared. At any time, these soldiers might be fired upon, captured, or separated from their group. They carried only the most essential tools with them at all times. A soldier would no more leave camp unprepared than we'd go to work naked.

If soldiers in earthly wars prepare themselves, how much more should we who engage a supernatural enemy?

Each of us must learn how to pack our own bags, to carry our own weapons. Some Christians put on the armor of Christ in theoretical terms. They recite today's Scripture passage as if the words themselves were magic.

I tend to take a more literal approach. As I consider my spiritual weapons, I try to review each piece of armor, meditating on the truth contained in the weapon. I think about my salvation, and the miracle of my coming to Christ. I think about how knowing God has protected my mind from foolish philosophy and the fads of men. I review my commitment to Jesus.

I think about the truth of the gospel, and how all truth must fall in line (literally, hang from) the truth of the Word of God. This truth hangs around my waist, close to my hands—providing support for every weapon I carry.

I think about how my relationship with God has given me new peace, and I meditate on my obligation to bring that peace to others. I pray for courage to share the gospel with whomever the Lord might bring into my path.

I think about the temptations I've endured over the past twenty-four hours, the temptations of pride, anger, selfishness, and I consider which bit of God's Word might counter the lies Satan has hurled my way. I try to use the Bible as an assault weapon in my battle.

I try to hide a bit of God's Word in my mind every day, before some crisis demands that I find it. I know the Word of God is an active weapon, tearing apart anything standing in its way. Like a soldier who cleans and readies his weapon, I try to store up my ammunition—the Word of God—and have it ready to use whenever the enemy exposes himself.

When I first became a Christian, I believed that conflict had to do with people. Now I know better. While some conflict comes from our own selfish humanity, some comes from the unseen world. How the enemy of our souls would love for us to hate and rebuke and destroy one another! In truth, we don't fight against people, but against Satan.

Though we cannot see him, he lives. Though he has been defeated, he still fights. We don't overcome Satan with lengthy arguments, or human struggle. We can't frighten him, or fire at him. God has given us superior weapons—the weapons of our faith. Will you use them?

Prayer ideas

As you consider the weapons of the faith, which do you feel unqualified to use? Do you need practice? Instruction? Ask God to begin teaching you how to pack your weapons. Ask him which weapon to begin with. Meditate and pray about that weapon until you fully understand its use.

WHAT DO YOU MEAN I CAN'T SEE THE PRESIDENT?

Jesus realized they wanted to ask him, so he said, "Are you asking your-selves what I meant? I said in just a little while I will be gone, and you won't see me anymore. Then, just a little while after that, you will see me again. Truly, you will weep and mourn over what is going to happen to me, but the world will rejoice. You will grieve, but your grief will suddenly turn to wonderful joy when you see me again. It will be like a woman experiencing the pains of labor. When her child is born, her anguish gives place to joy because she has brought a new person into the world. You have sorrow now, but I will see you again; then you will rejoice, and no one can rob you of that joy. At that time you won't need to ask me for anything. The truth is, you can go directly to the Father and ask him, and he will grant your request because you use my name. You haven't done this before. Ask, using my name, and you will receive, and you will have abundant joy." (John 16:19–24)

Many years ago Don Roberts, my brother, served as the Washington D.C. correspondent for King Broadcasting. His job involved reporting on the connections between local issues and the business of the White House and Congress. After moving to the D.C. area, it didn't take long for Don to confess his frustration with his new position.

"They keep the entire press corps in a tiny room in the White House. We sit jammed together for hours waiting for something to happen." Don shook his head as he explained his frustration. "Some days we'd stay all day and never see anyone about anything. Other days, we'd be lucky to get a typed press release at four in the afternoon. Talk about boring." Needless to say, Don soon took another job.

Though the Seattle news bureau expected my brother to report on the president, Don had no access to him. Don's only exposure to the president came as he watched the president take off and land in the helicopter on the back lawn. With the press corps, Don never spoke to the president personally, never shook his hand, never even sat in the same room with him.

As a reporter, Don had no right to enter the official business areas of the White House. As a person, he had no relationship with the president. Compared to the enormous stature of the president, Don was a nonperson.

Without Jesus, we'd have the same problem with God. We'd have no access. Our sin separates us from his holiness. In spite of all our effort, all our sorrow, all our restitution, we cannot make up for the sin in our own lives. Only Jesus' sacrifice can do that.

This passage in John records Jesus' words hours before his arrest and crucifixion. "All that is about to change," Jesus tells his friends. "Once you had no access. But now you are about to have full access. After my death and resurrection, you will be able to come before the Father in complete confidence, because of your relationship with me, you are family."

Remember those pictures of little John Kennedy Jr. crawling through under his father's desk? Little John, supremely confident in his father's love, had complete access to the president—not because of what he'd done, or because of his great contributions—but because of who he was. Little John Kennedy belonged with his daddy.

Jesus says the same thing about you. Before your decision to begin a faith life, you had no access. But now, because of your faith, you are part of the family of God. Because of Jesus, you belong with your daddy too. You can ask for anything—anything at all—and know that he hears you. Because of Jesus, you may ask boldly, confidently, knowing that Daddy hears your every word. Will you come to the Father with new confidence? You can, you know; you belong there.

Prayer ideas

Since you began your faith journey, how is your prayer life? Did you know your Heavenly Father longs to hear your voice? Begin today to pray boldly, knowing that you are the child of the King.

DON'T ASK UNLESS YOU PLAN TO LISTEN!

Then all the army officers, . . . and all the people, from the least to the greatest, approached Jeremiah the prophet. They said, "Please pray to the LORD your God for us. . . . Beg the LORD your God to show us what to do and where to go."

"All right," Jeremiah replied. "I will pray to the LORD your God, and I will tell you everything he says. I will hide nothing from you."

Then they said to Jeremiah, "May the LORD your God be a faithful witness against us if we refuse to obey whatever he tells us to do! Whether we like it or not, we will obey the LORD our God to whom we send you with our plea. For if we obey him, everything will turn out well for us."

Ten days later, the LORD gave his reply to Jeremiah . . . He (Jeremiah) said to them, "You sent me to the LORD, the God of Israel, with your request, and this is his reply: 'Stay here in this land. If you do, I will build you up and not tear you down; I will plant you and not uproot you. For I am sorry for all the punishment I have had to bring upon you. Do not fear the king of Babylon anymore, says the LORD. For I am with you and will save you and rescue you from his power. . . .'

When Jeremiah had finished giving this message from the Lord their God to all the people, Azariah . . . said to Jeremiah, "You lie! The Lord our God hasn't forbidden us to go to Egypt!" . . .

So Johanan and all the army officers and all the people refused to obey the Lord's command to stay in Judah. (Excerpted from Jeremiah 42:1–11; 43:1–4)

Once years ago, I got into a humdinger of a fight with a physician with whom I'd worked. I'd confronted him on a moral issue. I don't remember the whole conversation. Though I'd tried to be kind, I probably sounded blunt and accusative—personal faults I continue to struggle with.

In turn, he shouted and paced, cornered me against his bookcase and poked his finger into my chest, accusing me of terrible crimes against his honor. It was an ugly scene. In my mind, I was completely right. I'd caught him misleading people in a way that might cost human life. I went home weeping, completely humiliated. I thought we were friends.

It took more than a month for me to lick my wounds and begin to pray about what had happened. In the meantime, I received a letter from him, terminating our relationship. My devastation mounted. I took it to God in prayer.

I started with simple prayers. "Lord, I don't know what happened." With time, I moved on to personal prayers. "Lord, show me how to get through this." Eventually, still struggling with my emotions, I asked, "Lord, what do I do now?"

I feel as though the Lord answered me, and I didn't like his response. "Write a letter," he seemed to say. "Take complete responsibility for the event. Ask forgiveness. And then, when you close, explain again the gospel of forgiveness in Jesus Christ."

I didn't want to take responsibility. He was wrong—not me. How could I ask forgiveness for his angry behavior toward me? That couldn't be what the Lord wanted. I waited for a couple of weeks, thinking about the letter. Though I prayed hundreds of times to get out of the letter writing, his prompting didn't go away. Eventually I took pen to paper.

I don't know what happened as a result of that letter. The physician never responded. Still, in writing the letter, a miracle happened. When I did exactly as the Lord asked me to do, I was set free from the horrible memories of our disagreement. Instead of a movie-length version of what had happened, the whole scene was reduced to pictures and vague memories. I can actually meet the physician face-to-face, and not have the memory of our fight come screaming back to my consciousness. No matter what happened to him, I was set free.

In today's Scripture passage, the Jews have watched the Babylonians destroy their holy city. They're afraid to stay in the land of Israel, afraid the Babylonians will return. They believe they'll only be safe in Egypt. They ask Jeremiah to find out what God wants for them. When Jeremiah gives them God's message, their fear gets the better of them and they head for Egypt. In the end, the very Babylonian army they so feared destroys them in Egypt.

When we pray, the Lord expects us to ask for guidance. He loves to answer our questions. But, he also expects us to obey his instructions. Sometimes, his guidance surprises us. At other times, we find his direction downright revolting. No matter how odious, we must obey the leading of the Lord in prayer. As we do, we'll find his voice becomes ever clearer.

Will you ask for guidance? Will you obey?

Prayer ideas

Have you asked for guidance since you began your faith walk? Did you sense the Lord answering your questions? Did you obey? Ask the Lord to help you obey him. In prayer, commit yourself to obedience before you ask for guidance. And then, follow through!

WHO ME, PRAY?

"And now about prayer. When you pray, don't be like the hypocrites who love to pray publicly on street corners and in the synagogues where everyone can see them. I assure you, that is all the reward they will ever get. But when you pray, go away by yourself, shut the door behind you, and pray to your Father secretly. Then your Father, who knows all secrets, will reward you.

"When you pray, don't babble on and on as people of other religions do. They think their prayers are answered only by repeating their words again and again. Don't be like them, because your Father knows exactly what you need even before you ask him! Pray like this:

Our Father in heaven, may your name be honored. May your Kingdom come soon. May your will be done here on earth, just as it is in heaven. Give us our food for today, and forgive us our sins, just as we have forgiven those who have sinned against us. And don't let us yield to temptation, but deliver us from the evil one." (Matthew 6:5–13) [Some manuscripts add *For yours is the kingdom and the power and the glory forever. Amen.*]

I love to sew. For the first fifteen years of our marriage, I never bought a dress. I made every one—maternity dresses, church dresses, even work clothes. My husband, the original miser, told me I could have anything I could make. I sewed until he was sorry he ever said it.

Though I've never designed my own clothes, I enjoy using the commercial patterns provided by the big four pattern companies.

I have friends who think of sewing as punishment. Given a pattern, they obediently walk around a fabric store until they find the exact fabric shown on the pattern envelope, recreating the promotional picture detail for detail. They have yet to discover the freedom found in a single pattern. The possibilities are endless.

A single jacket pattern can be made long or short, heavy or light. It can become part of a suit, or worn with jeans. I can enhance the fabric before I cut out the pieces, or I can use it exactly as I find it on the bolt. I love the whole process—the endless possibilities—imagining a final result, and working with fabric and pattern until I create exactly what I'd imagined.

This is the trick most beginning seamstresses miss: one pattern has limitless potential. The pattern is designed only to get you started. The rest is up to you and your imagination.

The same is true for the Lord's Prayer. I don't think Jesus ever meant for these words to become the mumbled prayer of large audiences before a big event. He never intended the Lord's Prayer to become a kind of Christian Pledge of Allegiance, said by all and understood by none.

He had a pattern in mind. If you look carefully at his words, you'll see the pattern he wants us to learn. He gave us the pattern to create our own original prayers.

"Our Father, who art in heaven, may your name be honored." This honoring of the name, of the person of God, is nothing more than praise. Jesus encourages us to begin prayer by focusing on God and spending some time telling him how wonderful he is.

"May your kingdom come soon. May your will be done here on earth, just as it is in heaven." When you pray, take time to think about and reflect on God's sovereignty. Of course, we want to bring our needs to God. But we want to keep his providence, his plans in mind as we pray. I advise folks to ask for anything. But remind God that you want his best for you, whatever that might be. We want God's divine will to prevail over even our most earnest prayer requests.

"Give us our food for today . . ." In this part of the pattern, we lay our needs before God. I don't hold anything back here. I ask for big things—the healing of a friend who has cancer. And, I ask for small things—for help finding a wedding gift when I'm out of ideas. I've found, like many before me, that compared to God's power even my biggest concerns are small to him. I ask for anything I need, and he is faithful to answer my requests.

"And forgive us our sins . . ." In this section, Jesus teaches us to keep short accounts. When we mess up, we're instructed to go to God immediately and ask for forgiveness. Don't let everyday sins ferment. Big or small, clean them up. Get rid of them. In the same way, we talk with God every day about those who have hurt us. As we do, we forgive the injury and let go of our desire to retaliate. By forgiving others, we set ourselves free from the terrible anger and brooding that render our faith walk ineffective.

Next, we ask for protection from future sin. If you struggle with your temper, ask God to protect you from further outbursts. If you have a problem with pornography, make it an issue of prayer. Don't hide the things that tempt you; talk with God about them. Do it early. Do it often. Ask for divine help.

If you view this famous section of Scripture as a pattern for your own prayer, you'll find endless possibilities for meaningful and effective time with God. And in the end, your life will bring greater glory to the one who made you.

Prayer ideas

Take a 3 × 5 card and write down these cues: Praise. Submission. Needs. Forgiveness. Temptation. Use these words for one week as your own prayer pattern. See how your prayer life changes as you follow the pattern, letting God direct your daily prayer.

I Can't Love Them!

But if you are willing to listen, I say, love your enemies. Do good to those who hate you. Pray for the happiness of those who curse you. Pray for those who hurt you. If someone slaps you on one cheek, turn the other cheek. If someone demands your coat, offer your shirt also. Give what you have to anyone who asks you for it; and when things are taken away from you, don't try to get them back. Do for others as you would like them to do for you. (Luke 6:27–31)

You probably first learned the Golden Rule in kindergarten. Your teacher might have taught it to you after one child hit another, or after someone stole crayons from another student. This small bit of Scripture lies at the root of endless kindergarten lessons—like sharing, taking turns, and playing nicely together at recess. Unfortunately, before they turn the tassels on their graduation cap, most of the world's children dismiss the Golden Rule as archaic.

Instead, we retaliate. We submarine our enemies. We flash angry gestures. We honk. Or worse, we send our gang into rival areas of town and fire blindly into crowds. Sometimes, we dress children in vests filled with C4 and teach them to detonate themselves in hotels filled with tourists. Or we fly airplanes into buildings.

Loving our enemies doesn't come naturally. Retaliation does.

No amount of kindergarten teaching or congressional lawmaking will change the nature of men. Only the Holy Spirit can change men. He can make us yearn for peace badly enough to give up our desire for our own way. He can make us care about our enemies enough to pray for them—to actually bless them in prayer—rather than ask for their divine destruction.

Perhaps the most inspiring example of this kind of action happened outside Jerusalem on a dark Friday afternoon some two thousand years ago. There, on a small hill, a hateful group of soldiers killed an innocent man.

As the soldiers carried out the sentence, they jeered at him. They gambled for the few things he owned. They poked fun at him, and mocked his pain. As he suffered through the most agonizing and cruel method of capital punishment, they laughed. Then, as the moment to die approached, he prayed for the soldiers who killed him.

He asked for mercy for them. He expressed understanding for their behavior. Not once did he demand the Divine justice that might have been his. Though the soldiers were dead wrong, he prayed for their best.

In the final moments before Jesus died on the cross, he showed us how to love our enemies. He showed us how to pray for those who abuse us. Though he could have rebuked them, instead he prayed for them. Though he might have retaliated, instead he blessed them.

Jesus expressed God's kindness to the unkind, God's blessing to the unthankful. Even as he died, Jesus showed us how to live.

Prayer ideas

Has someone hurt you recently? Can you pray for them this morning? Have you hurt someone else? Do you need to ask forgiveness?

DAY 83

LOVE HIM?
ARE YOU KIDDING?

If I could speak in any language in heaven or on earth but didn't love others, I would only be making meaningless noise like a loud gong or a clanging cymbal. If I had the gift of prophecy, and if I knew all the mysteries of the future and knew everything about everything, but didn't love others, what good would I be? And if I had the gift of faith so that I could speak to a mountain and make it move, without love I would be no good to anybody. If I gave everything I have to the poor and even sacrificed my body, I could boast about it; but if I didn't love others, I would be of no value whatsoever.

Love is patient and kind. Love is not jealous or boastful or proud or rude. Love does not demand its own way. Love is not irritable, and it keeps no record of when it has been wronged. It is never glad about injustice but rejoices whenever the truth wins out. Love never gives up, never loses faith, is always hopeful, and endures through every circumstance. Love will last forever, but prophecy and speaking in unknown languages and special knowledge will all disappear. Now we know only a little, and even the gift of prophecy reveals little! But when the end comes, these special gifts will all disappear. It's like this: When I was a child, I spoke and thought and reasoned as a child does. But when I grew up, I put away childish things. Now we see things imperfectly as in a poor mirror, but then we will see everything with perfect clarity. All that I know now is partial and incomplete, but then I will know everything completely, just as God knows me now. There are three things that will endure—faith, hope, and love—and the greatest of these is love. (1 Corinthians 13:1–13)

Though I'm not sure why we did it, seven members of our church decided to ride the Seattle to Portland Bicycle Classic. The ride covers two hundred miles in two days—a feat which can't be accomplished by accident. It required training. I had no idea how much.

As we worked toward our goal, we had specific weekly objectives. Of course we wanted to increase our riding distance. Every week we increased our distance by ten percent. On the fourth week, we had a lazy week. Then again, we pushed our distance forward. As we approached the month of July, we rode more than 160 miles per week, giving us long hours in the saddle and days away from other obligations.

We also wanted to increase our speed. We set hourly distance goals during our rides. As we rode along, our ride leader continually pushed us to ride faster. We kept track of our average speed over the course of every ride, pushing the average up as the weeks went by. We had to complete one hundred miles in a reasonable length of time—or we wouldn't have enough rest for the second day of our Portland ride.

We learned a skill called drafting. By riding single file, very close together, we decreased the effort of riding through the air. By taking turns in the lead we shared the benefits, cutting our work by nearly thirty percent. We went farther using less energy. Drafting became a way of life.

We trained for emergencies as well. At first, it took three of us forty minutes to change a tube in a rear tire. We bruised our hands and scraped our skin—but we got faster. By the time we rode to Portland, we could change a flat in less than ten minutes.

We understood that we wouldn't be able to ride that far without concentrated work and directed training. We sacrificed other pursuits in order to succeed in this one area. We rode in the rain, in the wind, and in blistering heat. We rode through headaches and elbow aches and sore backsides. We did hills until our legs ached, and then we did them again.

We had a goal—and we chose to let everything else fall by the wayside in order to achieve this one success.

I can't tell you how thrilling it was to ride over the finish line in Portland. I couldn't believe I'd done it. The crowds cheered as the announcer read my finish time. I took my little embroidered patch with the pride of a gold medal winner. Afterwards, I smiled for two full days.

Today's famous Scripture passage, a description of love found in the second book of Corinthians, is often read at weddings. As you consider these words, remember that Paul wrote about love in the context of the body of Christ.

He wants members of the church to love one another with this kind of devotion, regardless of our contribution—whether you're Billy Graham, or the janitor at the Washtucna Community Church. Our love for one another should follow this lofty and divine pattern.

No matter how often you read this chapter, you will—like me—be struck by the awesome weight of the words. Who can love like this? How can we possibly do these things?

The answer? No human can.

But you can make love your highest ambition. Like our group of bicycle riders, you can set goals. You can push yourself. You can develop your skills. You can spend more time working at it. You can make sacrifices to let love grow in your life. You can ask for God's help.

And as you push toward this impossible goal, watch your Heavenly Father. Imitate his love. God's love takes the initiative. His love gives what's needed, whether or not the object of his love is thankful—or even aware of his gift. God sacrifices himself.

No price is too high for God's expression of love. In fact God's love is so profound, so ideal, that God identifies himself as being love. God is love, the Bible says.

More than any other words in the Bible, these words fill me with sorrow at my own failure. I have so far to go. If only I'd concentrate on growing love with the same fervor I ride my bike. Not for one race. Not for one year. But for a lifetime. Who might I become if I made love my highest goal?

Prayer ideas

*P*ray through each characteristic of love, one day at a time. As you concentrate on one word, ask God to show you more about that quality. Ask him to show you how you can grow in that area. Make a list. Write down some goals. Identify areas where your love is weak. Ask him for stronger love.

I Do Need a Shepherd!

The LORD is my shepherd; I have everything I need. He lets me rest in green meadows; he leads me beside peaceful streams. He renews my strength. He guides me along right paths, bringing honor to his name.

Even when I walk through the dark valley of death, I will not be afraid, for you are close beside me. Your rod and your staff protect and comfort me. You prepare a feast for me in the presence of my enemies. You welcome me as a guest, anointing my head with oil. My cup overflows with blessings. Surely your goodness and unfailing love will pursue me all the days of my life, and I will live in the house of the LORD forever. (Psalm 23)

When our oldest daughter was five, I looked up from nursing our newborn to find a swelling the size of a grapefruit on her neck. Though we knew she had a small, nonmalignant tumor, nothing could prepare me for the shock of seeing this sudden, overnight swelling. I called the doctor immediately.

After a week of antibiotics, they scheduled her surgery. The procedure, which we expected to take ninety minutes, took seven and a half hours. While we waited in the day surgery area, the janitor cleaned and mopped the waiting room. The hospital turned off the lights. All the nurses went home. We continued to wait.

Though we tried to stay calm, we felt terrified. We had no idea what had gone wrong. My husband and I took turns crying. Frequently I went to the door of the surgical area and pressed my nose against the window, looking for some sign of our daughter.

It was in that position, nose stuck on the glass, that the recovery nurse found me. The hospital had called her to come in and take care of Molly. "You must be the mama," she said touching my shoulder. "I'd recognize one anywhere." I started to cry. Again.

She took pity on me. "They're just finishing up in there," she said, gesturing to the operating room. "Normally, we don't allow parents in the recovery area. But there aren't any other patients back there at this hour. After you speak with the doctor, I'll come and get you. You'll see; Molly is doing just fine."

I can still picture Molly lying in that crib, her head wrapped in bandages, her fair skin blanched to a shocking white. Her lips seemed blue. She didn't move. How I longed to take her away from there. I wanted to protect her from all of those wires and tubes and pain.

That fierce desire—that almost animal instinct to care for my children is as close as I've ever come to understanding how God feels about us. It's as close as I'll ever come to knowing how a shepherd feels.

In his youth King David, who wrote this psalm, herded his father's sheep. He knew all there was to know about those woolly animals. He knew how easily they got themselves into trouble. He knew how they wandered off, how they'd drown if they tried to drink from fast-flowing streams. David knew the careful attention a good shepherd put into his work.

No wonder David used sheep and shepherds to show us our Heavenly Father's care for his children. Through the ages, people of faith have marveled at the profound truths hidden in these simple, yet meaningful verses.

The passage actually has two parts. In the first, God is the focus. Here, you'll see the care the shepherd lavishes on his sheep. In the second part, David becomes the focus. Here, David reviews the marvelous benefits of following his wonderful shepherd.

Look again at the passage and mark the statements about what the Lord does for us. Try highlighting the verbs in those statements. I found these: He leads (me). He lets (me rest). He renews (my strength). He guides (me). He protects and comforts (me). He prepares (a feast). He welcomes (me). He anoints (my head).

Take some time to think about each of these statements. Does one of them pop out at you? Do you need rest? Or strength? Or protection?

Could you use his healing touch? Do you need to feel more at home with him? Your shepherd is perfectly able to meet all those needs.

Surprisingly, Jesus uses this same image in John 10:11, when he said, "I am the good shepherd. The good shepherd lays down his life for the sheep."

Jesus wants to care for you. Ask for what you need. Then you can have his goodness and unfailing love chase you through your day. Your cup will overflow with blessings. Jesus is the good shepherd who lovingly cares for his sheep.

Prayer ideas

What keeps you from giving God all your needs? Do you have one need that you are particularly concerned about? Would you courageously ask God to meet it?

LIVING FACE DOWN

God blesses those who realize their need for him, for the Kingdom of Heaven is given to them. God blesses those who mourn, for they will be comforted. God blesses those who are gentle and lowly, for the whole earth will belong to them. God blesses those who are hungry and thirsty for justice, for they will receive it in full. God blesses those who are merciful, for they will be shown mercy. God blesses those whose hearts are pure, for they will see God. God blesses those who work for peace, for they will be called the children of God. God blesses those who are persecuted because they live for God, for the Kingdom of Heaven is theirs.

God blesses you when you are mocked and persecuted and lied about because you are my followers. Be happy about it! Be very glad! For a great reward awaits you in heaven. And remember, the ancient prophets were persecuted, too. (Matthew 5:3–12)

Zeb Osborn was the kind of guy who'd scare anybody. As a young man, he pulled his first armed robbery while AWOL from the marines. On his second day in prison, Zeb killed an aggressive inmate. Before long Zeb had done time in the most famous of American prisons. Eventually even the prison system gave up, labeling him an "incorrigible psychopath."

He finished his sentence and was out for less than a year before he robbed and shot a man in Greenville, South Carolina. Back in solitary, Zeb began reading *Run Baby Run*, the story of ex-gang leader Nicky Cruz.

As he read, the message of the book hit Zeb hard. Realizing the evil man he'd become, Zeb saw what a real man could be. That startling realization brought Zeb to tears. Weeping, he asked Jesus to forgive his sins, and to give him a new life.

Zeb asked for a Bible and began to read it. He began attending Bible studies in prison and joined other prisoners in outreach ministries to local youth. By a miraculous legal agreement, Zeb attended and graduated from Erskine Theological Seminary while still incarcerated. After leaving prison, he was ordained as a Baptist pastor in a church in his hometown.

Now a free man, Zeb continues to visit prisons, meeting personally with death row inmates. Zeb Osborn has gone from killing men to saving them, and his change is nothing short of miraculous.

But the whole thing began with a moment of utter emptiness. Seeing the self-centeredness of his life, Zeb mourned the waste. He recognized the loss. It was this spiritual death that brought him to spiritual life.

For Zeb Osborn, blessing began when he found himself face down—completely unable to help himself—before a mighty and loving God. He found God's blessing through his own mourning. His deep spiritual hunger drove him toward God.

Funny how the best gifts come to us when we arrive at the end of ourselves, isn't it?

Prayer ideas

Have you experienced that kind of utter emptiness before? Do you know what it is to come to God at the end of all of your resources—placing all your hope in him? Ask him to show you how faithful he can be—with those who need him most.

GRAFTED, NOT DRAFTED

God has appointed me as the apostle to the Gentiles. I lay great stress on this, for I want to find a way to make the Jews want what you Gentiles have, and in that way I might save some of them. For since the Jews' rejection meant that God offered salvation to the rest of the world, how much more wonderful their acceptance will be. It will be life for those who were dead! And since Abraham and the other patriarchs were holy, their children will also be holy. For if the roots of the tree are holy, the branches will be, too.

But some of these branches from Abraham's tree, some of the Jews, have been broken off. And you Gentiles, who were branches from a wild olive tree, were grafted in. So now you also receive the blessing God has promised Abraham and his children, sharing in God's rich nourishment of his special olive tree. But you must be careful not to brag about being grafted in to replace the branches that were broken off. Remember, you are just a branch, not the root.

"Well," you may say, "those branches were broken off to make room for me." Yes, but remember—those branches, the Jews, were broken off because they didn't believe God, and you are there because you do believe. Don't think highly of yourself, but fear what could happen. For if God did not spare the branches he put there in the first place, he won't spare you either.

Notice how God is both kind and severe. He is severe to those who disobeyed, but kind to you as you continue to trust in his kindness. But if you stop trusting, you also will be cut off. And if the Jews turn from their unbelief, God will graft them back into the tree again. He has the power to do it.

For if God was willing to take you who were, by nature, branches from a wild olive tree and graft you into his own good tree—a very unusual thing to do—he will be far more eager to graft the Jews back into the tree where they belong. (Romans 11:13–24)

My father-in-law, recently retired, loves nothing more than to putter around in the garden. For years he has grown his own vegetables. Every winter, he chops and stacks enough wood to keep our nation's capital warm—if only they used wood stoves. Sometimes, in the midst of his "messing around," he tries something just for the fun of it.

About fifteen years ago, the joy of learning prompted him to try grafting. Carefully, he collected the branches of a Golden Delicious apple tree and attached them to the freshly cut branch of a Gravenstein tree. With time, he got the knack of it and had some success. "It's all in the match. The new branch has to be placed just right," he told me. "That way the sap can flow from the tree into the new branch."

Of all the different methods of grafting, perhaps the most familiar is accomplished by cutting the branch of the recipient tree at a wide angle, exposing a large area of the inside of the branch. Then, a similarly cut donor branch is placed on top of the exposed branch. The two pieces are held together, often with electrical tape. Once the sap from the tree reaches the new branch, growth begins.

"So, what happens if the branch dies?" I asked Dave.

"You have to cut it off."

"Did that ever happen to you?"

"Oh yeah! Lots of times while I was learning. But you have to get the grafted branch off the tree; otherwise insects or disease can kill the tree. I always cut the branch back further than the original graft, and then either graft again, or seal it. If you don't get the dead branch off, instead of losing a branch, you lose the whole tree."

For David Nordberg, grafting was nothing more than an intellectual challenge. But, grafting plays a large part in our food industry. "Nowadays," Dave says, "you can buy trees at the garden center with three or four fruit varieties already grafted onto the trunk. Gardeners can save a lot of room that way. You can grow four different apples—all within an arm's length of one another."

It's interesting that Paul uses grafting to illustrate our relationship with Abraham's tree. By virtue of our faith in Jesus Christ, we have become part of the heritage of Abraham and the Jewish race. We take nourishment (much like a grafted branch takes sap) from God's special tree. Our leaves contribute food for the whole tree.

We belong. We take and we give.

Our relationship with the tree comes from God's own hand—not from anything we have done. We haven't been grafted because of our holiness, or accomplishment, or potential. We claim no honor in our position, only gratitude. How gracious and good is the gardener who chooses to include me in the rich life of this tree.

We'll look at some of that heritage in the section to come.

And while I rejoice in my position and my heritage, I take Paul's warning seriously. Continue to trust, he tells us. Don't let go. Don't give up. Don't take your faith lightly. By pressing forward in the faith, I keep my grafted branch healthy.

Prayer ideas

Have you considered the historical origin of the Christian faith? Did you recognize its Jewish roots? Would you ask God to help you be open to learning more about your new heritage?

DAY 87

ONE? YOU'RE KIDDING!

Don't forget that you Gentiles used to be outsiders by birth. You were called "the uncircumcised ones" by the Jews, who were proud of their circumcision, even though it affected only their bodies and not their hearts. In those days you were living apart from Christ. You were excluded from God's people, Israel, and you did not know the promises God had made to them. You lived in this world without God and without hope. But now you belong to Christ Jesus. Though you once were far away from God, now you have been brought near to him because of the blood of Christ.

For Christ himself has made peace between us Jews and you Gentiles by making us all one people. He has broken down the wall of hostility that used to separate us. By his death he ended the whole system of Jewish law that excluded the Gentiles. His purpose was to make peace between Jews and Gentiles by creating in himself one new person from the two group. Together as one body, Christ reconciled both groups to God by means of his death, and our hostility toward each other was put to death. He has brought this Good News of peace to you Gentiles who were far away from him, and to us Jews who were near. Now all of us, both Jews and Gentiles, may come to the Father through the same Holy Spirit because of what Christ has done for us.

So now you Gentiles are no longer strangers and foreigners. You are citizens along with all of God's holy people. You are members of God's family. We are his house, built on the foundation of the apostles and the prophets. And the cornerstone is Christ Jesus himself. We who believe are carefully joined together, becoming a holy temple for the Lord. Through him you Gentiles are also joined together as part of this dwelling where God lives by his Spirit. (Ephesians 2:11–22)

How could it happen? How could any nation turn its back while a maniacal leader kills six million Jews? I still find the Nazi extermination of Jews difficult to comprehend. But as I consider World War II, it helps me to look at a bigger picture.

Anti-Semitism, or the hatred of the Jewish people and their faith, didn't begin with Hitler. It began much earlier. Just how much earlier, who can tell?

We see evidence of a plot to murder Jews in the book of Esther, written five hundred years before Jesus' birth. And, it could be argued that Pharaoh himself was anti-Jewish, when he forced the nation of Israel into slavery. Later, his hatred and fear came to a boil as he began murdering Jewish newborns.

Hatred for the Jewish people has deep roots. Roman Emperors Tiberius and Caligula both conducted forced deportation of Jewish groups from the empire. Historians have records of church sermons preaching the separation of Christians and Jews written as early as the second century A.D. From there, incidents of hatred continued to grow.

Every family has skeletons. The Christian family is no different. Martin Luther (1483–1546) founded Protestantism in the sixteenth century. Frustrated by the reluctance of Jews to accept his new religion, Luther developed a bitter hatred for the Jewish people. Some of his writings describe Jews as ritual murderers and parasites. Three hundred years before Hitler, Luther believed the Jews should be expelled from Germany.

The root of such hatred might be found in Jewish law and tradition, which demands that devout Jews remain separate from Gentiles (non-Jews). Their dress and dietary laws make them stand out from their neighbors. All through history, the Jewish people have refused to blend in with the cultures around them.

Gentiles have considered this deliberate isolation a kind of superiority. Many find it offensive. This, added to the accusation of "Christ Killers," left Jews ripe for the hot hatred many have experienced.

For their part, the Jewish faith demanded separation from the Gentiles, who are not allowed to participate in Jewish sacrifices and feasts. Jews viewed themselves as the favorites of heaven. As a result, they sometimes did look down on the rest of the world.

Gentiles look down on Jews because of their peculiar habits.

Christians are not allowed these feelings of superiority or separation. We have been adopted into the Jewish family. Their rich inheritance has become ours. Though we do not follow the religious laws of the Jews, we consider their Old Testament Scriptures the foundation of our heritage as well.

In this New Testament passage, Paul tells us that the death of Jesus Christ has torn down the wall between Christians and Jews. Jesus' objective was not peace between the two peoples—but peace between all people and God. Only by faith, can any man—Gentile or Jew—come to God.

Because of Jesus, we are no longer considered Jews or Gentiles, but one new family—the family of faith. We must never forget that our salvation came through Jewish roots. As the story of God's work among people continues, it will return to its Jewish roots. The end is yet to come.

In the meantime, we've become one in the family of God—African Americans and Hispanics, men and women, Jews and Gentiles, American Indians and Asians. Every tongue and race and tribe and people is made one by faith in Jesus Christ.

We must begin to see people with spiritual rather than cultural eyes, for this is the way God views us. Once we come to Jesus, we become members of a new family: the family of Jesus Christ.

Prayer ideas

Have you considered your own feelings toward the Jewish people? Do your thoughts and emotions line up with Scriptures? Ask God to help you see people through spiritual eyes. If you have roots of racial bias, ask Jesus to let you see people of other races as he does. Ask him for help in befriending someone you might not have chosen before you began your faith walk.

A Flood to End All Floods

This is the history of Noah and his family. Noah was a righteous man, the only blameless man living on earth at the time. He consistently followed God's will and enjoyed a close relationship with him. . . . Now the earth had become corrupt in God's sight, and it was filled with violence. God observed all this corruption in the world, and he saw violence and depravity everywhere. So God said to Noah, "I have decided to destroy all living creatures, for the earth is filled with violence because of them. Yes, I will wipe them all from the face of the earth!

"Make a boat from resinous wood and seal it with tar, inside and out. Then construct decks and stalls throughout its interior. Make it 450 feet long, 75 feet wide, and 45 feet high. . . .

"Look! I am about to cover the earth with a flood that will destroy every living thing. Everything on earth will die! But I solemnly swear to keep you safe in the boat, with your wife and your sons and their wives. Bring a pair of every kind of animal—a male and a female—into the boat with you to keep them alive during the flood. . . . And remember, take enough food for your family and for all the animals."

So Noah did everything exactly as God had commanded him. . . . When Noah was 600 years old, on the seventeenth day of the second month, the underground waters burst forth on the earth, and the rain fell in mighty torrents from the sky. The rain continued to fall for forty days and forty nights....As the waters rose higher and higher above the ground, the boat floated safely on the surface. (Excerpted from Genesis 6 and 7)

In his lifetime, historians tell us that Thomas A. Edison patented more than one thousand inventions, including the Edison Universal Stock Printer, the automatic telegraph, the first commercial phonograph, the Edison storage battery, the first moving pictures, and the carbon-button transmitter used today in modern telephones.

No one would doubt that Edison possessed a keen imagination. Neighbors of his New Jersey laboratory dubbed him the "Wizard of Menlo Park." His creativity, sharp intellect, and intense curiosity combined to make Edison a highly successful inventor.

Even before the first long-lasting light bulb had been invented, Edison convinced rich and powerful men like the New York Vanderbilts and J. P. Morgan to invest in his industrial venture, the Edison Electric Light Company.

At the time, those observing Edison must have wondered about him. They must have wondered about his mental stability. He seemed always to be chasing the future. With his brilliant head in the clouds, and his finances in total disarray, I'd guess his neighbors often spoke behind his back. *Why doesn't he just get a job?*

Noah's neighbors must have wondered about him as well. Biblical experts suggest that none of Noah's neighbors had ever seen rain, because of what Genesis 2:5, 6 says:

> "When the Lord God made the heavens and the earth, there were no plants of grain growing on the earth, for the Lord God had not sent any rain. And no one was there to cultivate the soil. But water came up out of the ground and watered all the land."

Imagine the kind of comments Noah must have endured. "Hey, Noah, whatcha building there?"

"A boat."

"A boat?" (Chuckle, chuckle.) "That size? Whatever for?"

"God tells me it's gonna rain."

As Noah worked, he must surely have heard peals of laughter from onlookers. His friends must have worried about his mental stability. Even his children must have wondered about dear ol' dad. His wife must have endured endless jibes, and perhaps even some well-intentioned questions about Noah's mental condition.

On the outside, Noah and Edison appear similar. Furious activity occupied both men. They clearly envisioned something no one else had ever seen. Their ideas seemed impossible to their peers.

But the two could not be more different. While Edison dreamed of the future, Noah knew the future. While Edison's work anticipated changes in society, Noah responded to changes God had already begun.

God had given Noah clear instructions. No matter how outlandish the possibility of a flood must have seemed to him, Noah believed and obeyed.

Noah believed destruction was imminent. He believed God's plan would work, that the ark would float, that it would keep his family safe in the midst of a storm he could only imagine. And believing, Noah got out his tools and went to work.

In a way, we're like Noah. Because of sin, we know destruction is imminent. We believe that only our faith in Jesus Christ can take us through the storm of God's judgment. Believing, we place our faith in Jesus. Believing, we obey.

Obeying, we escape the destruction our neighbors will surely experience. God's wonderful kindness gave Noah a boat; his great mercy gave us Jesus Christ.

Prayer ideas

Read all three chapters about Noah in the book of Genesis. Ask God to help you see Noah's faith. Ask God about his plans for you. Do you see an impossible mission ahead?

ME? START A DYNASTY?

Then the Lord told Abram, "Leave your country, your relatives and your father's house, and go to the land that I will show you. I will cause you to become the father of a great nation. I will bless you and make you famous, and I will make you a blessing to others. . . . So Abram departed as the Lord had instructed him . . . He took his wife, Sarai, his nephew Lot, and all his wealth—his livestock and all the people who had joined his household at Haran—and finally arrived in Canaan. . . .

When Abram was ninety-nine years old, the Lord appeared to him and said, "I am God Almighty; serve me faithfully and live a blameless life. I will make a covenant with you, by which I will guarantee to make you into a mighty nation." At this, Abram fell face down in the dust. Then God said to him, "This is my covenant with you: I will make you the father of not just one nation, but a multitude of nations! What's more, I am changing your name. It will no longer be Abram; now you will be known as Abraham, for you will be the father of many nations. I will give you millions of descendants who will represent many nations. Kings will be among them! . . .

"Your part of the agreement," God told Abraham, "is to obey the terms of the covenant. You and all your descendants have this continual responsibility. This is the covenant that you and your descendants must keep: Each male among you must be circumcised; the flesh of his foreskin must be cut off. This will be a sign that you and they have accepted this covenant." . . .

On that very day Abraham took his son Ishmael and every other male in his household and circumcised them, cutting off their foreskins, exactly as God had told him. (Excerpted from Genesis 12 and 17)

In 1888, a Boston saloonkeeper's wife gave birth to a son. Like all mothers, she had dreams for her boy. She must have hoped that one day he'd have a successful career and a happy family. When he became a bank president at twenty-five, she must have nearly burst with pride. When he chose a wife from the mayor's children, she must have felt like all her dreams had come true.

Certainly, she could not have expected that he'd come to head one of the most powerful political dynasties this country had ever known.

But her son, Joseph Patrick Kennedy, did exactly that. Among his sons rose one president and two United States senators. Along with the Irish-Catholic heritage Kennedy passed along to his children, Joseph passed along vast wealth and fearsome political power. His quest for power began with preparing his oldest son for the presidency even before the beginning of World War II. When his oldest son died, Joseph immediately began grooming John Fitzgerald Kennedy for the position.

The dynasty of Joseph Kennedy includes more than the passing of money and influence. He had a reputation as a womanizer. In fact, he once invited his mistress, Gloria Swanson, to stay with his wife at the family home. Flaunting the laws of the nation, historians believe Kennedy ran liquor from Europe during prohibition. His dynasty included adultery and lawlessness.

At least three of his sons had adulterous relationships. In the book, *Jackie, Ethel and Joan: Women of Camelot* (Randy Taraborrelli, Warner Books, 2000), quotes Joseph Paolella (Secret Service Agent assigned to the Kennedy White House): "His womanizing was one of those things you didn't talk about to anyone but other agents. You just accepted it as part of the job."

Taraborrelli describes the additional duties of security: "An important part of his job during the Kennedy administration was to prevent Jackie from stumbling upon the President's indiscretions—not because she didn't know about them but rather to save the couple from an embarrassing situation."

Sons and grandsons in the Kennedy family have been charged with infidelity, drug possession, drug addiction, and selling mob protection in exchange for campaign contributions. Terms like Chappaquidick have become household names, connected to questionable Kennedy activities.

So, have I become a Kennedy basher? Not really.

Today's Scripture makes me consider the consequences of our choices. Abraham was a man who made choices, like Joseph Kennedy. When God called Abraham, he could have said, "Sorry, Lord. I have other plans."

Instead, Abraham yielded his hopes, his ambitions to the God of creation. He said, "Yes, Lord, I'll follow you. I'll enter into a permanent relationship with you."

Abraham chose to teach his children to follow God. Though he led an imperfect life, and his children failed as well, Abraham anchored his life with his relationship with God. Though he failed, he returned. Though he sinned, he confessed. Though he wandered, he came back to the calling of God. Though he doubted, he believed.

Abraham's legacy continues to this day. His faith and his determination to follow God have influenced many generations for good. His faith launched the nation of Israel, and paved the way for the birth of Christ.

One man's choice can lead to good, or evil. Which will you choose?

Prayer ideas

Think about your family. Have you experienced the consequences of someone else's choices? Ask God how your life can begin a new dynasty. Ask him what choices you can make to turn things in another direction.

WRESTLE WITH WHO?

When Isaac was forty years old, he married Rebekah . . . Isaac pleaded with the Lord to give Rebekah a child because she was childless. So the Lord answered Isaac's prayer and his wife became pregnant with twins . . . As the boys grew up, Esau became a skillful hunter, a man of the open fields, while Jacob was the kind of person who liked to stay at home. Isaac loved Esau in particular because of the wild game he brought home but Rebekah favored Jacob. (Excerpted from Genesis 25)

Esau hated Jacob because he had stolen his blessing, and he said to himself, "My father will soon be dead and gone. Then I will kill Jacob." But someone got wind of what Esau was planning and reported it to Rebekah. She sent for Jacob and told him, "Esau is threatening to kill you. This is what you should do. Flee to your uncle Laban in Haran. Stay there with him until your brother's fury is spent. When he forgets what you have done, I will send for you. . . ." (Genesis 27:41–45)

(Jacob goes to Haran and marries Laban's daughters. Years later, he returns to Caanan with four wives, thirteen children, many servants and extensive wealth. Afraid of his brother, Jacob sends a gift ahead and stays behind another night in the camp.)

But during the night Jacob got up and sent his two wives, two concubines, and 11 sons across the Jabbok River. After they were on the other side, he sent over all his possessions. This left Jacob all alone in the camp

and a man came and wrestled with him until dawn. When the man saw
that he couldn't win the match, he struck Jacob's hip and knocked it out
of joint at the socket. Then the man said, "Let me go, for it is dawn."

But Jacob panted, "I will not let you go unless you bless me."

"What is your name?" the man asked.

He replied, "Jacob."

"Your name will no longer be Jacob," the man told him. "It is now Israel,
because you have struggled with both God and men and have won." . . .

. . . for he said "I have seen God face to face, yet my life has been
spared." (Excerpted from Genesis 32:22–28, 30)

Chuck Colson, special counsel to President Richard Nixon,
was referred to as the White House "hatchet man."
According to The Prison Fellowship International website,
Colson was "a man feared by even the most powerful politicos during
his four years of service to Nixon." Some thought Colson "incapable of
humanitarian thought."

Colson agrees. He was willing to do anything at all for the sake of
the party or the president. In 1974, though suspected of being a partic-
ipant in the famous Watergate scandal, Colson pleaded guilty to
obstruction of justice in the case of Daniel Ellsberg. The judge sentenced Colson to serve one to four years in federal prison.

During the course of the investigation, Colson came to the end of
himself. In spite of Nixon's landslide win over McGovern, Colson's own
meteoric rise to power, and wide influence over the political landscape,
Colson felt empty. He had sacrificed nearly every other human pleasure
to obtain his position of power. Still, it didn't satisfy. Disgraced and
ostracized, Colson had nowhere to turn.

A friend told Colson about Jesus Christ, and explained the desperate need of all men to repent. Colson listened politely, but didn't
respond. Only later, when his future reached its darkest point, did
Colson find the humility he needed to confess his need for a Savior. He
submitted to Jesus Christ while parked in his friend's driveway.

Colson had been a trickster. And so was Jacob.

Both men found themselves driven, slaves to the god of power
and influence. Jacob took advantage of his brother's hunger to trick
Esau out of his inheritance. Unsatisfied with his brother's riches,

Jacob disguised himself as his brother in order to trick his father into giving him his older brother's blessing. Like Colson, Jacob wanted it all and would stop at nothing to accomplish his goal.

Both men learned the same lesson. Both realized that riches, influence, and the adulation of people mean nothing without the blessing of God. Without God, you are empty and without hope. Men may befriend you—but only for as long as your image remains untarnished.

The blessing of God lasts through any hardship.

Jacob was willing to wrestle all night with this God-man, in order to receive a divine blessing. It cost Jacob his hip socket. Colson wrestled too. When everyone else had abandoned him, he turned to Jesus. Only after Colson wrestled and overcame his pride, was he able to receive the blessing of relationship with Jesus Christ.

Jacob's wrestling was worth it. Though he walked away with a limp, he had a new position, a new name. He became father of the nation of Israel.

Colson walked away with a new name as well. He became a child of God. And in the process, he came away with a new nature. Colson's new nature founded Prison Fellowship International, which provides spiritual guidance and training for men living in prisons all over the world. His new nature now supervises more than 50,000 volunteers in more than eighty-eight countries.

His new nature gives him a passion for prisoners, a passion for the moral direction of our nation, and a passion for the written word. Colson has since authored numerous books, selling more than five million copies.

Both Colson and Jacob wrestled with God. Both came away changed. In the end, their new nature changed the world.

Have you wrestled with God lately?

Prayer ideas

Some consider Jacob's wrestling a picture of our wrestling with God in prayer. Have you experienced the intense struggle of desperate prayer? Do you need something only God can give? Are you willing to wrestle for what you need in prayer? Ask God to teach you this kind of determined prayer.

WHAT DO YOU MEAN, YOU DON'T LIKE ME?

So Jacob settled again in the land of Canaan, where his father had lived. . . . Now Jacob loved Joseph more than any of his other children because Joseph had been born to him in his old age. So one day he gave Joseph a special gift—a beautiful robe. But his brothers hated Joseph because of their father's partiality. The couldn't say a kind word to him. . . .

Soon after this Joseph's brothers went out to pasture their father's flocks at Shechem. When they had been gone for some time, Jacob said to Joseph, "Your brothers are over at Shechem with the flocks. I'm going to send you to them." . . .

When Joseph's brothers saw him coming, they recognized him in the distance and made plans to kill him. "Here comes that dreamer!" they exclaimed. "Come on, let's kill him and throw him into a deep pit. We can tell our father that a wild animal has eaten him. . . ."

Judah said to the others, "What can we gain by killing our brother? . . . Let's sell Joseph to one of those Ishmaelite traders. . . ." So when the traders came by, his brothers pulled Joseph out of the pit and sold him for twenty pieces of silver, and the Ishmaelite traders took him along to Egypt. . . .

Meanwhile in Egypt, the traders sold Joseph to Potiphar, an officer of Pharaoh, the king of Egypt. (Excerpted from Genesis Chapter 37)

I have a friend whose mother abandoned her family. Her father, an alcoholic and gambler, dragged my friend into town with him every weekend, leaving her to sit outside the card rooms while he played poker until daylight. In the dark, sitting unprotected on the street, she waited for her father.

I have another friend whose grandfather sexually abused her. For years, she endured the abuse, struggling to avoid contact with him; her family refused to believe her report. Again and again, she was forced to visit her grandfather, knowing what he would do to her there.

Stories of neglect and abuse surround us. They're so common in our culture that we've almost stopped listening to the children who grew up in these families. As adults we say to one another, "Aw, come on. Get over it."

But abuse and hatred didn't begin in the twentieth century. Families have been struggling since the beginning of time. And while God gives solid advice for avoiding trouble, his Word doesn't hide the effects of mismanaged families. Those stories are told in all their horror.

Of his thirteen children, Jacob preferred Joseph. Jacob's inability to control his feelings and his behavior set in motion a series of events which nearly ended Joseph's life. Why did Jacob prefer Joseph?

Joseph's grandfather (Laban) tricked Jacob into marrying both of his daughters. The two sisters competed with one another for Jacob's love, using their ability to bear children as a weapon in the battle. In their effort to win Jacob, each sister gave him her female servant as well, leaving Jacob with responsibility for two more "wives." Of these four women, Jacob loved Rebecca. She bore only two children, Joseph and Benjamin. Joseph was born into this embattled family as the twelfth child of an elderly father. His father loved him deeply.

From this household, poor Joseph became the unfortunate object of his brothers' deep resentment. Though he'd done nothing to deserve it, they wanted to kill him. When the opportunity arose, they sold young Joseph into slavery, sending him alone to a country far away. There, he had to fend for himself, having gone from chosen son to nameless slave.

Maybe you know someone who bears scars from this kind of child-hood—someone hurt by the very ones who should have cared the most. Perhaps you are a wounded child, grown now into a responsible adult, and yet, some mysterious happiness seems just out of your reach. You want to leave the pain behind, but you can't figure out how. You want to be free of resentment—and yet it simmers just below your awareness.

I have good news for you. Joseph's story has only just begun. Unfortunately, it gets worse before it gets better. But there is good news:

No matter how badly things look today, your story is not yet over.

And neither is Joseph's. We'll see how Joseph overcomes the trauma of his brothers' hatred. We'll watch him move beyond their evil schemes. Joseph manages to put his childhood behind him; he finds a successful and fulfilling life.

Though you may have an ugly past, don't quit now. Don't let yesterday's hurts disqualify you from today's success. Don't give up!

Prayer ideas

As you look at Joseph's difficult childhood, do you remember pain from your own past? Have you told Jesus about it? Have you told him how the memory makes you feel? Ask Jesus to heal your wounds and show you a new way of looking at things. He wants to help you with your hurts.

OH GREAT! PRISON!

Now when Joseph arrived in Egypt with the Ishmaelite traders, he was purchased by Potiphar, a member of the personal staff of Pharaoh, the king of Egypt. Potiphar was the captain of the palace guard. The LORD was with Joseph and blessed him greatly as he served in the home of his Egyptian master. Potiphar noticed this and realized that the LORD was with Joseph, giving him success in everything he did. So Joseph naturally became quite a favorite with him. Potiphar soon put Joseph in charge of his entire household and entrusted him with all his business dealings.

Now Joseph was a very handsome and well-built young man. And about this time, Potiphar's wife began to desire him and invited him to sleep with her. But Joseph refused.

She kept putting pressure on him day after day, but he refused to sleep with her, and he kept out of her way as much as possible. One day, however, no one else was around when he was doing his work inside the house. She came and grabbed him by his shirt, demanding, "Sleep with me!" Joseph tore himself away, but as he did, his shirt came off. . . . when her husband came home that night, she told him her story. "That Hebrew slave you've had around here tried to make a fool of me," she said. "I was saved only by my screams. He ran out, leaving his shirt behind!"

After hearing his wife's story, Potiphar was furious! He took Joseph and threw him into the prison where the king's prisoners were held. But the LORD was with Joseph there, too, and he granted Joseph favor with the chief jailer. Before long, the jailer put Joseph in charge of all the other prisoners and over everything that happened in the prison. (Genesis 39:1–22)

In the 1930s, few people in America believed Hitler would prove as serious a threat as our European Allies imagined. While we preached isolationism, Hitler began an expansion clearly outlawed by the treaties of World War I. Piece by piece, Hitler swallowed the countries nearest Germany. Most gave in without a fight.

Holland fought bravely for five days.

Cornelia ten Boom, a spinster living with her elderly father in Haarlem, Holland, believed that German occupation would create a kind of hell no one had yet imagined. It began with the forced extradition of all Dutch men to slave labor camps. It escalated with laws forcing Jewish citizens to wear the Star of David on their clothes. In November 1941, Cornelia watched soldiers destroy the fur shop of a Jewish friend, directly across the street from her home.

With the shop destroyed, the ten Booms realized the furrier could never return. They brought him into their home. Mr. Weil became the first of many Jewish citizens to escape Holland via Corrie's home.

Corrie and her family fed and housed many Jewish people looking for help. By making friends in the Dutch underground, Corrie obtained false identification and ration cards for her guests. She had a secret room installed upstairs. In this room she hid her Jewish guests during their stay with the family. Eventually, the police caught and tortured one of her messenger boys. His evidence led to the arrest of Corrie and her family.

At first, they were taken to a prison near The Hague where guards assigned Corrie to a bitterly cold cell with a straw mattress and a blanket scented with vomit from the previous owner. Corrie spent four months alone in this cell, living on a daily serving of thin porridge and a slice of black bread. Corrie used her formal hearing as an opportunity to tell her guards about the Good News of Jesus.

Corrie's father died within ten days of his imprisonment. Corrie and her sister Betsie lived in two other concentration camps before the war ended. In Ravensbruck, she and 1,400 other women lived in a barracks built for 400 prisoners. In dire hunger, amid endless mud and vermin, the prisoners lived selfish lives. Determined to share the love of God with her fellow prisoners, Corrie read the Bible out loud each evening. As she read, the women translated her Dutch words to their own language and passed the Bible reading along, until all the women in the barracks understood the reading.

Miraculously, prison officials released Corrie one week before all the prisoners in Ravensbruck were murdered. Corrie managed to return to Holland where she recovered with family. After the war, she opened a home where she ministered to people broken emotionally by the hardships they'd suffered. As people heard of Corrie's experiences they invited her to speak. For forty years, until her death in 1983, Corrie told audiences worldwide about the wonderful love of Jesus, and his sustaining power.

Both Corrie ten Boom and Joseph were sent to prison under false pretenses. Joseph went because he refused to sin against God; Corrie went because she refused to stand by while the German government killed innocent people.

But Joseph and Corrie had more in common than false accusations. Both rose above their circumstance. In the midst of their own troubles, they found a way to care about other people. Joseph took care of the other prisoners. The Bible tells us that Joseph eventually rose to high political power in Egypt, saving his entire family from starvation during severe famine.

Exhausted from hard labor, and depleted by illness and hunger, Corrie read the Bible to her fellow prisoners. After the war, Corrie shared Jesus with the whole world.

More than likely, you and I will never face an unjust prison sentence. But we might be falsely accused. Someone might accuse us of jealousy, or pride. Someone will pass along gossip about us. We'll undoubtedly be misunderstood, our motives misjudged.

When that happens, we'll face the same choices Joseph and Corrie faced. Will we turn inward, full of bitterness? Or will we focus on those around us, trying to see God's purpose in our situation?

God can help us choose wisely. Look to Jesus; the view is much better!

Prayer ideas

Have you ever been falsely accused? Misunderstood? Do you remember how you chose to respond? Ask God to help you make good choices in tough situations. Make a prayer commitment to look to him first when you find yourself in dark circumstances.

You Talkin' to Me?

In time, Joseph and each of his brothers died, ending that generation. But their descendants had many children and grandchildren. In fact, they multiplied so quickly that they soon filled the land. Then a new king came to the throne of Egypt who knew nothing about Joseph or what he had done. He told his people, "These Israelites are becoming a threat to us . . . We must find a way to put an end to this."

So the Egyptians made the Israelites their slaves and put brutal slave drivers over them . . . But the more the Egyptians oppressed them, the more quickly the Israelites multiplied! Then Pharaoh, the king of Egypt, gave this order . . . "When you help the Hebrew women give birth, kill all the boys as soon as they are born. . . ."

During this time, a man and woman from the tribe of Levi got married. The woman became pregnant and gave birth to a son. She saw what a beautiful baby he was and kept him hidden for three months. But when she could no longer hide him, she got a little basket . . . and waterproofed it . . . and put the baby in the basket and laid among the reeds along the edge of the Nile River. . . . Soon after this, one of Pharaoh's daughters came down to bathe in the river . . . The princess named him Moses, for she said, "I drew him out of the water." . . .

When the Lord saw that he had caught Moses' attention, God called to him from the bush, "Moses! Moses!"

"Here I am!" Moses replied. . . .

"The cries of the people of Israel have reached me, and I have seen how the Egyptians have oppressed them with heavy tasks. Now go, for I am sending you to Pharaoh. You will lead my people, the Israelites, out of Egypt." . . .

But Moses pleaded with the Lord, "O Lord, I'm just not a good speaker. I never have been and I'm not now . . . I'm clumsy with words."

"Who makes mouths?" the Lord asked him. . . . "Now go and do as I have told you. I will help you speak well, and I will tell you what to say." (Excerpted from Exodus 1—4)

Araminta Ross, called Minty by her family, was never the kind of person you'd expect to become a deliverer. As a young slave, Minty was frequently rented to nearby plantations. Before she turned five, she cleaned and cared for the households of white women. She often cared for newborn white babies, staying awake all night to be certain the babies slept. Whenever a newborn baby's cries awakened the mother, Minty experienced ferocious beatings.

Growing up, she watched as fellow slaves were removed from their families and sold to faraway plantations. She heard the cries of children taken from their mothers, and brothers torn from sisters. The nightmare of these separations followed her for the rest of her life.

Once, after her master caught a runaway slave, Minty was told to bind the slave's hands and feet. Knowing the owner intended to beat the slave, she refused. In a fit of rage, her master threw a heavy anvil. The iron weight crashed into her skull, leaving her comatose for days. Though she suffered from epilepsy for the rest of her life, Minty eventually recovered.

Broken physically, Minty grew more determined to gain her freedom. Working for other slave owners, Minty acquired some money. She married a freedman and took his last name which she combined with her mother's first name; Minty Ross became Harriet Tubman.

When her owner died, Harriet realized the time to escape had come. She asked her husband, John Tubman, to leave with her. He refused.

Through a long and perilous journey Harriet reached New Jersey. But Harriet found no joy in her freedom. In the book, *Harriet Tubman* (Franklin Watts, 1990) biographer Judy Bentley records Harriet's words: "I had seen their tears and sighs and I had heard their groans and I would give every drop of blood in my veins to free them . . . I would make a home for them in the North, and the Lord helping me, I would bring them all there."

In all, Harriet returned to Maryland nineteen times, helping more than three hundred slaves escape to freedom. Traveling at night, sometimes with the help of the Underground Railroad, Harriet slipped in and out of slave territory undetected.

Always, she depended on the Lord's help. Harriet believed God would continue to help her free others, putting her faith in these words: "The Lord told me to do this. I said, 'O Lord, I can't—don't ask me—take somebody else.' Then I could hear the Lord answer, 'It's you I want, Harriet Tubman'—just as clear as I heard him speak—and then I'd go again down South and bring up my brothers and sisters."

Once in a while, as with Moses and Harriet, the Lord asks his people to do impossible things. God said to Moses, "Go lead my people out of slavery." Can you imagine how it must have felt to hear those words? Moses knew the power of Pharaoh. He knew the determination of the Egyptians to keep their Jewish slaves. How could he help so many to escape?

How could Moses—himself a slave, a fugitive, an escaped convict—possibly achieve such a task? Moses tried to argue with God, just as Harriet Tubman did. "You can't ask me," they objected. "I can't possibly do it," they both said.

God had the same answer for both Moses and Harriet. "I want you."

God hadn't run out of trained slave-freeing professionals. He hadn't chosen impetuously. God had a plan. And when it comes to you, God has a plan as well. His plan for you may not be as grand as leading an entire nation out of slavery or as dangerous as sneaking into forbidden territory to release slaves.

But he has a task for you, one he has treasured and perfected since he began thinking about you. Will you accept your assignment? Will you depend on him to help you accomplish your task?

Prayer ideas

*A*sk God what task he has for you. Ask for his perfect timing. Ask him to teach you to depend on him as you obey.

BUT I AM AFRAID!

After the death of Moses the Lord's servant, the Lord spoke to Joshua son of Nun, Moses' assistant. He said, "Now that my servant Moses is dead, you must lead my people across the Jordan River into the land I am giving them. I promise you what I promised Moses: 'Everywhere you go, you will be on land I have given you—from the Negev Desert in the south to the Lebanon mountains in the north...No one will be able to stand against you as long as you live. For I will be with you as long as you live. For I will be with you as I was with Moses. I will not fail you or abandon you.

Be strong and courageous for you will lead my people to possess all the land I swore to give to their ancestors. Be strong and very courageous. Obey all the laws Moses gave you. Do not turn away from them and you will be successful in everything you do... Do not be afraid or discouraged. For the Lord your God is with you wherever you go. (Joshua 1:1–9)

Jim Elliot should have been afraid. The Auca Indians had already proven their willingness to kill. They had recently murdered others—a family and several Shell Oil Company executives. The Auca Indians had a reputation for murdering anyone who wandered into their territory.

In spite of the obvious danger, Jim Elliot, Ed McCully, Pete Fleming, Nate Saint, and Roger Youderian decided to bring the gospel to this remote tribe. During the weeks before their initial contact, the missionaries flew over the Auca village dropping gifts. The village responded with waves and smiles, leading the men to believe that they had become friends.

Hoping they'd be accepted, the men planned to land nearby and wait for the Auca to establish contact. If things went as planned, they would begin sharing the Good News of Jesus.

In January 1956 the five men landed their plane on a small river sandbar. Nate made several trips ferrying supplies to the river outpost before settling down with his companions to wait for tribal contact. Four days later, they had their first brief visit from Auca villagers. One week after landing, Elliot radioed his wife, saying they anticipated another visit from tribesmen.

His was the last transmission ever received from the men.

Days later, rescuers found the bodies of all five men lying a short distance from their airplane. They had been brutally massacred by Auca tribesmen.

Elliot should have been afraid. He knew the odds. But his fear didn't incapacitate him. It didn't keep him from making plans to try to reach this group of Indians for Christ. Why not? Where did Elliot find his bravery? I suspect all five men found courage in the same way that Joshua did. God's words to Joshua apply to us: "For the Lord your God is with you wherever you go."

Compare those words to those of Jesus in Matthew 28:20: "Teach these new disciples to obey all the commands I have given you. And be sure of this: I am with you always, even to the end of the age."

Our courage, like Joshua's, comes not from our expertise, not from our education, not from our physical prowess, not even from the promise of outward success. Rather, our courage comes from God's promise to go with us everywhere.

Over your lifetime of faith, God will ask many things of you. Some requests will be issues of simple obedience. Other requests may frighten you. A few may seem completely impossible—like poor Joshua who had to help a nation of slaves conquer the military giants of the land promised to the Jews.

Whatever God asks, you can count on his promise: He will go with you. Whether you succeed or fail, live or die, win or lose, God will go with you. That gives us courage!

Prayer ideas

Are you aware of Jesus' presence with you every day? Pray about ways you might remind yourself of his presence with you. Ask for courage when you need it.

BUT I WANTED TO BUILD IT!

Now when David was settled in his palace, he said to Nathan the prophet, "Here I am living in this beautiful cedar palace, but the Ark of the Lord's covenant is out in a tent!"

Nathan replied, "Go ahead with what you have in mind for God is with you."

But that same night, God said to Nathan, "Go and tell my servant David, 'This is what the Lord says. You are not the one to build me a temple to live in. I have never lived in a temple, from the day I brought the Israelites out of Egypt until now. My home has always been a tent, moving from one place to another. . . . This is what the Lord Almighty says: I chose you to lead my people Israel when you were just a shepherd boy, tending your sheep out in the pasture. I have been with you wherever you have gone, and I have destroyed all your enemies. Now I will make your name famous throughout the earth! And I have provided a permanent homeland for my people Israel, a secure place where they will never be disturbed. . . . And now I declare that the Lord will build a house for you— a dynasty of kings! For when you die, I will raise up one of your sons, and I will make his kingdom strong. He is the one who will build a house—a temple—for me. And I will establish his throne forever . . . '" (Excerpted from 1 Chronicles 17:1–12)

David said, "My son Solomon is still young and inexperienced, and the Temple of the Lord must be a magnificent structure, famous and glorious throughout the world. So I will begin making preparations for it now." So, David collected vast amounts of building materials before his death. (1 Chronicles 22:5)

Much has been written about King David, the second king of the nation of Israel. His story fills three Old Testament books. For generations, his courage and faithfulness, his unusual route to royalty, his moral failures and military victories have intrigued believers. Perhaps no other Old Testament character has so moved us as David. After all, God declared David a "man after his own heart."

Beginning in 1 Samuel, and continuing in 2 Samuel, God tells us about choosing a shepherd boy—the youngest in a family of boys to succeed a disobedient King Saul. On those pages, you read about the battle between David and a giant so fierce that no soldier in the nation would dare oppose him. You read about a shepherd boy who killed that giant with nothing more than a sling and stones, and faith in a mighty God.

These books tell about David's training in the house of King Saul, and about Saul's maniacal jealousy—pursuing the boy through the wilderness—determined to eliminate him as a threat to Saul's dynasty. They tell us about Saul's death and David's ascent to the throne.

An entire devotional could be based solely on the life of David. How can any writer stop with just one story? I chose an unusual focus for today's devotional.

When David faced the end of his life, his greatest desire was to build a temple for the Lord. His devotion to God needed expression. God had given him a kingdom, vanquished his enemies, and blessed him financially. God had given him wives and children and unbelievable riches. As David's kingdom increased, he never forgot his dependence on God. His gratitude burned inside of him, driving him to action. "Let me build you a home," he begged the Lord.

But God denied David's deepest desire. God refused him the thing he wanted more than anything else. God said simply, "Your son will build my temple."

For most of us who dare to dream, God's refusal would be a crippling blow. Feeling rejected, we might retaliate. We might thumb our nose at God. At the very least, we might say, "Okay, if that's the way you want it, God, let the kid do it all." Leaving the work for someone else, we might refuse to express interest or offer help.

But remember, David is a man after God's heart.

Though disappointed, David did the next best thing. He decided to lay the groundwork. He anticipated his son's needs. He amassed materials. He collected nearly four thousand tons of gold, forty thousand tons of silver, and so much iron and bronze that it couldn't be weighed. He gathered lumber and stone, and helped to assemble the skilled workers who would help his son with the project.

In fact, at the end of his life, David set apart everything others brought to him for the building of the temple. For us, that would be like returning all your Christmas gifts and giving the money to the church building fund—not once, but for the rest of your natural life.

When David's son Solomon set out to build the temple, most of the provisions had already been accumulated by the very man God had rejected as master contractor.

David did many wonderful things in his lifetime. He killed giants. He destroyed armies. He saved lives. He worshiped God publicly. But these things don't inspire me.

What inspires me about David is his devotion to God. Even when God denied David his dream, David submitted. David found a way to help someone else do what he longed to do himself. Denied the position of team leader, he chose the position of team financier. David had a submissive heart. A willing heart. A humble heart.

Someday, I hope to have a heart like David. I want to be a woman after God's own heart.

Prayer ideas

Have you ever had to let go of a dream? Do you remember how that felt? Ask God to help you hold your dreams with an open hand—willing at any time to let go of the things you desire most. Ask God to make your heart more like his. He'll do it. He is pleased to help.

WHAT MOTHER NAMES HER SON JEHOIAKIM?

During the third year of King Jehoiakim's reign in Judah, King Nebuchadnezzar of Babylon came to Jerusalem and besieged it with his armies. The Lord gave him victory over King Jehoiakim . . . Then the king (Nebuchadnezzar) ordered Ashpenaz, who was in charge of the palace officials, to bring to the palace some of the young men of Judah's royal family and other noble families, who had been brought to Babylon as captives. "Select only strong, healthy, and good-looking young men," he said. "Make sure they are well versed in every branch of learning, are gifted with knowledge and good sense, and have the poise needed to serve in the royal palace. Teach these young men the language and literature of the Babylonians." . . .

But Daniel made up his mind not to defile himself by eating the food and wine given to them by the king. He asked the chief official for permission to eat other things instead. Now God had given the chief official great respect for Daniel. But he was alarmed by Daniel's suggestion. . . .

Daniel talked it over with the attendant who had been appointed by the chief official . . . "Test us for ten days on a diet of vegetables and water," Daniel said. "At the end of ten days, see how we look compared to the other young men who are eating the king's rich food. . . ."

At the end of ten days, Daniel and his three friends looked healthier and better nourished than the young men who had been eating the food assigned by the king. (Excerpted from Daniel 1)

In 1923 a relatively obscure sprinter set a new English record for the 100-meter dash at the AAA track meet held in London, England. His remarkable athleticism and unusual running style drew the attention of every spectator in the stadium. Word of his feat spread, and soon all of Britain waited for the Paris Olympics of 1924, certain that Eric Liddell would win the gold in at least two events.

When he arrived in Paris, Liddell found the preliminary heats of the 100-meter dash and two relay races scheduled for Sunday, July 6. Eric, a faith-filled man, had always considered Sundays sacred. He told his track coach simply: "I'm not running."

In spite of international pressure, the promise of fame and the possibility of a medal, Eric refused to compromise. While others ran the 100-meter heats, Eric preached a sermon in a Paris church.

Unable to run his normal race, Eric began training immediately for the 200- and 400-meter dashes. He surprised spectators by winning the bronze medal in the 200-meter event. And then, Eric Liddell stunned the world by setting a new world record for the 400-meter race. In doing so, he won gold.

One year later, Eric returned to China, to his missionary parents and his birth home. Eventually Eric was ordained as a minister of the gospel. He married, and continued to minister—often by bicycle—in remote locations in China. During World War II, Liddell and several other missionaries managed to work inside a Japanese internment camp, where they served as teachers and sports administrators while presenting the gospel. Eric died in 1945 of a brain tumor. His last spoken words were, "It's complete surrender."

In our modern life, few people speak of convictions. But both Daniel and Eric Liddell had convictions. Both men believed in a higher standard, one established by God rather than man. By refusing to compromise, Daniel risked his life. By refusing to run on Sunday, Eric Liddell risked what he believed would be his only opportunity to win an Olympic medal.

In your new faith walk, you'll need to think about your own convictions. What values does the Word of God teach? Honesty? Sexual purity? Prayer? Giving? Generosity? All of these values can be translated into convictions like these:

- I will not lie for any reason—even if telling the truth means I might incriminate myself.

- I will not experience sex outside the boundaries of marriage.
- I commit to making my marriage my first priority.
- I will not look upon any lustful sexual material.
- I will not drink alcohol.
- I will not watch a soap opera. (The Lord led me to this silly one years ago.)

With the Holy Spirit's help, you'll establish convictions that will carry you through your entire life. Like Daniel and Eric Liddell, your convictions will be tested. But if you stand strong, you can count on God to bless your faithfulness.

Captured and deported from his home by the Babylonians, Daniel grew into the wisest of all advisors for three separate administrations. Through his convictions, Daniel introduced King Nebuchadnezzar to Israel's God. Daniel brought correction to Nebuchadnezzar's son. Daniel became an advisor to the Persian conqueror of the Babylonian nation. Daniel's influence spanned many cultures and kings, and his commitment to prayer influences Christians today, via the pages of the Bible.

Convictions. Our personal commitments do more than protect us from the influence of the world around us. They provide a means of influencing our culture. They provide an opportunity to share God with the people around us.

Without convictions, we bob endlessly, like a cork on the ocean—driven wherever the winds of our times take us.

Convictions stretch us, test us. Occasionally, they make us the object of ridicule. Often, they become the means of God's richest blessing in our lives.

Will you live by godly convictions?

Prayer ideas

Have you observed Christians who lived by godly convictions? Which of those inspired you? Ask God to help you build convictions into your life. Today, write down the conviction you sense God showing you. Ask his help to follow them.

A BIBLICAL CINDERELLA?

"Let us search the empire to find beautiful young virgins for the king. . . . Hegai, the eunuch in charge, will see that they are all given beauty treatments. After that, the young woman who pleases you most will be made queen instead of Vashti." . . . Esther, along with many other young women, was brought to the king's harem at the fortress of Susa and placed in Hegai's care. . . . Esther had not told anyone of her nationality and family background, for Mordecai had told her not to. Every day Mordecai would take a walk near the courtyard of the harem to ask about Esther and to find out what was happening to her. . . . the king loved her more than any of the other young women. He was so delighted with her that he set the royal crown on her head and declared her queen . . .

Some time later, King Xerxes promoted Haman . . . to prime minister, making him the most powerful official in the empire next to the king himself. All the king's officials would bow down before Haman to show him respect whenever he passed by . . . But Mordecai refused to bow or show him respect. . . . When Haman saw that Mordecai would not bow down or show him respect, he was filled with rage. So he decided . . . to destroy all the Jews throughout the entire empire of Xerxes.

Mordecai sent back this reply to Esther: "Don't think for a moment that you will escape there in the palace when all other Jews are killed. If you keep quiet at a time like this, deliverance for the Jews will arise from some other place, but you and your relatives will die. What's more, who can say but that you have been elevated to the palace for such a time as this?"

Then Esther sent this reply to Mordecai: "Go and gather together all the Jews of Susa and fast for me. Do not eat or drink for three days, night or day. My maids and I will do the same. And then, though it is against the law, I will go in to see the king. If I must die, I am willing to die. So Mordecai went away and did as Esther told him. (Excerpted from the book of Esther 1—4)

Pastor Dietrich Bonhoeffer never intended to become a political prisoner. He considered himself a student, an intellectual, who eventually served as leader of the Confessing Church Seminary at Zingst by the Baltic Sea. Bonhoeffer wanted nothing more than to prepare pastors to serve the church in Germany.

But history changed this quiet ambition. As the German government began its unprecedented campaign against German Jews, Bonhoeffer found himself an unwitting spokesman for Jewish rights. He became active in the Abwehr resistance circle, and an outspoken public defender of the Jewish people.

In his sermons and his writings, Bonhoeffer dared to confront the evil controlling his homeland. He became active in the Protestant resistance movement. He experienced great pressure to conform. Eventually the continuing deterioration of the situation in Germany forced him to another choice. Bonhoeffer began actively helping Jews escape to Switzerland.

This led to his arrest and imprisonment in 1943. Bonhoeffer spent two years in the Flossenburg concentration camp, where he was hanged on April 9, 1945—only weeks before the fall of the Third Reich.

Five centuries before the birth of Christ, in the Persian capital of Susa, King Xerxes chose a young Jewish woman to become his second queen. Though her ancestors had been exiled from the land of the Jews, Esther's family remained in Persia fifty years after the first of her people were allowed to return to Israel. Though far from home, from orphan to queen, Esther never forgot her people.

When Haman, a royal official, sought revenge for his injured pride, he planned to annihilate the Jews remaining in Persia. He tricked the Persian king into signing an unchangeable order to murder them—promising that those citizens who did the killing might confiscate the property of those they killed.

After three days of fasting and praying, Esther went before her king. With cunning, she appealed to his sense of justice. The outraged king ordered the death of Haman. Though the king could not reverse his prior order, he added another allowing the Jewish people to defend themselves from attack.

By faith, Esther asked God to help her change the course of history. By courage, Esther dared to confront evil. By wisdom, Esther found the best way to make her point.

By grace, she saved the lives of her people.

Two leaders: one an orphaned young woman, the other an intellectual, a pastor, a teacher. Neither chose the role they played in history.

But both recognized the face of evil in their land. Both found themselves with no choice but to stand against it.

You might think that of the two, only Esther succeeded. She saved her people.

I wonder if we really know the extent of our success here on earth. Perhaps we will only know when we arrive on the other side of life. Who knows how many people Bonhoeffer influenced? How many of those who read his work, or heard him speak took the opportunity to save someone destined for death? How much did Bonhoeffer's writing affect the Christians in the United States? Did their outcry change the American determination to remain neutral during World War II?

As you serve God, he may ask you to confront the evil around you. It will mean taking risks. It won't feel comfortable. It may not succeed in the way you hope.

But we cannot judge the success of our own involvement. Neither can we allow our fear of failure, or of discomfort, to determine our course. With the Lord's help, we must engage the enemy. Only he determines the outcome. Someday, when we see Jesus face-to-face, we'll know how well we did.

Will you take the risk?

Prayer ideas

Have you seen something evil in the world around you? Does it hurt you? Tell the Lord about what you see. Ask him if there is something you might do to make a difference.

HERE AM I, SEND ME!

In late autumn of the twentieth year of Artaxerxes' reign, I was at the fortress of Susa. . . . one of my brothers, came to visit me with some other men who had just arrived from Judah. I asked them about the Jews who had survived the captivity and about how things were going in Jerusalem. They said to me, "Things are not going well for those who returned to the province of Judah. . . . The wall of Jerusalem has been torn down and the gates have been burned."

When I heard this, I sat down and wept. In fact, for days I mourned, fasted, and prayed to the God of heaven. . . . Early the following spring . . . I was serving the king his wine. . . . So the king asked me, "Why are you so sad? You aren't sick, are you? You look like a man with deep troubles."

I replied, "Long live the king! Why shouldn't I be sad? For the city where my ancestors are buried is in ruins . . . If it please Your Majesty . . . send me to Judah to rebuild the city where my ancestors are buried." . . .

Three days after my arrival in Jerusalem, I slipped out during the night, taking only a few others with me. I had not told anyone about the plans God had put in my heart for Jerusalem. . . . But now I said to them, "You know full well the tragedy of our city. It lies in ruins, and its gates are burned. Let us rebuild the wall of Jerusalem and rid ourselves of this disgrace!" Then I told them about how the gracious hand of God had been on me, and about my conversation with the king. They replied at once, "Good! Let's rebuild the wall!" So they began the good work. (Excerpted from Nehemiah 1—2)

Needs.

We see them everywhere. Sometimes, overwhelmed, we turn away. We busy ourselves with our own concerns—trying to anesthetize our awareness of the pain around us. Sometimes, we ease our conscience by taking our leftovers to the Goodwill.

But once in a great while, a need drives us to action.

This happened when Dr. Bob Pierce experienced the overwhelming needs of the children orphaned in the Korean War. Unable to focus his attention elsewhere, he began to pray. In 1950, still riveted by the need, he formed a child-assistance agency. In order to continue providing long-term care, he established the first child sponsorship program in 1953.

In the fifty years since, that agency has grown into World Vision International, and World Vision Relief and Development. Today, this organization uses thousands of employees and volunteers to help in emergencies and alleviate suffering throughout East Africa, Liberia, Sierra Leone, the Balkan Republics, and the world.

Needs drove Bob Pierce. And they drove Nehemiah as well.

In the Old Testament, you'll discover two major conquerings of the Jewish nation. In those days, it was the custom of conquering nations to take the citizens of the land away from their homeland and place them in the home of the conquerors. Sometimes, natives of the conquering nations immediately replaced those exiles. By moving natives out and conquerors in, the new government ensured that no insurrection would occur in the new territory.

The Assyrians conquered the northern tribes of Israel and removed them out of the land in 722 B.C. The fall of Samaria (the capital of the Northern tribes) is described in 2 Kings 17. The Babylonians captured Judah more than one hundred years later in the fall of Jerusalem (the capital of Judah) in 597 B.C. When the Persians conquered the Babylonians just fifty years later, they inherited the Jews still living in the Babylonian territory.

Daniel was one of those moved from Jerusalem to Babylon. Nehemiah was probably a child of someone removed from Israel. Though they lived in a foreign land, the Jews never fully assimilated. They retained their religion and traditions. Eventually, after seventy years in captivity, the first of the captured Jews were allowed to return home. Some refused to return.

It was Nehemiah, a descendant of those transported from Judah, who discovered the desperate need of those living in his homeland. As cupbearer to the king, he held a rare position of prosperity and influence in the Persian kingdom. He was comfortable, well cared for. Still, he chose to leave his position behind in order to meet the need of his homeland.

Nehemiah didn't jump into action. Instead he prayed and fasted—went without food—as he tried to concentrate on hearing from the Lord. He waited. Nine months later, Nehemiah felt so moved by the need, so certain of his calling that he took action. He spoke to the king.

The book of Nehemiah tells the rest of the story. After traveling to Jerusalem, this one remarkable man united the citizens of Jerusalem and convinced them to help him accomplish his goal. Together they rebuilt the wall. His dependence on God and his determination to succeed continue to inspire readers even today.

The next time you see a need, will you run? Or will you pray? God uses his people to meet needs. He used Nehemiah to build a wall. He used Bob Pierce to save the children. Are you available?

Prayer ideas

Have you ever experienced pain over someone else's need? Could that pain have been God calling you to act? How would you know? When you see a need that moves you to action, ask God to make his way clear. Continue to pray until you are certain about the action God wants for you. Ask other believers to join you in prayer for the need.

Consider joining or starting a prayer group to pray for worldwide spiritual or physical needs.

AM I DONE YET?

After dark one evening, a Jewish religious leader named Nicodemus, a Pharisee, came to speak with Jesus. "Teacher," he said, "we all know that God has sent you to teach us. Your miraculous signs are proof enough that God is with you."

Jesus replied, "I assure you, unless you are born again, you can never see the Kingdom of God."

"What do you mean?" exclaimed Nicodemus. "How can an old man go back into his mother's womb and be born again?"

Jesus replied, "The truth is, no one can enter the Kingdom of God without being born of water and the Spirit. Humans can reproduce only human life, but the Holy Spirit gives new life from heaven. So don't be surprised at my statement that you must be born again. Just as you can hear the wind but can't tell where it comes from or where it is going, so you can't explain how people are born of the Spirit." (John 3:1–8)

Afterward Joseph of Arimathea, who had been a secret disciple of Jesus (because he feared the Jewish leaders), asked Pilate for permission to take Jesus' body down. When Pilate gave him permission, he came and took the body away. Nicodemus, the man who had come to Jesus at night, also came, bringing about seventy-five pounds of embalming ointment made from myrrh and aloes. Together they wrapped Jesus body in a long linen cloth with the spices, as is the Jewish custom of burial. (John 19:38–40)

On New Year's Day, my mother-in-law brought out a video-tape she'd made of a recent local newscast. The story featured a friend of mine who had just completed a medical mission to Afghanistan. As the camera focused on his snapshots from the trip, I heard my friend say, "The Afghan people shouldn't be dying of diseases caused by dirty water, or infected wounds. Their infants shouldn't die of malnutrition. We should care about them as much as we care about the poorest of our own people." The news story made me cry.

I first met this man the year I became a mother. At the time, he'd just begun his own medical practice. In those days, he looked like someone from the pages of a fashion magazine. In fact, for more than ten years, I'd never ever seen him without a tie.

Though he worked with people every day, he seemed uncomfortable with them—more than shy, less than arrogant—detached somehow, as though he didn't want to connect on a personal level. Kind and professional, he held his distance, rarely looking anyone in the eye. Whenever I spoke of spiritual things, he explained politely but firmly that he had no interest in "religion."

Several years ago, God turned this guy's life upside down. Intense trouble characterized both his personal and professional life. In the midst of it all, he made a decision to begin a faith journey. Once he chose to believe in Jesus Christ, his transformation was miraculous!

Today, his relaxed demeanor is characterized by a new vulnerability, a new and passionate desire to understand and care for people. He no longer carries the untouchable look of a model. Instead, his broad smile and gentle disposition invite confidence and trust. He has traveled across the world to provide free medical care in the name of Jesus. This man has been changed, as certainly as if someone new inhabits his old body.

It was that new man who went to serve in Afghanistan. And it was the new man, the new Nicodemus, who helped to bury Jesus. At first, Nicodemus was so afraid to be associated with Jesus that he visited by night, under cover of darkness. In the end, Jesus so changed him that he publicly helped bury Jesus' body. Nicodemus no longer cared what others thought. Jesus had changed his fear to courage—making him willing to take great risk to do the right thing.

The same thing happens to everyone who meets Jesus. Our association with the Spirit of God gives us new life, and over time we are made into new people.

Be patient with God and with yourself. In ten years you'll change too! Your transformation will be genuine. It will last for eternity. Enjoy the process. Trust the results.

Prayer ideas

Think about the one area you would like most to change. Tell God about your concerns and desires. Ask him for help. Then praise him for the changes he has already begun in your life.

HOW LONG CAN
I KEEP THIS UP?

"The Kingdom of Heaven can be illustrated by the story of ten brides-maids who took their lamps and went to meet the bridegroom. Five of them were foolish, and five were wise. The five who were foolish took no oil for their lamps, but the other five were wise enough to take along extra oil. When the bridegroom was delayed, they all lay down and slept. At midnight they were roused by the shout, `Look, the bridegroom is coming! Come out and welcome him!'

"All the bridesmaids got up and prepared their lamps. Then the five foolish ones asked the others, 'Please give us some of your oil because our lamps are going out.'

But the others replied, 'We don't have enough for all of us. Go to a shop and buy some for yourselves.'

"But while they were gone to buy oil, the bridegroom came, and those who were ready went in with him to the marriage feast, and the door was locked. Later, when the other five bridesmaids returned, they stood outside, calling, 'Sir, open the door for us!'

But he called back, 'I don't know you!'

"So stay awake and be prepared, because you do not know the day or hour of my return." (Matthew 25:1–13)

Not too long ago, I had quite a surprise. My husband and I joined friends for a walk up to the marina office in Nanaimo, British Columbia. There, above the harbor, on the glass door of a gift shop, I encountered a map of Vancouver Island nearly as tall as I am.

I scanned the map for the bay where we'd docked our boats. It shouldn't be hard to find, I thought. After all, I'd spent most of the morning pouring over marine charts covering the route between Telegraph Harbor and Nanaimo. I scanned Vancouver's east side but couldn't find Nanaimo. I looked again, more slowly this time, starting from the northern tip of the island.

To my surprise, I found Nanaimo along the lower edge—not far from my knee. All this time, I thought Nanaimo was on the northern end of Vancouver Island.

How could I be so mistaken in my geography? Embarrassed, it occurred to me that in all our cruising, I'd been looking at highly magnified charts of small sections of the island. I knew Nanaimo only from where I believed it to be—having never actually located it on a full-scale drawing of the entire island. After so many days on the water, we'd barely left home.

All my life, I've wanted to take our boat to Alaska. On the gift shop map, I traced my finger north, toward Alaska, and imagined the miles of water separating Vancouver Island and Ketchikan. Looking at this map, I began to doubt my own dreams.

How would I hold out on a voyage covering such a vast expanse of water? From this dock in Nanaimo, how would it feel to face so many miles of cruising still before me?

The Christian life is something like a long voyage. None of us knows the exact course of our journey, or how long our trip will take. We plan our provisions and plot our course. But we're on the ship for the long haul—no matter how long we must wait to reach port.

Some of us will go on to heaven from this life. Others will live to see the Lord's return. But we must all be faithful. We must plan for every contingency, and never let the length of the voyage take us by surprise. We must be patient and prepared, working faithfully as we wait for the certain return of our Savior.

We know that with preparation and patience, we will go the distance.

Prayer ideas

Ask God to help you settle in for the long haul. Ask him to show you a church where you can serve faithfully, give regularly, and grow continually. Ask for patience as you realize the length of the journey you have yet to travel.

ACKNOWLEDGMENTS

Sometimes, I think of myself as a Certificate of Deposit. Over the years, literally hundreds of God's servants have taken the time to deposit their gifts into my soul. I could never mention all of them.

But for those of you just beginning this journey, I'd like to give you a glimpse of the ways I've been blessed by God through people: In 1975, I was saved by the fasting prayers of my college roommates, Karen and Nancy. In those early years, Pastor Charles Anderson faithfully laid the groundwork for my growth in Christ. Doug Tutmarc gave me my first glimpse of humble Christian service. Wayde Goodall gave me my first opportunity to teach. Gwen Ellis and Marge Stewart taught my first Young Married Sunday School Class. They showed me that strong women contribute to the body of Christ.

In 1979, Linda Hickling challenged me to read through the Bible in a year. I've been in the Bible ever since.

For more than twenty summers, fine Bible teachers at Cannon Beach Conference Center have challenged me to read and study the Bible for myself. Dr. David Jeremiah challenged me to write for publication. Petey Prater prayed me through my first editor appointment. Dr. Art Hunt challenged me to help plant a brand-new church in Puyallup, Washington. Together with the original leadership team at Lighthouse (lovingly titled the Dumb Dirty Dogs), I learned much about servant leadership. D. J. Young taught me how to nurture a committee through a task. Kim Carlson taught me to play worship piano, and Pastor Marcus Robinson gave me the chance to practice what I'd learned in a real service. Gwen Christopherson taught me to play without guilt. The Reflections Drama Team taught me to lead with love and laughter.

My walking ladies have taught me to show love tangibly.

My husband, Kim Nordberg, has never wavered in his commitment to me, and to our children. In the process of working out our marriage, we've been forced to grow up together. Because of our commitment to the Lord, we are learning to walk our talk.

I am a writer because Kim pays the bills.

For the opportunity to write this manuscript, I owe a debt of thanks to my friend and editor Dan Penwell. There are no words to thank Jeannie St. John Taylor—my writing friend—who supports my work with prayer, wise advice, and an occasional shoulder to cry upon.

Of course, God prompted all of these men and women to invest in my life. Because of the faithfulness of both God and men, I've done some investing of my own. It is my prayer that this book helps you begin your life of faith.

Perhaps someday, by God's wonderful grace, you will remember this book as part of my investment in your account. May you yield huge dividends!